# A GUIDE
## TO THE STUDY AND READING
## OF NORTH CAROLINA HISTORY

by *Hugh Talmage Lefler*

*Kenan Professor of History*

*The University of North Carolina at Chapel Hill*

*THIRD EDITION*

*The University of North Carolina Press · Chapel Hill*

*A GUIDE TO THE STUDY AND READING
OF NORTH CAROLINA HISTORY*

# CONTENTS

# ABBREVIATIONS

*Agr. Hist.—Agricultural History*
*AHA—American Historical Association*
*AHR—American Historical Review*
*Am. Anthrop.—American Anthropologist*
*Am. Antiq. Soc. Proc.—Proceedings of the American Antiquarian Society*
*Am. Cath. Hist. Rev.—American Catholic Historical Review*
*Am. Cath. Hist. Soc. Rec.—Records of the American Catholic Historical Society*
*Am. Ch. Mo.—American Church Monthly*
*Am.-Ger. Rev.—American-German Review*
*Am. Jew. Hist. Soc. Publ.—American Jewish Historical Society Publications*
*Am. Jour. Int. Law—American Journal of International Law*
*Am. Lit.—American Literature*
*Am. Phil. Soc. Proc.—American Philosophical Society Proceedings*
*Art and Archaeol.—Art and Archaeology*
*Conf. Vet.—Confederate Veteran*
*Cornhill Mag.—Cornhill Magazine,* London
*D.A.R. Mag.—Daughters of the American Revolution Magazine*
*Ga. Hist. Quar.—Georgia Historical Quarterly*
*Ind. Mag. Hist.—Indiana Magazine of History*
*JHUS—Johns Hopkins University Studies*
*Jour. Negro Ed.—Journal of Negro Education*
*Jour. Negro Hist.—Journal of Negro History*
*Jour. Sou. Hist.—Journal of Southern History*
*JSHP—James Sprunt Historical Publications,* Chapel Hill
*Luth. Ch. Rev.—Lutheran Church Review*

*Luth. Quar.*—*The Lutheran Quarterly*
*Mag. Hist.*—*Magazine of History*
*MVHR*—*Mississippi Valley Historical Review*
*Nat. Geog. Mag.*—*National Geographic Magazine*
*NCB*—*North Carolina Booklet*
NCC&D—North Carolina Department of Conservation and Development
*NC Hist. Com. Publ.*—*North Carolina Historical Commission Publications*
*NCHR*—*North Carolina Historical Review*
*N.C. Lit. and Hist. Assoc.*—*North Carolina Literary and Historical Association*
*NCLR*—*North Carolina Law Review*
*Pa. Law Rev.*—*Pennsylvania Law Review*
*Pa. Mag. Hist.*—*Pennsylvania Magazine of History*
*Peabody Jour. of Ed.*—*Peabody Journal of Education*
*P. E. Church Hist. Mag.*—*Protestant Episcopal Church Historical Magazine*
*Scot. Hist. Rev.*—*Scottish Historical Review*
*Sou. Atl. Quar.*—*South Atlantic Quarterly*
*S.C. Hist. Mag.*—*South Carolina Historical Magazine*
*SIS*—*Southern Indian Studies*
TCHS—Trinity College Historical Society
*Tenn. Mag. Hist.*—*Tennessee Magazine of History*
*Tyler's Quar. Hist. Mag.*—*Tyler's Historical and Genealogical Magazine*
*Va. Law Rev.*—*Virginia Law Review*
*Va. Quar. Rev.*—*Virginia Quarterly Review*
*WMQ*—*William and Mary Quarterly*

*A GUIDE TO THE STUDY AND READING
OF NORTH CAROLINA HISTORY*

# I. / SOURCES FOR THE STUDY
## AND WRITING
## OF NORTH CAROLINA HISTORY:
## STATE AND LOCAL

North Carolina is rich in materials for the writing, teaching, and study of the state's history. It has some of the best manuscript collections in the nation, notably that of the Southern Historical Collection in The University of North Carolina Library at Chapel Hill, the Flowers Collection of Southern historical materials at Duke University, and the official manuscript archives in the Department of Archives and History at Raleigh. It also has several noteworthy manuscript collections for the study of church history, among the most outstanding being those of the Southern Presbyterian Church at Montreat and the Moravian collection at Winston-Salem. The state's one hundred counties also have local manuscript archives of varying quantity, importance, and value. An excellent guide to these local records is to be found in *The Historical Records of North Carolina*, 3 vols. (Raleigh, 1938-1939), edited by C. C. Crittenden and Dan Lacy.

Most valuable of all collections of printed sources for North Carolina history before 1789 are the *Colonial Records of North Carolina*, 10 vols. (Raleigh, 1886-1890), edited by W. L. Saunders, followed by *State Records of North Carolina*, 16 vols. (Winston, Goldsboro, Charlotte, 1895-1905), edited by Walter Clark, with four index volumes (Goldsboro, Charlotte, Raleigh, 1909-1914), edited by Stephen B. Weeks. This series, one of the best published by any state, includes: legislative journals; laws; royal instructions to governors; letters of governors, missionaries, and other people; the census of 1790; lists of taxables; extracts from newspapers; official documents of various kinds, and a great variety of miscellaneous documents. *The Colonial Records of North Carolina* has been out of print for many years. Under the auspices of the State Department of Archives and History, a new set of colonial records will be published within the next decade or so. This new collection will contain many new documents; it will correct the numerous errors in the older set; it will be better organized, more carefully edited, and better indexed. Volume I of the new series, *North Carolina Charters and Constitutions, 1578-1698,* edited by Mrs. Mattie Erma Edwards Parker, was published in 1963, in connection with the tercentenary celebration of the Carolina Charter. *Records of the Moravians in North Carolina,* edited by Adelaide L. Fries (7 vols.; 1752-1822), Douglas L. Rights (Volume VIII, 1823-1837), Minnie J. Smith (Volume IX, 1838-1847), and Kenneth G. Hamilton (Volume X, 1841-1851), contain a wealth of information on the economic, social, religious, and cultural life of the North Carolina Piedmont area for more than a century and a quarter. J. Bryan Grimes, *Abstract of North Carolina Wills* (Raleigh, 1910) and *North Carolina Wills and Inventories* (Raleigh, 1912) are useful for social and economic history, particularly for the colonial era, since they give detailed lists of the worldly goods of many North Carolinians, especially those of the planter class.

The role of the North Carolina delegates in Continental Congress (1774-1789) may be traced in E. C. Burnett (ed.), *Letters of Members of the Continental Congress,* 8 vols. (Washington, 1921-1936), while the activity of the state's delegates in the Constitutional Convention of 1787 may be followed in Max Farrand (ed.), *The Records of the Federal Convention of 1787,* 4 vols. (Washington, 1911-1937). Jonathan Elliot (ed.), *The Debates in the Several State Conventions on the Adoption of the Federal Constitution,* IV (Washington, 1836), contains the proceedings of the Convention at

Hillsborough in 1788. There are no extant records of the debates in the Fayetteville Convention of 1789 which ratified the Constitution.

The North Carolina Historical Commission (now the State Department of Archives and History) has published scores of documentary volumes, including the papers of John Steele, Archibald D. Murphey, Thomas Ruffin, John Gray Blount, William A. Graham, Willie P. Mangum, John W. Ellis, Zebulon B. Vance, and the official papers of many of the recent governors. Many of these volumes are listed at the proper place in the Chapter Bibliographies below. The *Manual of North Carolina* for 1913, edited by R. D. W. Connor, is an invaluable source for a study of North Carolina political history since it lists governors, state legislators, congressmen, and other public officials from 1664 to 1913. It also gives election returns for president and governor, 1836-1912, and votes on various conventions and constitutional amendments. Very useful is a more recent publication (Chapel Hill, 1962), compiled by Donald R. Matthews and staff, *North Carolina Votes: General Election Returns by County for President of the United States, 1868-1960; Governor of North Carolina, 1868-1960; United States Senator from North Carolina, 1914-1960.*

Hundreds of North Carolinians have had biographical sketches written about them though extremely few have had full-length biographies. Some two hundred of the state's most prominent citizens have had sketches in the authoritative *Dictionary of American Biography,* 22 vols. (New York, 1928-1958). A few of the most outstanding colonial figures have been written up in the English *Dictionary of National Biography,* 63 vols. (London, 1882-1959). There is a brief sketch of all North Carolinians who have served in the Congress of the United States in the *Biographical Directory of the American Congress, 1774-1961* (Washington, 1961). S. A. Ashe (ed.), *Biographical History of North Carolina from Colonial Times to the Present,* 8 vols. (Greensboro, 1905-1917), is the most ambitious undertaking of its kind in the state's history. It contains over six hundred biographical essays, chiefly about political leaders. W. J. Peele (ed.), *Lives of Distinguished North Carolinians, with Illustrations and Speeches* (Raleigh, 1898) contains fifteen lengthy sketches of some of the state's most famous political and military leaders. Scores of biographical sketches have also appeared in the *North Carolina Booklet* (Raleigh, 1901-1926).

Some excellent biographical studies and many good articles on almost every aspect of North Carolina history have appeared in the *North Carolina Historical Review* which has been published under the auspices of the North Carolina Historical Commission (now the State Department of Archives and History) since 1924. This quarterly journal, one of the best of its kind, is indispensable for a thorough study of North Carolina history. Many excellent articles have also appeared in the Trinity College Historical Society *Papers* at what is now Duke University, in the *James Sprunt Studies in History and Political Science* at The University of North Carolina, in the *Johns Hopkins University Studies,* in the *Journal of Southern History,* and in the *American Historical Review.* Some articles and documents relating to North Carolina have also been printed in the *Mississippi Valley Historical Review* (now the *Journal of American History*), the *William and Mary Quarterly,* the *Journal of Negro History,* the *Proceedings of the American Antiquarian Society* (Worcester, Mass.), the *South Atlantic Quarterly,* and the *Annual Reports* of the American Historical Association. Many short articles on North Carolina History are found in J. T. Adams (ed.), *Dictionary of American History,* 6 vols. (2nd ed. rev. and enl.; New York, 1961).

The *North Carolina Booklet,* published under the auspices of the North Carolina Society, Daughters of the American Revolution (Raleigh, 1901-1926) contains many articles on various phases of state and local history. See the *Index to "North Carolina Booklet,"* compiled by Grace Stowell (Greensboro, 1922). Many interesting articles on North Carolina history, biography, and local history have appeared and continue to appear in the *State* magazine (Raleigh, since 1933) and in the leading Sunday newspapers. An extremely valuable source of information about economic and social conditions in the state is *The University of North Carolina News Letter,* formerly published semi-monthly, October-May, and now published quarterly, by the Institute for Research in Social Science at The University of North Carolina (Chapel Hill, since 1914).

One of the most popular and useful books on North Carolina ever published was the North Carolina volume in the American Guide Series. A new *North Carolina Guide,* based on the original (1939) and edited by Blackwell P. Robinson (Chapel Hill: The University of North Carolina Press, 1955), is valuable, especially for local history.

Some of the best historical research which has been done in North Carolina history remains unpublished. It is to be found in masters' theses and doctoral dissertations at The University of North Carolina and Duke University. These scholarly studies, typed and bound, are in the libraries of these two institutions.

Perhaps the finest source for the study of governmental aspects of the state's history is "hid away" in the official and semi-official publications of the state government. These include printed reports of all branches of the government— executive, legislative, and judicial, as well as reports of all state boards and agencies. Included in these publications are the reports of railroads, plank roads and canal companies, navigation companies, and other enterprises in which the state owned stock. Also included, though not financed by the government, are such things as digests and codes, commercially published, but containing legal material of great value. Of invaluable service to the researcher in state history will be Mary Thornton (compiler), *Official Publications of the Colony and State of North Carolina, 1749-1939: A Bibliography* (Chapel Hill: The University of North Carolina Press, 1954), and Mary Thornton (compiler), *A Bibliography of North Carolina, 1589-1956* (Chapel Hill: The University of North Carolina Press, 1958). An extremely important book is H. G. Jones *For History's Sake: The Preservation and Publication of North Carolina History, 1663-1903* (Chapel

Hill, 1966). Also useful to the researcher are: *North Carolina Newspapers on Microfilm: A Checklist of Early North Carolina Newspapers available on Microfilm from the State Department of Archives and History,* edited by H. G. Jones and Julius H. Avant (3rd ed.; Raleigh, 1965) and *Union List of North Carolina Newspapers 1751-1900* edited by H. G. Jones and Julius H. Avant (Raleigh, 1963). An extremely helpful volume, especially for local history, is William S. Powell's *The North Carolina Gazetteer* (Chapel Hill, 1968), 580 pp.

## II. / SELECT LIST OF BOOKS
##    AND ARTICLES
##    RELATING TO
##    NORTH CAROLINA HISTORY

Adam, Margaret I. "The Causes of the Highland Emigrations of 1783-1803," *Scot. Hist. Rev.,* XVII (1919-1920) , 73-89.

Adams, Percy G. "John Lawson's Alter Ego—Dr. John Brickell," *NCHR,* XXXIV, No. 3 (July, 1957), 313-326.

Adams, Randolph G. "An Effort to Identify John White," *AHR,* XLI (1935) , 87-91.

Adams, W. J. "Evolution of Law in North Carolina," *NCLR,* II, No. 3 (April, 1924), 133-145.

Albertson, Catherine S. *In Ancient Albemarle.* Raleigh, 1914. 170 pp.
——. "Enfield Farm Where the Culpeper Rebellion Began," *NCB,* XII (April, 1913), 224-231.
——. "The first Albemarle Assembly [1665]—Hall's Creek, near Nixonton," *NCB,* XII (January, 1913), 202-207.
——. *Roanoke Island in History and Legend.* Elizabeth City, 1934. 28 pp.

Alden, John R. *John Stuart and the Southern Colonial Frontier.* Ann Arbor, 1944. 384 pp.
——. *The South in the Revolution, 1763-1789.* Baton Rouge, 1957. 442 pp.

Alderman, Edwin A. "Charles Brantley Aycock—An Appreciation," *NCHR,* I, No. 3 (July, 1924) , 243-250.

Alderman, Ernest H. "The North Carolina Colonial Bar," *JSHP*, I (1913), 5-13.

Alexander, C. B. "Richard Caswell's Military and Later Public Services," *NCHR*, XXIII, No. 3 (July, 1946), 287-312.
———. "Richard Caswell: Versatile Leader of the Revolution," *NCHR*, XXIII, No. 2 (April, 1946), 119-141.
———. "The Training of Richard Caswell," *NCHR*, XXIII, No. 1 (January, 1946), 13-31.

Alexander, Violet G. "The Confederate States Navy Yard at Charlotte, North Carolina, 1862-1865," *NCB*, XXIII (1926), 28-37.

Allcott, John V. "Architectural Developments at 'Montrose' in the 1850's," *NCHR*, XLII, No. 1 (January, 1965), 85-95.
———. *Colonial Homes in North Carolina.* Raleigh, 1963. 75 pp.

Allen, Talbot M. "Samuel Johnston in Revolutionary Times," TCHS, *Papers,* V (1905), 39-49.

Allen, W. C. "Whigs and Tories," *NCB*, II, No. 5 (1902), 3-24.

Allred, Fred J. and Alonzo T. Dill. (eds.). "The Founding of New Bern: A Footnote," *NCHR*, XL, No. 3 (July. 1963), 361-374.

Amis, Moses N. *Historical Raleigh from Its Foundation in 1792.* Raleigh, 1902. 230 pp.

Anderson, Mrs. John H. "The Confederate Arsenal at Fayetteville, North Carolina," *Conf. Vet.,* XXXVI (June, 1928), 222-223, 238.
———. *North Carolina Women of the Confederacy.* Fayetteville, 1926. 141 pp.
———. "What Sherman Did to Fayetteville," *Conf. Vet.,* XXXII (April, 1924), 138-140.

Andrews, Alexander B. "Richard Dobbs Spaight," *NCHR*, I, No. 2 (April, 1924), 95-120.

Andrews, Charles M. "Captain Henry Wilkinson," *Sou. Atl. Quar.,* XV (July, 1916), 172-202.
———. *The Colonial Period of American History,* Vol. III,

New Haven, 1937. 354 pp. Chs. V and VI: "Carolina, The Beginnings" and "The Two Carolinas: Later Years," 182-267.

———— (ed.). *Narratives of the Insurrections, 1675-1690.* New York, 1915. 414 pp. (For N.C., see 143-164.)

————, and Evangeline Andrews (eds.). *The Journal of a Lady of Quality.* New Haven, 1921. 341 pp., reprint, 1934 and 1939.

Anscombe, Francis C. *I Have Called You Friends: The Story of Quakerism in North Carolina.* Boston, 1959. 407 pp.

Applewhite, Marjorie M. "Sharecropper and Tenant in the Courts of North Carolina," *NCHR,* XXXI, No. 2 (April, 1954), 134-149.

Archdale, John. *A New Description of that Fertile and Pleasant Province of Carolina.* London, 1707. 32 pp.

Armytage, W. H. G. "The Editorial Experience of Joseph Gales, 1786-1794," *NCHR,* XXVIII, No. 3 (July, 1951), 332-361.

Arnett, A. M. *Claude Kitchin and the Wilson War Policies.* Boston, 1937. 341 pp.

————. "Claude Kitchin Versus the Patrioteers," *NCHR,* XIV, No. 1 (January, 1937), 20-30.

————. *The Story of North Carolina.* Chapel Hill, 1933. Book for young readers. 496 pp.

Arnett, Ethel S. *Confederate Guns Were Stacked at Greensboro.* Greensboro, 1965. 173 pp.

————. *William Swaim, Fighting Editor. The Story of O. Henry's Grandfather.* Greensboro, 1963. 401 pp.

Arthur, J. P. *Western North Carolina, 1730 to 1913.* Raleigh, 1914. 710 pp.

Asbury, Francis. *The Journals of the Rev. Francis Asbury, Bishop of the Methodist Episcopal Church, from August 7, 1771 to December 7, 1815.* 3 vols. New York, 1821.

Ashe, S. A. (ed.). *Biographical History of North Carolina*

*from Colonial Times to the Present.* 8 vols., Greensboro, 1905-1917. Contains 620 sketches, 122 of them by Ashe. Other volumes were planned. Manuscripts are at Duke.

————. "Early Times on the Cape Fear," *NCB,* XIII (January, 1914), 152-174.

————. *History of North Carolina.* 2 vols. Raleigh, 1908; Greensboro, 1925.

————. "Our Own Pirates: Blackbeard and Bonnett," *NCB,* II, No. 2 (1902), 3-23.

————. "Social Conditions in North Carolina in 1783," *NCB,* X, No. 4 (1911), 200-222.

————. "Some New Light on John Paul Jones," *Sou. Atl. Quar.,* XVII, No. 1 (January, 1918), 44-57.

————. "The State of Franklin," *NCB,* XIV (July, 1914), 28-49.

————. "A Turning Point in the Life of the People of the State; the Legislation of 1848," *NCB,* XXII (1923), 12-31.

————. "Was Lederer in Bertie County?" *NCB,* XV (1915), 33-38.

Atchison, Ray M. " 'The Land We Love:' A Southern Post-Bellum Magazine of Agriculture, Literature, and Military History," *NCHR,* XXXVII, No. 4 (October, 1960), 506-515.

————. " 'Our Living and Our Dead:' A Post-Bellum North Carolina Magazine of Literature and History," *NCHR,* XL, No. 4 (October, 1963), 423-433.

Attmore, William. "Journal of a Tour to North Carolina, 1787," ed. by Lida T. Rodman, *JSHP,* XVII, No. 2 (1922), 1-46.

Avery, Myron H., and Kenneth S. Boardman (eds.). "Arnold Guyot's Notes on the Geography of the Mountain District of Western North Carolina," *NCHR,* XV, No. 3 (July, 1938), 251-318.

Aydlett, A. Laurence. "The North Carolina State Board of Public Welfare," *NCHR,* XXIV, No. 1 (January, 1947), 1-34.

Bailey, Ralph E. *Guns over the Carolinas: The Story of Nathanael Greene.* New York, 1967. 224 pp.

Bailyn, Bernard. "The Blount Papers: Notes on the Merchant 'Class' in the Revolutionary Period," *WMQ,* XI, No. 2 (April, 1954), 98-104.

Baker, Howard F. "National Stocks in the Population of the United States as Indicated by the Surnames in the Census of 1790," *AHA, Annual Report* (1931), 126-134.

Baldwin, Alice M. "Twenty-Five Years in North Carolina," *NCHR,* XXVI, No. 2 (April, 1949), 236-242.

Baldwin, Simeon. "The Contributions of North Carolina to the Development of American Institutions." *NCB,* XIV (January, 1915), 141-154.

Bancroft, Frederic. *Slave-Trading in the Old South.* Baltimore, 1931; New York, 1959. 415 pp.

Barbee, David R. "Hinton Rowan Helper," *Tyler's Quar. Hist. and Gen. Mag.,* XV (1934), 145-172, 228-231.

Bardolph, Richard. "Inconstant Rebels: Desertion of North Carolina Troops in the Civil War," *NCHR,* XLI, No. 2 (April, 1964), 163-189.
———. "A North Carolina Farm Journal of the Middle Fifties," *NCHR,* XXV, No. 1 (January, 1948), 58-90.

Barnes, A. M. "Locke's Grand Model: Historical Review of the First Form of Government of the Carolina Colonies," *Lawyer and Banker,* XIII (July, 1920), 210-215.

Barnhart, John D. "Southern Contributions to the Social Order of the Old North-West," *NCHR,* XVII, No. 3 (July, 1940), 237-248.

Barnwell, John. "The Tuscarora Expedition," *S.C. Hist. Mag.,* IX (January, 1908), 28-58.

Barrett, John G. *The Civil War in North Carolina.* Chapel Hill, 1963. 484 pp.
———. "General Sherman's March through North Carolina," *NCHR,* XLII, No. 2 (April, 1965), 192-207.

——. *North Carolina As a Civil War Battleground, 1861-1865.* Raleigh, 1960. 99 pp.

——. "Sherman and Total War in the Carolinas," *NCHR,* XXXVII, No. 3 (July, 19960), 367-381.

——. *Sherman's March through the Carolinas.* Chapel Hill, 1956. 325 pp.

Barringer, Paul B. *The Natural Bent: The Memoirs of Dr. Paul Barringer.* Chapel Hill, 1949. 280 pp.

——. "The Influence of Peculiar Conditions in the Early History of North Carolina," *N.C. Lit. and Hist. Assoc. Proc.,* XVIII (1919), 13-25.

Barry, Richard S. "Fort Macon: Its History," *NCHR,* XXVII, No. 2 (April, 1950), 163-177.

Barton, Lew. *The Most Ironic Story in American History: An Authoritative Documented History of the Lumbee Indians of North Carolina.* Pembroke, N.C., 1967. xvii, 142 pp.

Bartram, John. "Diary of a Journey through the Carolinas, Georgia, and Florida, 1765-1766." Annotated by Francis Harper. *Transactions of the American Philosophical Society, 1942-1943.* Philadelphia, 1943. 242 pp.

Bartram, William. *Travels through North & South Carolina.* Philadelphia, 1791. Edited with commentary and an annotated index by Francis Harper. New Haven, 1958. lxi, 727 pp.

Bassett, John Spencer. *Anti-Slavery Leaders of North Carolina.* Baltimore, 1898. 74 pp.

——. "The Case of State *vs.* Will," TCHS, *Papers,* II (1898), 12-20.

——. "The Congressional Career of Thomas L. Clingman, TCHS, *Papers,* IV (1900) 31-47.

——. *The Constitutional Beginnings of North Carolina.* Baltimore, 1894. 73 pp.

——. "The County of Clarendon," *NCB,* II, No. 9 (February, 1903), 1-20.

———. "Edward Graham Daves," TCHS, *Papers,* I (1897), 53-55.

——— (ed.). "General Slade's Journal of a Trip to Tennessee," TCHS, *Papers,* VI (1906), 37-56.

———. *History of Slavery in the State of North Carolina.* Baltimore, 1899. 111 pp.

———. "The Influence of Coast Line and Rivers on North Carolina," *AHA, Annual Report,* 1908, 1, 58-61.

———. "Landholding in Colonial North Carolina," TCHS, *Papers,* II (1898), 44-61.

———. "Naming the Carolinas," *Sewanee Review,* II, No. 3 (1894), 343-352.

———. "North Carolina Methodism and Slavery," TCHS, *Papers,* IV (1900), 1-11.

———. "Old Durham Traditions," TCHS, *Papers,* VI (1906), 27-36.

———. "The Regulators of North Carolina," *AHA, Annual Report,* 1894, 141-212.

———. "Running the Blockade from Confederate Ports," TCHS, *Papers,* II (1898), 62-67.

———. *Slavery and Servitude in the Colony of North Carolina.* Baltimore, 1896. 86 pp.

———. "Some New Material Relating to the Mecklenburg Resolves—May 31, 1775," TCHS, *Papers,* V (1905), 67-70.

——— (ed.). "Some Unpublished Letters of Nathaniel Macon," TCHS, *Papers,* VI (1906), 53-55.

———. "Suffrage in the State of North Carolina, 1776-1881," *AHA, Annual Report,* 1894, 269-285.

——— (ed.). *The Writings of Colonel William Byrd of Westover of Virginia.* New York, 1901. IX-LXXXVIII, 461 pp.

Bates, Whitney K. "Northern Speculators and Southern State Debts, 1790," *WMQ,* XIX, No. 1 (January, 1962), 30-48.

Battle, George Gordon. "The State of North Carolina *vs.* Negro Will, a slave of James S. Battle; a cause célèbre of ante bellum times." *Va. Law Rev.* (April, 1920), 515-530.

Battle, Kemp P. "History of the Supreme Court of North Carolina," 103 *N.C. Reports.* Raleigh, 1899. 309-342.

――――. *History of the University of North Carolina.* 2 vols. Raleigh, 1907-1912.

―――― (ed.). "Letters and Documents Relating to the Early History of the Lower Cape Fear," *JSHP,* No. 4 (1903), 135 pp.

―――― (ed.). "Letters of Nathaniel Macon, John Steele and William Barry Grove," *JSHP,* No. 3 (1902), 122 pp.

――――. "The Trial of James Glasgow and the Supreme Court of North Carolina," *NCB,* III (May, 1903), 1-11.

Battle, William J. (ed.). *Kemp Plummer Battle: Memories of an Old-Time Tar Heel.* Chapel Hill, 1945. 296 pp.

Bean, W. G. "Anti-Jeffersonianism in The Ante-Bellum South," *NCHR,* XII, No. 2 (April, 1935), 103-124.

Bell, John L., Jr. "Baptists and the Negro in North Carolina during Reconstruction," *NCHR,* XLII, No. 4 (October, 1965), 391-401.

――――. "The Presbyterian Church and the Negro in North Carolina during Reconstruction," *NCHR,* XL, No. 1 (January, 1963), 15-36.

Benjamin, Marcus. "John Henry Bonner," *Sou. Atl. Quar.,* III, No. 2 (April, 1904), 166-174.

Bergeron, Paul H. (ed.). "My Brother's Keeper: William H. Polk Goes to School," *NCHR,* XLIV, No. 2 (April, 1967), 188-204.

Berkeley, Edmund, and Dorothy S. Berkeley (eds.). "The Manner of Living of the North Carolinians, by Francis Veale, December 19, 1730," *NCHR,* XLI, No. 2 (April, 1964), 239-245.

Bernheim, G. D. *The History of the Evangelical Lutheran Synod and Ministerium of North Carolina.* Philadelphia, 1902. 191 pp.

――――. *History of the German Settlements and the Lutheran Church in North and South Carolina.* Philadelphia, 1872. 557 pp.

Bernstein, Leonard. "The Participation of Negro Delegates in the Constitutional Convention of 1868," *Jour. Negro Hist.*, XXXIV, No. 4 (October, 1949), 391-409.

Best, James Arthur. "The Adoption of the Federal Constitution by North Carolina," TCHS, *Papers*, V (1905), 12-36.
———. "North Carolina in the French and Indian War." *Trinity Archive*, XV (1902), 382-388.

Betts, Robert E. "The Lost Colony," *Cornhill Mag.*, CLVII (1938), 50-67.

Betz, Eva (Kelly). *William Gaston, Fighter for Justice.* New York, 1964. 190 pp.

Biggs, Joseph. *A Concise History of the Kehukee Baptist Association.* . . . Tarboro, 1834. 300 pp.

Bivins, J. F. "The Life and Character of Jacob Thompson," TCHS, *Papers*, II (1898), 53-91.

Black, Robert C. *The Railroads of the Confederacy.* Chapel Hill, 1952. 360 pp.

Black, Wilfred W. (ed.). "Civil War Letters of E. N. Boots from New Bern and Plymouth," *NCHR*, XXVII, No. 2 (April, 1959), 205-223.

Blackwelder, Fannie Farmer. "The Bar Examination and Beginning Years of Legal Practice in North Carolina, 1820-1860," *NCHR*, XXIX, No. 2 (April, 1952), 159-170.
———. "Legal Education in North Carolina, 1820-1860," *NCHR*, XXVIII, No. 3 (July, 1951), 271-297.
———. "Legal Practice and Ethics in North Carolina, 1820-1860," *NCHR*, XXX, No. 3 (July, 1953), 329-353.
———. "The North Carolina Records Management Program," *NCHR*, XXXVI, No. 3 (July, 1959), 340-357.
———. "Organization and Early Years of the North Carolina Bar Association," *NCHR*, XXXIV, No. 1 (January, 1957), 36-57.

Blackwelder, Ruth. "The Attitude of North Carolina Moravians toward the American Revolution," *NCHR*, IX, No. 1 (January, 1932), 1-21.

Blades, Thomas E., and John W. Fike. "Career of a Flag," *NCHR*, XVI, No. 4 (October, 1949), 439-445.

Blair, Marian H. (ed.). "Civil War Letters of Henry W. Barrow to John W. Fries," *NCHR*, XXIV, No. 1 (January, 1957), 68-85.

Blanchard, J. C. "North Carolina in the First National Congress." *Trinity Archive*, XV (1902), 382-388.

Blauch, L. E. "An Early Normal College in the South," *Peabody Jour. Ed.*, VIII (1931), 297-304.

Bleeker, Sonia. *The Cherokee: Indians of the Mountains.* New York, 1952. 159 pp.

Bloom, Leonard. "The Acculturation of the Eastern Cherokees: Historical Aspects," *NCHR*, No. 4 (October, 1942), 322-357.

Blythe, W. LeGette. *William Henry Belk: Merchant of the South.* Chapel Hill, 1950. 225 pp.

Bolton, C. K. *Scotch-Irish Pioneers in Ulster and America.* Boston, 1910. 398 pp.

Bond, B. W. *The Quit Rent System in the American Colonies.* New Haven, 1919. 492 pp.

Bonner, James C. "Plantation Experiences of a New York Woman," *NCHR*, Nos. 3 and 4 (July and October, 1956), 384-412, 529-546.

Bost, W. T. "A Reporter Reviews Fifty Years of North Carolina History," *NCHR*, XXVII, No. 2 (April, 1950), 205-217.

Bowles, Elisabeth Ann. *A Good Beginning: The First Four Decades of The University of North Carolina at Greensboro.* Chapel Hill, 1967. 193 pp.

Boyd, Julian P. (ed.). "A North Carolina Citizen on the Federal Constitution, 1788," *NCHR*, XVI, No. 1 (January, 1939), 36-53.
———. "The Sheriff in Colonial North Carolina," *NCHR*, V, No. 2 (April, 1928), 151-180.

Boyd, W. K. "Ad Valorem Taxation," TCHS, *Papers,* V (1905), 1-11.

———. "Antecedents of the North Carolina Convention of 1835," *Sou. Atl. Quar.* (January-April, 1910), 1 29.

——— (ed.). *The Autobiography of Brantley York.* TCHS, *Monographs.* Durham, 1910. 139 pp.

———. "Currency and Banking in North Carolina, 1709-1836," TCHS, *Papers,* X (1914), 52-86.

———. "Dennis Heartt," TCHS, *Papers,* II (1898), 34-43.

———. "Early Relations of North Carolina and the West," *NCB,* VII, No. 3 (1908), 193-209.

———. "Federal Politics in North Carolina, 1824-1836," *Sou. Atl. Quar.,* XVIII (January-April, 1949), 41-51, 167-174.

———. "The Finances of the North Carolina Literary Fund," *Sou. Atl. Quar.,* XIII, No. 3 (July, 1914), 361-370.

———. "Fiscal and Economic Conditions in North Carolina during the Civil War," *NCB,* XIV (April, 1915), 195-219.

———. *History of North Carolina: The Federal Period.* Chicago, 1919. 407 pp.

———. "John S. Cairnes, Ornithologist," TCHS, *Papers,* I (1897), 53-55.

——— (ed.). "A Journal and Travel of James Meacham, Part I, May 19-August 31, 1789," TCHS, *Papers,* IX (1912), 66-95; Part II, TCHS, *Papers,* X (1914), 87-102.

——— (ed.). "Letters of Nathaniel Macon to Judge Charles Tait," TCHS, *Papers,* VIII (1908-1909), 3-5.

——— (ed.). "Letters of Sylvius," TCHS, *Papers,* XI (1915), 5-46.

——— (ed.). *The Memoirs of W. W. Holden,* TCHS, *Monographs,* II, Durham, 1911. 199 pp.

———. "Methodist Expansion in North Carolina after the Revolution," TCHS, *Papers,* XII (1916), 37-55.

——— (ed.). *Military Reminiscences of General William R. Boggs, CSA.* Durham, 1913. 115 pp.

———. "Nathaniel Macon in National Legislation," TCHS, *Papers,* III (1900), 72-88.

——— (ed.). "News, Letters, and Documents Concerning

North Carolina and The Federal Constitution," TCHS, *Papers,* XIV (1922) , 75-95.

―――. "The North Carolina Fund for Internal Improvements," *Sou. Atl. Quar.,* XV, No. 1 (January, 1916) , 52-67.

―――. "North Carolina on the Eve of Secession," *AHA, Ann. Report* (1910) , 165-177.

―――― (ed.). "Selections from the Correspondence of Bedford Brown, Part I 1832-1856," TCHS, *Papers,* VI (1906) , 66-92; Part II, TCHS, *Papers,* VII (1907) , 16-31.

―――― (ed.) . *Some Eighteenth Century Tracts Concerning North Carolina.* Raleigh, 1927.

―――. *The Story of Durham, City of the New South.* Durham, 1925. 345 pp.

―――― (ed.). *William Byrd's Histories of the Dividing Line Betwixt Virginia and North Carolina.* Raleigh, 1929. xi, xxvii, 341 pp; rev. ed., with new introduction by Percy G. Adams, New York, 1967. xxxix, 340 pp.

―――. "William W. Holden," TCHS, *Papers,* III (1899) , 39-78, 90-130.

―――, and Charles A. Krummel (eds.) . "German Tracts Concerning the Lutheran Church in North Carolina during the Eighteenth Century," *NCHR,* VII, Nos. 1 and 2 (January and April, 1930) , 79-147, 225-282.

Bradbeer, William W. "North Carolina State Currency," *NCB,* XIX (July, 1919), 36-46.

Bradlee, F. B. C. *Blockade Running during the Civil War. . . . Essex Inst. Hist. Soc. Coll.,* LXII (Jan.-Oct., 1926) , 33-64, 129-160, 321-352.

Bradsher, A. B. "The Manufacture of Tobacco in North Carolina," TCHS, *Papers,* VI (1906) , 12-21.

Branson, Lanier. *Eugene Cunningham Branson: Humanitarian.* Charlotte, 1967. 183 pp.

Braverman, Howard. "Calvin H. Wiley's *North Carolina Reader,*" *NCHR,* XXIX, No. 4 (October, 1952) , 500-522.

Brewer, James H. "Legislation Designed to Control Slavery

in Wilmington and Fayetteville," *NCHR*, XXX, No. 2 (April, 1953), 155-166.

Brickell, John. *The Natural History of North Carolina.* Dublin, 1737. 408 pp.; reprint. Raleigh, 1911. 417 pp.

Bridenbaugh, Carl. *Myths and Realities: Societies of the Colonial South.* Baton Rouge, 1952. 208 pp. (See Chapter Three for Carolina.)

Bridges, Earley W. *The Masonic Governors of North Carolina.* Greensboro, 1937. 279 pp.

Brigham, C. S. *Bibliography of American Newspapers, 1690-1820. Am. Antiq. Soc. Proc.,* N.S. XXVIII, No. 2 (1919), 291-322. (See Part X, for N.C. references).

Brink, Wellington. *Big Hugh [Bennett] the Father of Soil Conservation.* New York, 1951. 167 pp.

Brooks, A. L. "David Caldwell and his 'Log College,'" *NCHR*, XXVIII, No. 4 (October, 1951), 399-407.
———. *A Southern Lawyer: Fifty Years at the Bar.* Chapel Hill, 1950. 214 pp.
———. *Walter Clark: Fighting Judge.* Chapel Hill, 1944. 278 pp.
———, and Hugh T. Lefler (eds.). *The Papers of Walter Clark,* 2 vols. Chapel Hill, 1948, 1950.

Brooks, E. C. "Charles Brantley Aycock," *Sou. Atl. Quar.,* XI, No. 3 (July, 1912), 279-282.

Brown, C. K. "A History of the Piedmont Railroad Company," *NCHR,* III, No. 2 (April, 1926), 198-222.
———. "The Southern Railway Security Company, an Early Instance of a Holding Company," *NCHR,* VI, No. 2 (April, 1929), 158-170.
———. *The State Highway System of North Carolina, Its Evolution and Present Status.* Chapel Hill, 1931. 260 pp.
———. *A State Movement in Railroad Development.* Chapel Hill, 1928. 300 pp.

Brown, Douglas S. *The Catawba Indians: The People of the River.* Columbia, S.C., 1967. 400 pp.

Brown, John P. *Old Frontiers: The Story of the Cherokee Indians from Earliest Times to the Date of Their Removal to the West, 1838.* Kingsport, 1938. 570 pp.

Brown, Louis A. (ed.). "The Correspondence of David Olando McRaven and Amanda Nantz McRaven, 1864-1865," *NCHR,* XXVI, No. 1 (January, 1949), 41-98.

Brown, Louise F. *The First Earl of Shaftesbury.* New York, 1931. 350 pp.

Brown, Norman D. "A Union Election in Civil War North Carolina," *NCHR,* XLIII, No. 4 (October, 1966), 381-400.

Brown, Roy M. *Public Poor Relief in North Carolina.* Chapel Hill, 1929. 184 pp.

Brown, W. Burlie. "The State Literary and Historical Association, 1900-1950," *NCHR,* XXVIII, No. 2 (April, 1951), 156-197.

Browning, James B. "The Free Negro in Ante-Bellum North Carolina," *NCHR,* XV, No. 1 (January, 1938), 23-33.
———. "The North Carolina Black Code," *Jour. Negro Hist.,* XV, No. 4 (October, 1930), 461-473.

Bryan, W. A. "Some Social Traits of the Quakers of Rich Square," TCHS, *Papers,* VII (1907), 64-70.
———. "Some Social Traits of the Rich Square Quakers, with New Garden Document," II, TCHS, *Papers,* VIII (1908-1909), 6-14.

Bryson, Herman. *Gold Deposits in North Carolina,* Raleigh, 1936. 157 pp.
———. *The Story of the Geologic Making of North Carolina.* Raleigh, 1928. 42 pp.

Bullock, C. J. *Essays on the Monetary History of the United States.* New York, 1900. 292 pp. (Chapter II, "Paper Currency in North Carolina.")

Burgess, Margaret Elaine. *Negro Leadership in a Southern City* [Durham], Chapel Hill, 1962. 231 pp.

Burkhead, L. S. "History of the Difficulties of the Front Street

Methodist Church, Wilmington, N.C. for the Year 1865," TCHS, *Papers*, VIII (1908-1909) , 35-118.

Burnett, E. C. *The Continental Congress.* New York, 1941. 757 pp.

———— (ed.) . *Letters of Members of the Continental Congress.* Washington, 1921-1931. 8 vols. (See Vols. II-VII for North Carolina references.)

————. "Southern Statesmen and the Confederation," *NCHR,* XIV, No. 4 (October, 1937) , 343-360.

Burwell, Mrs. M. A. "Shipwreck Off Hatteras, 1812," *NCB,* XXI (1922) , 90-100.

Caldwell, Bettie D. *Founders and Builders of Greensboro, 1808-1908.* Greensboro, 1925. 356 pp.

Caldwell, Joseph. *Autobiography and Biography of the Rev. Joseph Caldwell, First President of the University of North Carolina.* Chapel Hill, 1860. 68 pp.

————. *Letters on Popular Education, Addressed to the People of North Carolina.* Hillsborough, 1832. 54, 48 pp.

————. *The Numbers of Carlton Addressed to the People of North Carolina, on a Central Railroad through the State.* New York, 1828. 232 pp.

Camp, Cordelia. *Governor Vance: A Life for Young People.* Asheville, 1961. 58 pp.

————. *The Influence of Geography Upon Early North Carolina.* Raleigh, 1963. 31 pp.

————, and Eddie W. Wilson. *The Settlement of North Carolina.* Cullowhee, N.C., 1942. 44 pp.

Cannon, John. "Henry McCulloch and Henry McCulloh," *WMQ,* XV, No. 1 (January, 1958) , 71-73.

Cappon, Lester J. "Iron-Making—A Forgotten Industry of North Carolina," *NCHR, IX, No.* 4 (October, 1932), 331-348.

Carlton, Luther M. "The Assassination of John Walter Stephens," TCHS, *Papers,* II (1898), 1-11.

Carpenter, B. F. "The Legal Regulation of Public Morals in Colonial North Carolina," TCHS, *Papers,* II (1898), 68-75.

Carr, Elias. *Resources and Advantages of North Carolina.* Raleigh, 1893. 22 pp.

Carr, John W. "The Manhood Suffrage Movement in North Carolina," TCHS, *Papers,* XI (1915), 47-78.

Carraway, Gertrude. *Crown of Life: History of Christ Church, New Bern, North Carolina, 1715-1940.* New Bern, 1940. 245 pp.

———. *Historic New Bern Guide Book.* 11th edition. New Bern, 1957. 75 pp.

———. "History Is an Important Product," *NCHR,* XXXV, No. 2 (April, 1958), 182-190.

———. *Years of Light: History of St. John's Lodge, No. 3., A-F and A-M.* New Bern, 1944. 256 pp.

Carrier, Lyman. *The Beginnings of Agriculture in America.* New York, 1923. 323 pp.

Carroll, K. L. "The Nicholites of North Carolina," *NCHR,* XXXI, No. 4 (October, 1954), 453-462.

Carson, W. W. "Agricultural Reconstruction in North Carolina after the Civil War," *AHA Annual Rept.* (1921), 217-225.

Caruthers, E. W. *Revolutionary Incidents: And Sketches of Characters Chiefly in the "Old North State,"* Philadelphia, 1854. 431 pp.

———. *A Sketch of the Life and Character of the Rev. David Caldwell.* Greensboro, 1842. 302 pp.

Cash, W. J. *The Mind of the South.* New York, 1941. 429 pp.

Catesby, Mark. *The Natural History of Carolina, Florida and the Bahama Islands.* 2 vols. London, 1731 (contains 220 colored plates).

Cathey, C. O. *Agriculture in North Carolina Before the Civil War.* Raleigh, 1966. 46 pp.

———. *Agricultural Developments in North Carolina, 1783-1860.* Chapel Hill, 1956. 229 pp.

————. "The Impact of the Civil War on Agriculture in North Carolina," J. C. Sitterson (ed.). *Studies in Southern History*. Chapel Hill, 1957, pp. 97-110.

————. "Sidney Weller: Ante-Bellum Promoter of Agricultural Reform," *NCHR*, XXXI, No. 1 (January, 1954), 1-17.

Catterall, Helen T. (ed.). *Judicial Cases concerning American Slavery and the Negro*. Washington, 1929. (Vol. III. "Cases from the Courts of North Carolina, South Carolina, and Tennessee.")

Chaffin, Nora. "A Southern Advocate of Methodist Unification in 1865," *NCHR*, XVIII, No. 1 (January, 1941), 38-47.

————. *Trinity College, 1839-1892: The Beginnings of Duke University*. Durham, 1950. 584 pp.

Chambers, Lenoir. "The South on the Eve of the Civil War," *NCHR*, XXXIX, No. 2 (April, 1962), 181-194.

Chambers, William N. "As the Twig is Bent: The Family and the North Carolina Years of Thomas Hart Benton, 1752-1801," *NCHR*, XXVI, No. 4 (October, 1949), 385-416.

————. *Old Bullion Benton, Senator from the New West, 1782-1855*. Boston, 1956. 517 pp.

Chappell, Mack. "The Cupola House and Its Associations," *NCB*, XV (April, 1916), 203-217.

Chavis, John. "The Influence of John Chavis and Lunsford Lane on the History of North Carolina," *Jour. Negro Hist.*, XXV (1940), 14-24.

Cheek, Roma. *Sleeping Tar-Heels*. Durham, 1956. 95 pp.

Cheshire, Joseph B. "The Fundamental Constitutions of Carolina, and Religious Liberty in the Province of North Carolina," *P. E. Church Hist. Mag.*, I (1932), 221-264.

————. *Nonnulla, Stories, and Traditions, More or Less Authentic, About North Carolina*. Chapel Hill, 1930. 255 pp.

————. *Sketches of Church History in North Carolina*. Wilmington, 1892. 456 pp.

Chesnutt, Helen M. *Charles Waddell Chesnutt: Pioneer of the Color Line.* Chapel Hill, 1952. 324 pp.

Clapp, J. C., and J. C. Leonard. *Historic Sketches of the Reformed Church in North Carolina.* Philadelphia, 1908. 327 pp.

Clark, Ernest J. "Aspects of the North Carolina Slave Code, 1715-1860," *NCHR*, XXXIX, No. 2 (April, 1962), 148-164.

Clark, Rosamond. "A Sketch of Fort Dobbs," *NCB*, XIX (April, 1920), 133-138.

Clark, Walter. "The Edenton Tea-Party," *Mag. Hist.* IX (February, 1909), 86-91.

———— (ed.). *Histories of the Several Regiments and Battalions from North Carolina in the Great War, 1861-1865. Written by Members of the Respective Commands.* 5 vols. Raleigh, 1901.

————. "History of the Superior and Supreme Courts of North Carolina," *NCB*, XVIII (1918), 79-104.

————. "Indian Massacre and the Tuscarora War," *NCB*, II, No. 5 (1902), 3-16.

————. *North Carolina at Gettysburg, and Pickett's Charge a Misnomer.* Raleigh, 1921. 31 pp.

————. "North Carolina in the World War," *Proc. of N.C. Bar Assoc.* (1923), 57-72.

————. "North Carolina Troops at Gettysburg," *NCB*, XXII (1923), 71-108.

————. "The Raising, Organization, and Equipment of North Carolina Troops During the Civil War," *N.C. Lit. and Hist. Assoc. Proc.*, XXVIII (1919), 104-111.

————. "The State Motto and Its Origin," *NCB*, IX (January, 1910), 179-182.

Clarke, Desmond. *Arthur Dobbs Esquire, 1689-1765: Surveyor General of Ireland, Prospector and Governor of North Carolina.* Chapel Hill, 1957. 232 pp.

Clewell, J. H. *History of Wachovia in North Carolina.* New York, 1902. 365 pp.

Clonts, F. S. "Travel and Transportation in Colonial North Carolina," *NCHR,* III, No. 1 (January, 1926), 16-35.

Clowes, Chorley E. "John Stark Ravenscroft [1772-1830], First Bishop of North Carolina," *Am. Ch. Mo.,* XXIII (March, 1928), 37-47.

Coates, Albert. "A Century of Legal Education," *NCLR,* XXIV (1946), 307-401.

———. "Punishment for Crime in North Carolina," *NCLR,* XVII (1939), 205-232.

Coe, Joffre. "The Formative Cultures of the Carolina Piedmont," *Am. Phil. Soc. Trans.,* Vol. LIV (August, 1964). 130 pp.

Cobb, Collier. "Early English Survivals on Hatteras Island," *NCB,* XIV (October, 1914), 91-99.

Coffin, Levi. *Reminiscences of Levi Coffin.* Cincinnati, 1876. 712 pp.

Cole, A. C. *The Whig Party in the South.* Washington, 1913. 392 pp.

Collins, Herbert. "The Idea of a Cotton Textile Industry in the South, 1870-1890," *NCHR,* XXXIV, No. 3 (July, 1957), 358-392.

Collins, W. H. *The Domestic Slave Trade in the Southern States.* New York, 1904. 154 pp.

"Colonial Coast Forts on the South Atlantic Coast," *Artillery Jour.,* LXX (January, 1929), 41-62.

Conkin, Paul. "The Church Establishment in North Carolina, 1765-1776." *NCHR,* XXXII, No. 1 (January, 1955), 1-30.

Connor, H. G. "The Convention of 1835," *NCB,* VII, No. 2 (October, 1908), 89-110.

———. "The Granville Estate and North Carolina," *Pa. Law Rev.* (1914), 671-697.

———. "James Iredell, 1751-1799," *NCB,* XI, No. 4 (April, 1912), 201-250.

———. "Thomas Jordan Jarvis and the Rebuilding of North

Carolina," *N.C. Lit. and Hist. Assoc. Proc.*, XVI (1916), 81-97.

Connor, R. D. W. *Ante-Bellum Builders of North Carolina.* Greensboro, 1914. 149 pp.

———. *The Beginnings of English America: Sir Walter Raleigh's Settlements on Roanoke Island, 1584-1587.* Raleigh, 1907. 39 pp.

———. *Canova's Statue of Washington.* Raleigh, 1910. 96 pp.

———. "Captain Blakeley in the War of 1812," *The North Carolina Review,* April 6, 1913.

——— (ed.). *A Documentary History of the University of North Carolina, 1776-1799* (edited by L. R. Wilson and Hugh T. Lefler) 2 vols., Chapel Hill, 1953.

———. *Cornelius Harnett: An Essay in North Carolina History.* Raleigh, 1909. 209 pp.

———. "The Early Settlers of North Carolina; A Refutation of the Character assigned to them in *Old Virginia and Her Neighbors,*" *The North Carolina Review,* October 2, 1910.

———. "The Genesis of Higher Education in North Carolina," *NCHR,* XXVIII, No. 1 (January, 1951), 1-14.

———. "Governor Samuel Johnston of North Carolina," *NCB,* XI, No. 4 (1912), 259-285.

———. *History of North Carolina: The Colonial and Revolutionary Periods.* Chicago, 1919. 519 pp.

———. "John Harvey," *NCB,* VIII, No. 1 (1908), 3-42.

———. "John Motley Morehead," *NCB,* XII, No. 3 (1913), 173-192.

———. *Makers of North Carolina History.* 2nd ed. Raleigh, 1930. 350 pp. For young readers.

———. *North Carolina: Rebuilding An Ancient Commonwealth.* 2 vols. Chicago, 1929.

———. "North Carolina As a Proprietary," *The South in the Building of the Nation.* 12 vols. Richmond, 1909. I, 413-440.

——— (ed.). *North Carolina Manual, 1913.* Raleigh, 1913. 1053 pp.

———. "North Carolina's Priority in the Demand for Independence," *Sou. Atl. Quar.*, VIII, No. 3 (July, 1909), 235-254.

——. "The Peabody Education Fund," *Sou. Atl. Quar.*, IV, No. 2 (April, 1905), 169-181.

——. *Race Elements in the White Population of North Carolina.* Raleigh, 1920. 115 pp.

——. *Revolutionary Leaders of North Carolina.* Greensboro, 1916. 125 pp.

——. "Samuel A'Court Ashe," *NCHR*, III, No. 1 (January, 1926), 132-134.

——. "The Settlement of the Cape Fear," *Sou. Atl. Quar.*, VI, No. 3 (July, 1907), 272-287.

——. "The Voyage of Verrazzano: The First Exploration of the North Carolina Coast by Europeans," *NCB*, XVI (April, 1917), 209-218.

——. "Walter Hines Page: A Southern Nationalist," *Journal of Social Forces*, II, No. 2 (January, 1924), 164-168.

——. "William Gaston, A Southern Federalist of the Old School and His Yankee Friends, 1788-1844," *Am. Antiq. Soc. Proc.* (October, 1933). 68 pp.

——, and Clarence Poe (eds.). *Life and Speeches of Charles Brantley Aycock.* New York, 1912. 369 pp.

Cook, Florence. "Procedure in the North Carolina Colonial Assembly, 1731-1770," *NCHR*, VIII, No. 3 (July, 1931), 258-283.

Cook, Raymond A. "The Man Behind the Birth of a Nation [Thomas Dixon]" *NCHR*, XXXIX, No. 4 (October, 1962), 519-540.

Cooke, Charles S. "The Governor, Council, and Assembly in Royal North Carolina," *JSHP*, XII, No. 1 (January, 1912), 7-40.

Cooke, W. D. (comp.). *Revolutionary History of North Carolina.* New York, 1853. 236 pp.

Coon, Charles L: "The Beginnings of the North Carolina City Schools, 1867-1887," *Sou. Atl. Quar.*, XII, No. 3 (July, 1913), 235-247.

——— (ed.). *The Beginnings of Public Education in North*

*Carolina: A Documentary History, 1790-1840.* 2 vols. Releigh, 1908.

———. "North Carolina in the School Geographies 110 Years Ago," *NCHR,* III, No. 1 (January, 1926), 36-51.

——— (ed.). *North Carolina Schools and Academies, 1790-1840: A Documentary History.* Raleigh, 1915. lii, 846 pp.

———. "School Support and Our North Carolina Courts," *NCHR,* III, No. 3 (July, 1926), 399-438.

Cooper, Arthur W. *Smith Island and the Cape Fear Peninsula.* Raleigh, 1964. xv, 80 pp.

Corbitt, D. L. "Congressional Districts of North Carolina, 1789-1934," *NCHR,* XII, No. 2 (April, 1935), 173-188.

———. *Explorations, Descriptions, and Attempted Settlements of Carolina, 1584-1590.* Raleigh, 1948; revised ed., 1953. 154 pp.

———. *The Formation of North Carolina Counties, 1663-1943.* Raleigh, 1950. xix, 323 pp.

———. "Judicial Districts of North Carolina, 1746-1934," *NCHR,* XII, No. 1 (January, 1936), 45-61.

——— (ed.). "Letters from Hugh Lackey, Raleigh Hatter, 1843," *NCHR,* XXV, No. 2 (April, 1948), 179-192.

———. "The North Carolina Gazette," *NCHR,* XII, No. 1 (January, 1936), 45-61.

——— (ed.). *Public Papers and Letters of Cameron Morrison, Governor of North Carolina, 1921-1925.* Raleigh, 1927. xlviii, 365 pp.

——— (ed.). *Public Papers and Letters of Angus Wilton McLean, Governor of North Carolina, 1925-1929.* Raleigh, 1931. xxvii, 921 pp.

——— (ed.). *Public Papers and Letters of Oliver Max Gardner, Governor of North Carolina, 1929-1933.* Raleigh, 1937. lxiii, 788 pp.

——— (ed.). *Addresses, Letters, and Papers of John Christoph Blucher Ehringhaus, Governor of North Carolina, 1933-1937.* Raleigh, 1950. xxi, 509 pp.

——— (ed.). *Addresses, Letters, and Papers of Clyde Roark Hoey, Governor of North Carolina, 1937-1941.* Raleigh, 1944. xxxi, 869 pp.

—————— (ed.). *Public Addresses, Letters, and Papers of Joseph Melville Broughton, Governor of North Carolina, 1941-1945.* Raleigh, 1950. xx, 718 pp.

—————— (ed.). *Public Addresses and Papers of Robert Gregg Cherry, Governor of North Carolina, 1945-1949.* Raleigh, 1951. lxii, 1058 pp.

—————— (ed.). *Public Addresses, Letters, and Papers of William Kerr Scott, Governor of North Carolina, 1949-1953.* Raleigh, 1957. xxxii, 626 pp.

—————— (ed.). *Public Addresses, Letters, and Papers of William Bradley Umstead, Governor of North Carolina, 1953-1954.* Raleigh, 1957. xxxi, 414 pp.

—————— (ed.). "The Robert J. Miller Letters, 1813-1831," *NCHR,* XXV, No. 4 (October, 1948), 485-521.

—————— *Secretaries of the U.S. Navy: Brief Sketches of Five North Carolinians,* Raleigh, 1958. 18 pp.

——————, and Elizabeth Wilborn (eds.). *Civil War Pictures.* Raleigh, 1961. Third printing, 1967. (90 pp.) Seventy-five pictures and seventeen pages of text.

—————— . "Thomas Macknight," *NCHR,* II, No. 4 (October, 1925), 502-525.

Corkran, David H. *The Cherokee Frontier: Conflict and Survival, 1740-62.* 302 pp. Norman, Oklahoma, 1962.

—————— . "Cherokee Pre-History," *NCHR,* XXXIV, No. 4 (October, 1957), 455-466.

—————— . "The Unpleasantness at Stecoe," *NCHR,* XXXII, No. 3 (July, 1955), 358-375.

Couch, W. T. (ed.). *Culture in the South.* Chapel Hill, 1934. 711 pp.

—————— . "Twenty Years of Southern Publishing," *Va. Quar. Rev.,* XXVI (April, 1950), 171-185.

Coulter, E. M. *The Confederate States of America, 1861-1865.* Baton Rouge, 1950. 644 pp.

—————— . "The Granville District," *JSHP,* XIII, No. 1 (1913), 35-56.

—————— . "Sherman and the South," *NCHR,* VII, No. 1 (January, 1931), 41-54.

————. *The South during Reconstruction, 1865-1877.* Baton Rouge, 1947. 426 pp.

Coxe, Daniel. *A Description of the English Province of Carolina.* London, 1722. 122 pp.

Coyle, John G. "Cornelius Harnett," *Am. Irish Hist. Soc. Jour.,* XXIX (1931), 148-156.

Crabtree, Beth. *North Carolina Governors, 1585-1958: Brief Sketches.* Raleigh, 1958. 137 pp.

Craig, Alberta R. "Old Wentworth Sketches," *NCHR,* XI, No. 3 (July, 1934), 185-204.

Craig, Barbara. *The Wright Brothers and Their Development of the Airplane.* Raleigh, 1960. 23 pp.

Craig, D. I. *History of the Development of the Presbyterian Church in North Carolina.* Richmond, 1907. 192 pp.

Craig, James H. *The Arts and Crafts in North Carolina, 1696-1840.* Old Salem, 1965. 480 pp.

Craig, Marjorie (ed.). "Home-life in Rockingham County in the 'Eighties and 'Nineties," *NCHR,* XXXIII, No. 4 (October, 1956), 510-528.

Crane, V. W. *The Southern Frontier, 1670-1732.* Durham, 1928. 391 pp.

Craven, Avery O. *The Civil War in the Making, 1815-1860.* Baton Rouge, 1959. 115 pp.
————. *The Coming of the Civil War.* New York, 1942. 491 pp.; rev. ed. Chicago, 1957.
————. *The Growth of Southern Nationalism, 1848-1861.* Baton Rouge, 1953. 433 pp.

Craven, Charles. "The Robeson County Uprising against the KKK," *Sou. Atl. Quar.,* LVII, No. 4 (October, 1958), 433-442.

Craven, Wesley Frank. *The Southern Colonies in the Seventeenth Century, 1607-1689.* Baton Rouge, 1949. 451 pp.

Creecy, R. B. *Grandfather's Tales of North Carolina History.*

Raleigh, 1901. 301 pp. (93 sketches of history, biography, and legend.)

———. "What I Know about 'Shocco Jones,'" TCHS, *Papers,* II (1898), 29-33.

Crenshaw, Ollinger. "The Psychological Background of the Election of 1860 in the South," *NCHR,* XIX, No. 3 (July, 1942), 260-279.

Crittenden, C. C. *The Commerce of North Carolina, 1763-1789.* New Haven, 1937. 196 pp.

———. "Inland Navigation in North Carolina, 1763-1789," *NCHR,* VIII, No. 2 (April, 1931), 145-154.

———. "Means of Communication in North Carolina, 1763-1789," *NCHR,* VIII, No. 4 (October, 1931), 373-383.

———. "North Carolina Newspapers before 1790," *JSHP,* XX, No. 1 (1928), 1-83.

———. "Overland Travel and Transportation in North Carolina, 1763-1789," *NCHR,* VIII, No. 3 (July, 1931), 239-257.

———. "The Seacoast in North Carolina History, 1763-1789," *NCHR,* VII, No. 4 (October, 1930), 433-442.

———. "Ships and Shipping in North Carolina, 1763-1789," *NCHR,* VIII, No. 1 (January, 1931), 1-13.

———. "The Surrender of the Charter of Carolina," *NCHR,* I, No. 4 (October, 1924), 383-402.

———, and Dan Lacy (eds.). *The Historical Records of North Carolina.* 3 vols. Raleigh, 1938-1939.

Cronon, E. David. "Josephus Daniels as a Reluctant Candidate," *NCHR,* XXXIII, No. 4 (October, 1956), 457-482.

Cross, A. L. *The Anglican Episcopate and the American Colonies.* New York, 1902. 368 pp.

Cross, Tom Peete. "Witchcraft in North Carolina," *Studies in Philology,* XVI, No. 3 (July, 1910), 217-287.

Crowell, John F. *Personal Recollections of Trinity College, North Carolina, 1887-1894.* Durham, 1939. (Preface by C. L. Raper). 280 pp.

Cumming, W. P. "The Identity of John White Governor of

Roanoke and John White the Artist," *NCHR*, XV, No. 3 (July, 1938), 197-203.

―――. "Naming Carolina," *NCHR*, XXII, No. 1 (January, 1945), 34-42.

―――. *North Carolina in Maps*. Raleigh, 1966. 36 pp.

―――. *The Southeast in Early Maps*. Princeton, 1958; Chapel Hill, 1962. 275 pp. 67 maps.

Cunningham, H. H. *Doctors in Gray: The Confederate Medical Service*. Baton Rouge, 1958. 338 pp.

―――. "Edmund Burke Haywood and Raleigh's Confederate Hospitals," *NCHR*, XXXV, No. 2 (April, 1958), 153-166.

―――. "Organization and Administration of the Confederate Medical Department," *NCHR*, XXXI, No. 3 (July, 1954), 385-409.

Cunningham, Noble E., Jr., "Nathaniel Macon and the Southern Protest against National Consolidation," *NCHR*, XXXII, No. 3 (July, 1953), 376-384.

Curtis, Robert S. *The History of Livestock in North Carolina*. Raleigh, 1956. 116 pp.

Curtis, Zeb F. "William J. Yates," TCHS, *Papers*, II (1898), 21-28

Cutten, George B. *The Silversmiths of North Carolina*. Raleigh, 1948. 93 pp.

Dailey, Douglas C. "The Elections of 1872 in North Carolina," *NCHR*, XL, No. 3 (July, 1963), 338-360.

Dalzell, George W. *Benefit of Clergy in America & Related Matters*. Winston-Salem, 1955. 299 pp.

Daniels, Jonathan. *Prince of Carpetbaggers* [Milton S. Littlefield]. Philadelphia, 1958. 319 pp.

―――. *A Southerner Discovers the South*. New York, 1938. 346 pp.

―――. *Tar Heels: A Portrait of North Carolina*. New York, 1941. 347 pp.

―――. "The University of North Carolina." *Holiday*, V (June, 1949), 98-105, 152-153.

Daniels, Josephus. "Charles Brantley Aycock—Historical Address," *NCHR*, I, No. 3 (July, 1924), 251-276.

———. *Editor in Politics*. Chapel Hill, 1941. 644 pp.

———. *Tar Heel Editor*. Chapel Hill, 1939. 544 pp.

———. *The Wilson Era*. 2 vols. Chapel Hill, 1944.

Daves, E. G. "Raleigh's New Fort in Virginia 1585," TCHS, *Papers*, I (1897), 27-52.

Davidson, Chalmers. "Catawba Springs—Carolina's Spa," *NCHR*, XXVIII, No. 4 (October, 1951), 414-425.

———. *Piedmont Partisan: The Life and Times of Brigadier-General William Lee Davidson*. Davidson, N.C., 1951. 190 pp.

———. "Three Hundred Years of Carolina History," *NCHR*, XL, No. 2 (April, 1963), 213-220.

Davidson, Elizabeth Huey. *Child Labor Legislation in the Southern Textile States*. Chapel Hill, 1939. 302 pp.

———. "The Child-Labor Problem in North Carolina, 1883-1903," *NCHR*, XIII, No. 2 (April, 1936), 105-121.

———. "Child-Labor Reforms in North Carolina Since 1903," *NCHR*, XIV, No. 2 (April, 1937), 109-134.

———. "Early Development of Public Opinion against Southern Child Labor," *NCHR*, XIV, No. 3 (July, 1937), 230-250.

———. "The Establishment of the English Church in Continental American Colonies," TCHS, *Papers*, XX (1936), 94 pp.

Davidson, Philip G. "Industrialism in the Ante-Bellum South," *Sou. Atl. Quar.*, XXVII, No. 1 (January, 1928), 405-425.

———. *Propaganda and the American Revolution, 1763-1783*. Chapel Hill, 1941. xvi, 460 pp.

———. "Sons of Liberty and Stamp Men," *NCHR*, IX, No. 1 (January, 1932), 38-56.

Davis, Burke. *The Cowpens-Guilford Courthouse Campaign*. Philadelphia, 1962. 208 pp.

Davis, Jedith Roan. "Reconstruction in Cleveland County," TCHS, *Papers,* X (1914), 5-31.

Davis, Junius. "Some Facts about John Paul Jones." Part I, *Sou. Atl. Quar.,* IV (October, 1905), 378-391; Part II, *Sou. Atl. Quar.,* V (January, 1906), 50-64.

Davis, Lambert. "North Carolina and the University Press," *NCHR,* XLIII, No. 2 (January, 1959), 149-156.

Davis, Sallie. "North Carolina's Part in the Revolution," *Sou. Atl. Quar.,* II, No. 4 (1903), 314-324; III (January-July, 1904), 27-38, 154-165.

Dedmond, Francis B. (ed.). "Editor Hayne to Editor Kingsbury: Three Significant Unpublished Letters," *NCHR,* XXXII, No. 1 (January, 1955), 92-101.

De Filipis, M. "Italian Account of Cherokee Uprisings at Fort Loudoun and Fort Prince George, 1760-1761," *NCHR,* X, No. 3 (July, 1943), 247-258.

Delaney, Norman C. "Charles Henry Foster and the Unionists of Eastern Carolina," *NCHR,* XXXVII, No. 3 (July, 1960), 348-366.
———. "The Outer Banks of North Carolina during the Revolutionary War," *NCHR,* XXXVI, No. 1 (January, 1959), 1-16.

Delap, Simeon A. "The Populist Party in North Carolina," TCHS, *Papers,* XIV (1922), 40-74.

DeMond, Robert O. *The Loyalists in North Carolina during the Revolution.* Durham, 1940. 286 pp.

Dent, Sanders. "Francis Lister Hawks," TCHS, *Papers,* I (1897), 56-65.
———. "The Origin and Development of the Ku Klux Clan," TCHS, *Papers,* I (1897), 27-52.

De Santis, Vincent P. "President Garfield and the 'Solid South,'" *NCHR,* XXXVI, No. 4 (October, 1959), 442-465.

Des Champs, Margaret B. "John Chavis As a Preacher to the Whites," *NCHR,* XXXII, No. 2 (April, 1955), 165-172.

De Vorsey, Louis, Jr. *The Indian Boundary in the Southern Colonies, 1763-1775.* Chapel Hill, 1966. xii, 267 pp.

Deyton, Jason B. "The Toe River Valley to 1865," *NCHR,* XXIV, No. 4 (October, 1947), 423-466.

Dickson, William. "A Picture of the Last Days of the Revolutionary War in North Carolina," *NCB,* XXI (1922), 59-67.

Dill, Alonzo T. "Eighteenth Century New Bern," *NCHR,* XXII, Nos. 1, 2, 3, 4 (January, April, July, October, 1945), 1-21, 152-175, 292-319, 460-489; XXIII, Nos. 1, 2, 3, 4, (January, April, July, October, 1946), 47-78, 142-171, 325-359, 405-535.

———. *Governor Tryon and His Palace.* Chapel Hill, 1955. 304 pp.

———. "Public Buildings in Craven County, 1722-1835," *NCHR,* XX, No. 4 (October, 1943), 301-326.

———. "Tryon's Palace—A Neglected Niche of North Carolina History," *NCHR,* XIX, No. 2 (April, 1942), 119-167.

———, and Fred J. Allred (eds.). "The Founding of New Bern: A Footnote," *NCHR,* XLI, No. 3 (July, 1963), 361-374.

———. "Some Early Physicians of the Albemarle," *NCB,* IX (July, 1911), 17-25.

———. "The Indian Tribes of Eastern North Carolina," *NCB,* VI (July, 1906), 3-26.

Dillard, Richard. *The Historic Tea-Party of Edenton, October 25th, 1774.* 6th ed. Edenton, 1925. 170 pp.

———. "Some North Carolina Heroines of the Revolution," *NCB,* VIII (April, 1909), 325-333.

Dirket, A. L. "The Noble Savage Convention Epitomized in Lawson's *A New Voyage to Carolina,*" *NCHR,* XLIII, No. 4 (October, 1957), 455-466.

Dodd, W. E. *The Cotton Kingdom.* New Haven, 1921. 161 pp.

———. *The Life of Nathaniel Macon.* Raleigh, 1903. 443 pp.

———. "North Carolina in the Revolution," *Sou. Atl. Quar.,* I, No. 2 (1902), 156-161.

————. *The Old South: Struggles for Democracy.* New York, 1937. 312 pp.

Doran, Joseph I. "Sir Walter Raleigh, Chief Governor of Virginia and Founder of Roanoke Colony," *Pa. Soc. Col. Governor's Publ.,* I (1916), 52-72.

Dorris, Jonathan T. "Pardoning North Carolinians," *NCHR,* XXIII, No. 3 (July, 1946), 360-401.

Dortch, Hugh. "Lest We Forget: North Carolina's Commemoration of the War Between the States," *NCHR,* XXXVI, No. 2 (April, 1959), 163-167.

Douglas, Clarence D. "Conscription and the Writ of Habeas Corpus in North Carolina During the Civil War," TCHS, *Papers,* XIV (1922), 5-39.

Douglass, Elisha P. *Rebels and Democrats: The Struggle for Equal Political Rights and Majority Rule during the American Revolution.* Chapel Hill, 1955. 368 pp.

————. "Thomas Burke, Disillusioned Democrat," *NCHR,* XXVI, No. 2 (April, 1949), 150-186.

Douty, H. M. "Early Labor Organizations in North Carolina, 1800-1900," *Sou. Atl. Quar.,* XXXIV, No. 3 (July, 1935), 260-268.

Dowd, Clement. *The Life of Zebulon B. Vance.* Charlotte, 1897. 493 pp.

Drake, William E. *Higher Education in North Carolina before 1860.* New York, 1964. 283 pp.

Draper, Lyman. *King's Mountain and Its Heroes.* Cincinnati, 1881. 612 pp. reprint. Marietta, Georgia, 1954.

————. "The Revolutionary War in North Carolina: Narrative of John Hodges Drake of Nash County," *Publ. Southern Hist. Assoc.,* IV (1900), 14-21.

Driver, Carl. *John Sevier, Pioneer of the Old Southwest.* Chapel Hill, 1932. 240 pp.

Dumond, D. L. (ed.). *Southern Editorials on Secession.* New York, 1931. xxxiii, 529 pp.

Dunaway, W. F. *The Scotch-Irish of Colonial Pennsylvania.* Chapel Hill, 1944. 273 pp.

Dunbar, Gary S. *Geographical History of the North Carolina Outer Banks.* Baton Rouge, 1956. 249 pp.

Dunlap, Lily Doyle. "Old Waxhaw," *NCB,* XIX (April, 1920), 139-144.

Dunn, Charles W. "A North Carolina Gaelic Bard," *NCHR,* XXXVI, No. 4 (October, 1959), 473-475.

Durden, Robert F. "The Battle of the Standards in 1896 and North Carolina's Place in the Mainstream," *Sou. Atl. Quar.,* LXIII, No. 3 (Summer, 1964), 336-350.
——. "Governor Daniel L. Russell Explains His 'South Dakota Bond Scheme,'" *NCHR,* XXXVIII, No. 4 (October, 1961), 527-533.
——. *Reconstruction Bonds & Twentieth Century Politics: South Dakota v. North Carolina, 1904.* Durham, 1962. 274 pp.

Dykeman, Wilma. *The French Broad.* New York, 1955. 371 pp.

Earnhart, Hugh G. (ed.). "Aboard a Blockade Runner: Some Civil War Experiences of Jerome Du Shane," *NCHR,* XLIV, No. 4 (October, 1967), 392-399.

Eaton, Clement. "Edwin A. Alderman—Liberal of the New South," *NCHR,* XXIII, No. 2 (April, 1946), 206-221.
——. *Freedom of Thought in the Old South.* Durham, 1940. 343 pp.
——. *A History of the Old South.* New York, 1949. 636 pp.
——. *A History of the Southern Confederacy.* New York, 1954. 351 pp.
——. *The Mind of the Old South.* Baton Rouge, 1964. 271 pp.

Ebert, Charles H. V. "Furniture Making in High Point," *NCHR,* XXXVI, No. 3 (July, 1959), 330-339.

Edmonds, Helen G. *The Negro and Fusion Politics in North Carolina, 1894-1901.* Chapel Hill, 1951. 260 pp.

Edmonds, W. R. Revised by D. L. Corbitt. *The North Carolina State Flag.* Raleigh, 1913. (Sixth printing, Raleigh, 1966), 15 pp.

Eliason, Norman E. *Tarheel Talk: An Historical Study of the English Language in North Carolina to 1860.* Chapel Hill, 1956. 324 pp.

Ellen, John C. "Newspaper Finance in North Carolina's Piedmont and Mountain Region during the 1850's," *NCHR,* XXXVII, No. 4 (October, 1960), 488-505.

Eller, Ernest M. *"The House of Peace," being a Historical, Legendary, and Contemporary Account of the Moravians and their Settlement of Salem in North Carolina.* New York, 1937. 257 pp.

Elliot, Jonathan (ed.). *The Debates in the Several State Conventions on the Adoption of the Federal Constitution.* Washington, 1836-1845. Vol. IV, 1-25.

Elliott, Robert N., Jr. "James Davis and the Beginning of the Newspaper in North Carolina," *NCHR,* XLII, No. 1 (January, 1965), 1-20.
——. "The Nat Turner Insurrection As Reported in the Northern Press," *NCHR,* XXXVIII, No. 1 (January, 1961), 1-18.
——. *The Raleigh Register, 1799-1863.* Chapel Hill, 1955. 133 pp.

Emmerson, John C. *Steam Navigation in Virginia and Northeastern North Carolina Waters, 1826-1836.* Portsmouth, Va. 453 pp.

Emmons, Ebenezer. *Geological Report of the Midland Counties of North Carolina.* New York, 1856. xx, 351 pp.
——. *The Swamp Lands of North Carolina.* Raleigh, 1860. 95 pp.

Epler, Blanche N. "A Bit of Elizabethan England in America," *Nat. Geog. Mag.,* LXIV (1938), 695-730.

*Equal Protection of the Laws in North Carolina, Report of the North Carolina Advisory Committee of the United States*

*Commission on Civil Rights, 1959-1962.* Washington, 1963. 251 pp.

Ervin, Paul R. "Civil Rights in North Carolina," *NCLR,* Vol. 42, No. 1 (December, 1963) , 30-49.

Ervin, Sam J., Jr. "Federalism and Federal Grants-in-Aid," *NCLR,* Vol. 43, No. 3 (April, 1965), 487-501.

―――――. "The Provincial Agents of North Carolina," *JSHP,* XVI, No. 2 (1919), 63-67.

Eutsler, Roland B. "The Cape Fear and Yadkin Railroad," *NCHR,* II, No. 4 (October, 1925) , 427-441.

Evans, William McKee. *Ballots and Fence Rails: Reconstruction on the Lower Cape Fear.* Chapel Hill, 1967. 314 pp.

Ewing, Cortez A. M. "Two Reconstruction Impeachments," *NCHR,* XV, No. 3 (July, 1938) , 204-230.

Falk, Stanley L. "The Warrenton Female Academy of Joseph Mordecai, 1809-1818," *NCHR,* XXXV, No. 3 (July, 1955) , 281-298.

Fanning, David. *The Narrative of Colonel David Fanning.* Richmond, 1861. 92 pp. (See also *State Records,* XXII, 180-239.)

Faris, James J. "The Lowrie Gang—An Episode in the History of Robeson County," TCHS, *Papers,* XV (1925) , 55-93.

Farish, Hunter D. "An Overlooked Personality in Southern Life" [Samuel A. Hale], *NCHR,* XII, No. 4 (October, 1935) , 341-353.

Farmer, Fannie Memory. "The Bar Examination and Beginning Years of Legal Practice in North Carolina, 1820-1860," *NCHR,* XXIX, No. 2 (April, 1952) , 159-170.

―――――. "Legal Education in North Carolina, 1820-1860," *NCHR,* XXVIII, No. 3 (July, 1951), 271-353.

―――――. "Legal Practice and Ethics in North Carolina, 1820-1860," *NCHR,* XXX, No. 3 (July, 1953), 329-353.

Farrison, William E. "The Negro Population of Guilford

County, North Carolina, before the Civil War," *NCHR,* XXI, No. 4 (October, 1944), 319-329.

Faust, A. B. "The Graffenried Manuscripts," *Ger.-Am. Annals,* N.S. XI (September, 1913), 205-312.
———. *The German Element in the United States.* 2 vols. New York, 1909.
———. *Lists of Swiss Emigrants in the Eighteenth Century to the American Colonies.* 2 Vols. Washington, 1920-1925.

Ferguson, Robert L. "Colonel William J. Hicks," TCHS, *Papers,* VII (1907), 48-54.

Ferrell, John A. "The North Carolina Campaign against Hookworm Disease," *Sou. Atl. Quar.,* XI, No. 2 (April, 1912), 128-135.

Few, W. P. "Washington Duke," *Sou. Atl. Quar.,* IV, No. 3 (July, 1905), 203-208.

Fisher, Clyde O. "The Relief of Soldiers' Families in North Carolina during the Civil War," *Sou. Atl. Quar.,* XVI (January, 1917), 60-72.

Fiske, John. *Old Virginia and Her Neighbors.* 2 vols. Boston, 1897.

Fitch, W. E. *The First Founders in America. . . .* New York, 1913. 40 pp.
———. *Some Neglected History of North Carolina.* New York, 1905. 307 pp.

Flanagan, Beecher. *A History of State Banking in North Carolina to 1866.* Nashville, Tennessee. 253 pp.

Fleer, Jack D. *North Carolina Politics.* Chapel Hill, 1968. 163 pp.

Fleming, John K. *History of the Third Creek Presbyterian Church, Cleveland, North Carolina, 1787-1966.* Raleigh, 1967. 199 pp.

Fletcher, Inglis. *Lusty Wind for Carolina.* Indianapolis, 1944. 509 pp. Novel.

Flowers, Robert L. "Fort Hamby on the Yadkin," TCHS, *Papers,* I (1897), 1-9.

——. "John Joseph Bruner," TCHS, *Papers,* III (1899), 1-7.

——. "Matthew Whitaker Ransom: A Senator of the Old Regime," *Sou. Atl. Quar.,* IV, No. 2 (April, 1905), 159-168.

Folk, Edgar E. "W. W. Holden and the Election of 1858," *NCHR,* XXI, No. 4 (October, 1944), 294-318.

——. "W. W. Holden and the *North Carolina Standard,* 1843-1848: A Study in Political Journalism," *NCHR,* XIX, No. 1 (January, 1942), 22-47.

Ford, H. J. *The Scotch-Irish in America.* Princeton, 1915. 607 pp.

Ford, Paul M. "Calvin H. Wiley's View of the Negro," *NCHR,* XLI, No. 1 (January, 1964), 1-20.

Ford, W. C. "Early Maps of Carolina," *Geographical Rev.,* XVI (1926), 264-273.

——. "Dr. S. Millington Miller and the Mecklenburg Declaration," *AHR,* XXXI, No. 3 (April, 1906), 548-558.

Fordham, Jeff B. "Iredell's Dissent in Chisholm v. Georgia: Its Political Significance," *NCHR,* VIII, No. 2 (April, 1931), 155-167.

——, and William H. Hoyt. "Constitutional Restrictions Upon Public Debt in North Carolina," *NCLR,* Vol. 16 (1937-1938), 329-363.

Foreman, Grant. *Indian Removal: The Emigration of the Five Civilized Tribes of Indians.* Norman, Okla., 1932; reprint, 1953. 415 pp.

Foster, W. O. "The Career of Montfort Stokes in North Carolina," *NCHR,* XVI, No. 3 (July, 1939), 237-272.

Fox, Luther A. "Decline and Revival of the Lutheran Consciousness in the Carolinas," *Luth. Ch. Rev.,* XXXI (October, 1912), 658-677.

——. "Patriotism of the Germans in the Colonial South," I, *Luth. Ch. Rev.,* XXXVIII (Jan.-April, 1919), 10-17, 160-166.

Franklin, Earl R. "Henry Clay's Visit to Raleigh," TCHS, *Papers,* VII (1907), 55-63.

———. "The Instruction of United States Senators by North Carolina," TCHS, *Papers,* VII (1907), 5-15.

Franklin, John Hope. "The Free Negro in the Economic Life of Ante-Bellum North Carolina," *NCHR,* XIX, Nos. 3 and 4 (July and October, 1942), 239-259, 358-374.

———. *The Free Negro in North Carolina, 1790-1860.* Chapel Hill, 1943. 271 pp.

Franklin, W. Neil. "Agriculture in Colonial North Carolina," *NCHR,* III, No. 4 (October, 1926), 539-574.

———. "Some Aspects of Representation in the American Colonies," *NCHR,* VI, No. 1 (January, 1929), 38-66.

Frech, Laura P. "The Wilmington Committee of Public Safety and the Loyalist Risings of February, 1776," *NCHR,* XLI, No. 1 (January, 1964), 21-33.

Freel, Margaret Walker. *Our Heritage: The People of Cherokee County, North Carolina, 1540-1955.* Asheville, 1957. 407 pp.

Freud, Susanne H., and Alice B. Keith (trans. and eds.). "Prince Bernhard's Travels in the Carolinas, December, 1825," *NCHR,* XXVI, No. 4 (October, 1949), 446-459.

Frick, George Frederick, and Raymond Stearns. *Mark Catesby: The Colonial Audubon.* Urbana, Illinois, 1961. 137 pp.

Fries, Adelaide L. "Der North Carolina land und colonie établissement," *NCB,* IX (August, 1910), 199-214.

———. "The Lure of Historical Research," *NCHR,* I, No. 2 (April, 1924), 121-137.

———. "The Moravian Contribution to Colonial North Carolina," *NCHR,* VII, No. 1 (January, 1930), 1-14.

———. "North Carolina Certificates of the Revolutionary War Period," *NCHR,* IX, No. 3 (July, 1932), 229-241.

———. "One Hundred Years of Textiles in Salem," *NCHR,* XXVII, No. 1 (January, 1950), 1-19.

——— (ed.). *Records of the Moravians of North Carolina.* 8 vols. Raleigh, 1922-1954.

———. (ed.). "Report of the Brethren Abraham Steiner and Friederich Christian von Schweinitz of their Journey to the Cherokee Nation and in the Cumberland Settlements in the State of Tennessee, from 28th October to 28th December, 1799," *NCHR,* XXI, No. 4 (October, 1944), 330-375.

———. *The Road to Salem.* Chapel Hill, 1944. 316 pp.

———. *The Town Builders, Winston-Salem.* Raleigh, 1915. 19 pp.

——— (ed.). "Travel Journal of Charles A. Van Vleck, 1826," *NCHR,* VIII, No. 2 (April, 1931), 187-206.

Frome, Michael. *Strangers in High Places: The Story of the Great Smoky Mountains.* Garden City, N. Y., 1966. 394 pp.

Ganyard, Robert L. "Radicals and Conservatives in Revolutionary North Carolina: A Point at Issue, the October Election, 1776," *WMQ,* XXIV, No. 4 (October, 1967), 568-587.

———. "Threat from the West: North Carolina and the Cherokee, 1776-1778," *NCHR,* XLV, No. 1 (January, 1968), 47-66.

Garber, Paul N. *John Carlisle Kilgo, President of Trinity College, 1894-1910.* Durham, 1937. 412 pp.

———. *The Romance of American Methodism.* Greensboro, 1931. 343 pp.

Gardner, Dillard S. *The Continuous Revision of Our State Constitution.* Raleigh, 1957. 23 pp.

Gass, W. Conrad. "Kemp Plummer Battle and the Development of Historical Instruction at the University of North Carolina," *NCHR,* XLV, No. 1 (January, 1968), 1-22.

Gaston, William. "Judge Gaston and the Constitution of North Carolina," *Am. Cath. Hist. Records* (July, 1910), 293-296.

Gatewood, Willard B., Jr. "Eugene Clyde Brooks: Educational Journalist in North Carolina, 1906-1923," *NCHR,* XXXVI, No. 3 (July, 1957), 307-329.

————. *Eugene Clyde Brooks, Educator and Public Servant.* Durham, 1968. 279 pp.

————. "Eugene Clyde Brooks and Negro Education in North Carolina, 1919-1923, *NCHR,* XXXVIII, No. 3 (July, 1961), 362-379.

————. "North Carolina and Federal Aid to Education: Public Reaction to the Blair Bill, 1881-1890," *NCHR,* XL, No. 4 (October, 1963), 465-488.

————. "North Carolina's Role in the Establishment of the Great Smoky Mountains National Park," *NCHR,* XXXVII, No. 2 (April, 1960), 165-184.

————. "Politicians and Piety in North Carolina: The Fundamentalist Crusade at High Tide, 1925-1927," *NCHR,* XLII, No. 3 (July, 1965), 275-290.

————. *Preachers, Pedagogues & Politicians: The Evolution Controversy in North Carolina, 1920-1927.* Chapel Hill, 1966. 268 pp.

Gehrke, William H. "The Ante-Bellum Agriculture of the Germans in North Carolina," *Agric. Hist.,* IX (1935), 143-160.

————. "The Beginnings of the Pennsylvania German Element in Rowan and Cabarrus Counties," *Pa. Mag. Hist.,* LVIII (1934), 342-369.

————. "Negro Slavery among the Germans in North Carolina," *NCHR,* XIV, No. 4 (October, 1937), 307-432.

————. "The Transition from the German to the English Language in North Carolina," *NCHR,* XII, No. 1 (January, 1935), 1-19.

Gibbons, J. P. "Bart F. Moore on Secession and Reconstruction," TCHS, *Papers,* II (1898), 75-82.

Gibson, George H. "Attitudes in North Carolina Regarding the Independence of Cuba," *NCHR,* XLIII, No. 1 (January, 1966), 43-65.

————. "Opinion in North Carolina Regarding the Acquisition of Texas and Cuba, 1835-1855," *NCHR,* XXXVII, Nos. 1 and 2 (January and April, 1960), 1-21, 185-201.

——. "Twenty-Seven Tickets," *NCHR*, XXXVII, No. 4 (October, 1960) , 477-487.

Gibson, John M. "Walter Hines Page has been 'forgiven,' " *Sou. Atl. Quar.*, XXXII (1933), 283-293.

Gilbert, Dorothy. *Guilford, A Quaker College*. Greensboro. 1937. 359 pp.
—— (ed.). "Joe Cannon's North Carolina Background," *NCHR*, XXIII, No. 4 (October, 1946) , 471-482.

Gilpatrick, D. H. "Contemporary Opinion of Hugh Williamson," *NCHR*, XVII, No. 1 (January, 1940) , 26-36.
——. *Jeffersonian Democracy in North Carolina, 1789-1816*. New York, 1931. 257 pp.
——. "North Carolina Congressional Elections, 1803-1810," *NCHR*, X, No. 3 (July, 1933), 168-185.

Glasgow, Tom. "H.M.S. 'Tiger,' " *NCHR*, XLIII, No. 2 (April, 1966) , 115-121.

Gobbel, L. L. *Church-State Relationships in Education in North Carolina Since 1776*. Durham, 1938. 251 pp.
——. "The Militia of North Carolina in Colonial and Revolutionary Times," TCHS, *Papers*, XIII (1919) , 35-61.

Golden, Harry. "The Jewish People of North Carolina," *NCHR*, XXXII, No. 2 (April, 1955) , 194-216.

Goodloe, D. R. "North Carolina and the Georgia Boundary," *NCB*, III, No. 12 (April, 1904), 1-22.

Goodpasture, A. V. "Pepys and the Proprietors of Carolina," *Tenn. Hist. Mag.*, VI (October, 1920) , 166-176.

Govan, Thomas P. "An Ante-Bellum Attempt to Regulate the Price and Supply of Cotton," *NCHR*, XVII, No. 4 (October, 1940) , 302-312.

Graham, Edward K. "The Poetry of John Charles McNeill," *Sou. Atl. Quar.*, VI, No. 1 (January, 1907) , 81-86.

Graham, Ian C. C. *Colonists from Scotland: Emigration to North America, 1707-1783*. Ithaca, New York, 1956. 213 pp.

Graham, William A. "The North Carolina Union Men of

Eighteen Hundred and Sixty-One," *NCB*, XI (July, 1911), 3-16.

Grantham, Dewey W., Jr. "The Southern Senators and the League of Nations, 1918-1920," *NCHR*, XXVI, No. 2 (April, 1949), 187- 205.

Gray, L. C. *History of Agriculture in the Southern United States to 1860.* 2 vols. Washington, 1933.

Green, F. M. *Constitutional Development of the South Atlantic States, 1776-1960.* Chapel Hill, 1930. 328 pp.
———. "Electioneering 1802 Style," *NCHR*, XX, No. 3 (July, 1943), 238-246.
———. "George Davis, North Carolina Whig and Confederate Statesman," *NCHR*, XXIII, No. 4 (October, 1946), 449-470.
———. "Gold Mining: A Forgotten Industry in Ante-Bellum North Carolina," *NCHR*, XIV, Nos. 1 and 2 (January and April, 1937), 1-19, 135-155.
———. "Listen to the Eagle Scream: One Hundred Years of the Fourth of July in North Carolina," *NCHR*, XXXI, Nos. 3 and 4 (July and October, 1954), 295-320, 529-549.
———. "Resurgent Southern Sectionalism, 1933-1955," *NCHR*, XXXIII, No. 3 (April, 1956), 222-240.

Green, Paul. *The Highland Call.* Chapel Hill, 1941. 280 pp. Pageant.
———. *The Lost Colony.* Chapel Hill, 1939. 138 pp. Symphonic drama.

Greene, E. B., and V. D. Harrington. *American Population before the Federal Census of 1790.* New York, 1932. 228 pp.

Greene, G. W. *The Life of Nathanael Greene, Major General in the Army of the Revolution.* 3 vols. New York, 1867-1871.

Greene, Jack P. "The North Carolina Lower House and the Power to Appoint Public Treasurers, 1711-1775," *NCHR*, XL, No. 1 (January, 1963), 37-53.
———. *The Quest for Power: The Lower Houses of As-*

*sembly in the Southern Royal Colonies, 1689-1776.* Chapel Hill, 1963. 528 pp.

———. "The Publication of the Official Records of the Southern Colonies," *WMQ*, XIV, No. 3 (July, 1957), 268-280.

Griffin, Clarence W. "History and Progress of the Western North Carolina Historical Association," *NCHR*, XXXIII, No. 2 (April, 1956), 202-212.

Griffin, Richard W. "Reconstruction of the North Carolina Textile Industry, 1865-1885," *NCHR*, XLI, No. 1 (January, 1964), 34-53.

Grimes, J. Bryan. *The History of the Great Seal of the State of North Carolina, 1616-1909.* Revised by D. L. Corbitt. (Eighth printing, Raleigh, 1966.) 32 pp.

———. "Notes on Colonial North Carolina, 1700-1750," Raleigh, 1905. 69 pp.

Grissom, W. L. *History of Methodism in North Carolina. . . .* Nashville, 1905. 373 pp.

———. "Some First Things in North Carolina Methodism," TCHS, *Papers*, IX (1912), 22-32.

Groome, Bailey T. *Mecklenburg in the Revolution, 1740-1783.* Charlotte, 1931. 114 pp.

Guess, W. C. "County Government in Colonial North Carolina," *JSHP*, XI, No. 1 (1911), 7-39.

Gulick, John. *Cherokees at the Crossroads.* Chapel Hill, 1960. xv. 202 pp.

Haislip, Bryan. *A History of the Z. Smith Reynolds Foundation.* Winston-Salem, 1967. 119 pp.

Hamer, P. M. "Anglo-French Rivalry in the Cherokee Country, 1754-1757," *NCHR*, II, No. 3 (July, 1925), 303-322.

———. "Fort Loudoun in the Cherokee War, 1758-1761," *NCHR*, II, No. 4 (October, 1925), 442-458.

Hamilton, John B. (ed.). "Diary of Thomas Miles Garrett at the University of North Carolina, 1849," *NCHR*, Nos. 1, 2, 3, 4 (January, April, July, October, 1961), 64-93, 241-262, 380-410, 534-563.

Hamilton, J. G. de R. "Benjamin Sherwood Hedrick," *JSHP*, X, No. 1 (1910) , 1-42.

————— (ed.) . *The Correspondence of Jonathan Worth.* 2 vols. Raleigh, 1929.

—————. "The Elections of 1872 in North Carolina," *Sou. Atl. Quar.*, XI, No. 2 (April, 1912) , 143-152.

—————. "The Freedmen's Bureau in North Carolina," *Sou. Atl. Quar.*, VIII, Parts I and II, 53-67, 154-163.

—————. "George Patterson: North Carolinian by Adoption," *NCHR*, XXX, No. 2 (April, 1953) , 191-199.

—————. *History of North Carolina,* Vol. III, *North Carolina Since 1860.* Chicago, 1919. 434 pp.

————— (ed.) . "Letters of John Rust Eaton [1794-1815]," *JSHP*, IX (1910) , 25-59

—————. "The North Carolina Convention of 1865-1866," *N.C. Lit. and Hist. Assoc. Proc.*, XIV (1914), 56-68.

—————. "The North Carolina Courts and the Confederacy," *NCHR*, IV, No. 4 (October, 1927) , 366-403.

————— (ed.) . *The Papers of Randolph Shotwell.* 3 vols. Raleigh, 1929-1936.

————— (ed.) . *The Papers of Thomas Ruffin,* 2 vols. Raleigh, 1918-1920.

————— (ed.). *The Papers of William A. Graham.* 4 vols. Raleigh, 1957-1961.

—————. "Party Politics in North Carolina, 1835-1860," *JSHP*, XV, (1916) , 17-29.

—————. "The Preservation of North Carolina History," *NCHR*, IV, No. 1 (January, 1927) , 3-21.

—————. "The Prison Experiences of Randolph Shotwell," *NCHR*, II, Nos. 2, 3, 4 (April, July, October, 1925) , 147-161, 332-350, 459-474.

—————. *Reconstruction in North Carolina.* Raleigh, 1906. 264 pp.

—————. "Southern Members of the Inns of Court," *NCHR*, X, No. 4 (October ,1933), 273-286.

—————. "The Union League in North Carolina," *Sewanee Rev.*, XX (October, 1912) , 143-152.

Hamilton, Kenneth G. "The Moravians and Wachovia," *NCHR*, XLIV, No. 2 (April, 1967), 144-153.

Hamilton, Mary H. "Heraldry and Its Usage in the Colony of North Carolina," *NCB*, XIV (July, 1914), 3-27.

Hamilton, Peter J. *The Colonization of the South*. Philadelphia, 1904. xxiii, 494 pp.

Hamilton, William B. *Fifty Years of the South Atlantic Quarterly*. Durham, 1952. 397 pp.
———. "The Research Triangle of North Carolina: A Study in Leadership for the Common Weal," *Sou. Atl. Quar.*, LXV, No. 2 (April, 1966), 254-278.

Hamlin, Griffith A. "Educational Activities of the Disciples of Christ in North Carolina, 1852-1902," *NCHR*, XXXIII, No. 3 (July, 1956), 310-331.

Hammer, Carl, Jr. *Rhinelanders on the Yadkin: The Story of the Pennsylvania Germans in Rowan and Cabarrus*. Salisbury, 1943. 130 pp; 2nd ed. [rev.] Salisbury, 1965. 134 pp.

Hammond, Mrs. John D. "The Work of the General Education Board in the South," *Sou. Atl. Quar.*, XIV, No. 4 (October, 1915), 348-357.

Hamnett, W. L., and D. C. Thornton. *Tar Heel Wildlife*. Raleigh, 1953. 98 pp.

Hanna, C. A. *The Scotch-Irish*. 2 vols., New York, 1902.

Hariot, Thomas. *A Brief and True Report of the New Found Land of Virginia*. London, 1588. 33 pp.

Harlan, Louis R. *Separate and Unequal: Public School Campaigns and Racism in the Southern Seaboard States*. Chapel Hill, 1958. xii, 290 pp.

Harman, Henry E. "John Charles McNeill and His Work," *Sou. Atl. Quar.*, XV, No. 4 (October, 1916), 301-308.

Harmon, George D. "Benjamin Hawkins and the Federal Factory System," *NCHR*, IX, No. 2 (April, 1932), 138-152.
———. "The Military Experiences of James A. Peifer, 1861-

1865," *NCHR,* XXXII, Nos. 2 and 3 (July and October, 1955) , 385-409, 544-572.

———. "The North Carolina Cherokees and the New Echota Treaty of 1835," *NCHR,* VI, No. 3 (July, 1929) , 239-253.

Harper, Roland M. "A Statistical Study of the Croatans," *Rural Sociology,* II (1937) , 444-456.

Harrell, Isaac. "Gates County to 1860," TCHS, *Papers,* XII (1916), 56-106.

———. "North Carolina Loyalists," *NCHR,* III, No. 4 (October, 1926) , 575-590.

Harrill, Fannie G. "Old Fort Dobbs," *D.A.R. Mag.,* XLV (December, 1914) , 299-303.

Harrington, J. C. "Archeological Exploration of Fort Raleigh National Historic Site," *NCHR,* XXVIII, No. 3 (April, 1949) , 127-149.

———. "Evidence of Manual Reckoning in the 'Cittie of Raleigh,' " *NCHR,* XXVI, No. 1 (January, 1956), 1-11.

———. "The Manufacture and Use of Bricks at the Raleigh Settlement on Roanoke Island," *NCHR,* XLIV, No. I (January, 1969) , 1-17.

———. *Search for the Cittie of Raleigh.* Washington, 1962. 63 pp.

Harris, Bernice Kelly. "A Land More Large Than Earth," *NCHR,* XXXIX, No. 2 (April, 1962) , 175-180.

Haskins, J. A. "George Washington in Guilford," *NCB,* XIX (January, 1920) , 107-115.

Hathaway, J. R. B. *The North Carolina Historical and Genealogical Register.* 3 vols. Edenton, 1900-1903. *Index and Digest . . . with Genealogical Notes and Annotations,* ed. by Worth S. Ray. Austin, Texas, 1945. (Genealogies of sixty North Carolina families.)

Hawks, F. L. *History of North Carolina.* 2 vols. Fayetteville, 1857-1858.

Hayden, Harry. *The Story of the Wilmington Rebellion.* Wilmington, 1936. 32 pp.

Haywood, C. Robert. "The Mind of the North Carolina Advocates of Mercantilism," *NCHR,* XXXIII, No. 2 (April, 1956), 139-165.

———. "The Mind of the North Carolina Opponents of the Stamp Act," *NCHR,* XXIX, No. 3 (July, 1952), 317-343.

Haywood, M. deL. *The Beginnings of Freemasonry in North Carolina and Tennessee.* Raleigh, 1906. 86 pp.

———. "Canova's Statue of Washington," *Sou. Atl. Quar.,* I, No. 3 (July, 1902), 278-287.

———. "An Early Peace Society in North Carolina, 1819-1822," *NCB,* VII (April, 1908), 290-300.

———. "Governor Charles Eden," *NCB,* III, No. 8 (December, 1903), 1-24.

———. *Governor William Tryon and His Administration in the Province of North Carolina, 1765-1771.* Raleigh, 1903. 233 pp.

———. "Grand Masters Spaight, Jenkins, and Clark," *NCB,* XXI (1922), 68-76.

———. *Lives of the Bishops of North Carolina.* Raleigh, 1910. 270 pp.

———. "Sir Richard Everard, Baronet, Governor of the Colony of North Carolina, 1725-1731," *NCB,* XIV (July, 1914), 50-61.

———. "The State Navy of North Carolina in the War of the Revolution," *NCB,* XVII (July, 1917), 48-56.

———. "Story of Queen's College or Liberty Hall," *NCB,* XI (January, 1912), 278-287.

———. "Thomas and Henry John Burgess, Church of England Missionaries in the Provinces of Virginia and North Carolina during the Eighteenth Century," *NCB,* XXIII (1926), 63-73.

*Heads of Families: First Census of the United States—1790: North Carolina.* Washington, 1908. Reprint, Spartanburg, S.C. 1961.

Heard, Alexander. *A Two-Party South?* Chapel Hill, 1952. 334 pp.

———, and Donald S. Strong. *Southern Primaries and Elections, 1920-1949.* Tuscaloosa, Ala., 1950. 206 pp.

Hecht, Arthur. "Postal History of North Carolina, 1789-1795," *NCHR*, XXXV, No. 2 (April, 1958), 125-152.

Heckman, Oliver S. "The Presbyterian Church of the United States of America in Southern Reconstruction, 1860-1880," *NCHR*, XX, No. 3 (July, 1943), 219-237.

Helper, Hinton Rowan. *The Impending Crisis of the South: How to Meet It.* New York, 1857. 420 pp.

Henderson, Archibald. *The Campus of the First State University.* Chapel Hill, 1949. 421 pp.

―――. *The Conquest of the Old Southwest: The Romantic Story of the Early Pioneers into Virginia, the Carolinas, Tennessee, and Kentucky, 1740-1790.* New York, 1920. 395 pp.

―――. *Cradle of Liberty: Historical Essays Concerning the Mecklenburg Declaration of Independence.* . . . Charlotte, 1955. 53 pp.

―――. "Early Drama and Professional Entertainment in North Carolina," *Reviewer*, V (July-October, 1925), 47-57, 68-77.

――― (ed.). "Herman Husband's Continuation of the *Impartial Relation*," *NCHR*, XVIII, No. 1 (January, 1941), 48-81.

―――. "John Steele [1764-1815]," *NCB*, XVIII, Nos. 3 and 4 (January and April, 1919), 123-133, 159-177.

―――. "The Mecklenburg Declaration of Independence," *Jour. Sou. Hist.*, VI, No. 4 (1912), 781-788.

―――. *North Carolina, the Old North State and the New.* 3 vols. Chicago, 1941.

―――. "North Carolina and the Ulster Scot," *NCB*, XXIII (1926), 51-56.

―――. "The Origin of the Regulation in North Carolina," *AHR*, XXI, No. 2 (January, 1916), 320-332.

―――. *The Revolution in North Carolina in 1775: Transylvania, Craven, Anson, and Mecklenburg.* Chapel Hill, 1916. 18 pp.

――― (ed.). "Robert Henry's Narrative," TCHS, *Papers*, III (1899), 16-24.

————. *The Star of Empire: Phases of the Westward Movement in the Old Southwest.* Durham, 1919. 86 pp.

————. "The Treaty of Long Island of Holston, July, 1777," *NCIIR,* VIII, No. 1 (January, 1931), 55-116.

————. *Washington's Southern Tour, 1791.* Boston, 1923. 339 pp.

Hendren, Linville L. "De Graffenreid and the Swiss and Palatine Settlement of New Berne, N.C.," TCHS, *Papers,* IV (1900), 64-71.

Hendrick, B. J. *The Training of an American: The Earlier Life and Letters of Walter Hines Page, 1855-1913.* New York, 1928. 444 pp.

Herbert, H. A., and others. *Why the Solid South? or Reconstruction and Its Results.* Baltimore, 1890. 452 pp. (See Article by Zebulon B. Vance, 70-84.)

Herndon, G. Melvin. "Indian Agriculture in the Southern Colonies," *NCHR,* XLIV, No. 3 (July, 1967), 283-297.

Herring, Harriet. "Cycles of Cotton Mill Criticism," *Sou. Atl. Quar.,* XXVIII, No. 2 (July, 1929), 113-125.

————. *Passing of the Mill Village.* Chapel Hill, 1949. 137 pp.

————. *Welfare Work in Mill Villages.* Chapel Hill, 1929. 406 pp.

Hesseltine, W. B. *Civil War Prisons: A Study in War Psychology.* Columbus, Ohio, 1930. 290 pp.

Heyman, Max L. " 'The Great Reconstructor,' General E. R. S. Canby and the Second Military District," *NCHR,* XXXI, No. 1 (January, 1955), 52-80.

Hicks, John D. "The Farmers' Alliance in North Carolina," *NCHR,* II, No. 2 (April, 1925), 162-187.

————. *The Populist Revolt: A History of the Farmers' Alliance and the People's Party.* Minneapolis, 1931. 473 pp.

————, and John D. Barnhart. "The Farmers' Alliance," *NCHR,* VI, No. 3 (July, 1929), 254-280.

Higginbotham, Don. *Daniel Morgan, Revolutionary Rifleman.* Chapel Hill, 1961. 239 pp.

High, James. "Henry McCulloh, Progenitor of the Stamp Act," *NCHR*, XXIX, No. 1 (January, 1952), 24-38.

Hill, D. H. *North Carolina in the War Between the States, Bethel to Sharpsburg.* 2 vols. Raleigh, 1926.

Hilldrup, R. L. "The Salt Supply of North Carolina during the American Revolution," *NCHR*, XXII, No. 4 (October, 1945), 393-417.

Hines, E. A. "Hugh Williamson, M.D., LL.D., North Carolina Physician, Statesman, and Historian," *Am. Med. Hist.*, VII (1935), 323-326.

Hinshaw, C. R., Jr. "North Carolina Canals before 1860," *NCHR*, XXV, No. 1 (January, 1948), 1-57.

Hinshaw, Ida C. "Cornwallis in North Carolina: Episodes of the Revolutionary Period," *Jour. Sou. Hist.*, No. 4 (October, 1912), 385-389.

Hirsch, Charles B. *The Experiences of the S. P. G. in Eighteenth Century North Carolina.* Ann Arbor, Mich. 384 pp.

Hixon, Iva May. "Academic Requirements of Salem College, 1854-1909," *NCHR*, XXVII, No. 4 (October, 1950), 419-429.

Hobbs, S. H., Jr. *North Carolina, Economic and Social.* Chapel Hill, 1930. 403 pp.
———. *North Carolina: An Economic and Social Profile.* Chapel Hill, 1958. 380 pp.

Hodge, F. W. *Handbook of American Indians North of Mexico.* 2 vols., Washington, 1907-1910.

Hodges, Luther H. *Businessman in the State House: Six Years As Governor of North Carolina.* Chapel Hill, 1962. 324 pp.

Hoffman, Ural. "Major W. A. Graham," *TCHS, Papers,* VI (1906), 22-26.

Hoffman, William S. *Andrew Jackson and North Carolina Politics.* Chapel Hill, 1958. 134 pp.

———. "The Downfall of the Democrats: The Reaction of North Carolinians to Jacksonian Land Policy," *NCHR,* XXXIII, No. 2 (April, 1956) , 166-180.

———. "The Election of 1836 in North Carolina," *NCHR,* XXXI, No. 1 (January, 1955) , 31-51.

———. "John Branch and the Origin of the Whig Party in North Carolina," *NCHR,* XXXV, No. 3 (July, 1958) , 299-315.

———. *North Carolina in the Mexican War, 1846-1848.* Raleigh, 1959. 48 pp.; 2nd printing, Raleigh, 1963.

Holder, Edward M. "Social Life of the Early Moravians in North Carolina," *NCHR,* XI, No. 3 (July, 1934), 167-184.

Holder, Rose Howell. *McIver of North Carolina.* Chapel Hill, 1957. 283 pp.

Holladay, Edward M. "Social Conditions in Colonial North Carolina," *NCB,* III, No. 4 (1910) , 5-30.

Holman, C. Hugh. *Thomas Wolfe.* Minneapolis, 1960. 47 pp.
———. *The World of Thomas Wolfe.* New York, 1962. 187 pp.

Holmes, John S. *Common Forest Trees of North Carolina, How to Know Them; A Pocket Manual.* Chapel Hill, 1922. 76 pp.

Holt, Bryce R. "The Supreme Court of North Carolina and Slavery," TCHS, *Papers,* XVII (1927) , 7-77.

Hooker, Richard J. (ed.) . *The Carolina Backcountry on the Eve of the Revolution. The Journal and other Writings of Charles Woodmason, Anglican Itinerant.* Chapel Hill, 1953. xxxix, 305 pp.

House, Robert B. "Aycock and Universal Education," *NCHR,* XXXVII, No. 2 (April, 1960), 211-216.
———. *The Light that Shines: Chapel Hill 1912-1916.* Chapel Hill, 1964. 216 pp.
———. "On Autobiography," *NCHR,* XXIV, No. 2 (April, 1947) , 200-206.

————. "Preserving North Carolina's World War Records As a State Enterprise," *Sou. Atl. Quar.*, XIX, No. 2 (April, 1920), 109-117.

———— (ed.). *Public Letters and Papers of Thomas Walter Bickett, Governor of North Carolina, 1917-1921.* Raleigh, 1923.

Howell, Andrew J., Jr. *The Book of Wilmington.* Wilmington, 1930. 206 pp.

Howerton, R. T., Jr. "The Rose of Sharon Baptist Church," TCHS, *Papers*, VII (1907), 39-47.

*How They Began: The Story of North Carolina County, Town, and Other Place Names.* New York, 1941. 73 pp.

Hoyle, Bernadette. *Tar Heel Writers I Know.* Winston-Salem, 1956. 215 pp.

Hoyt, Elizabeth S. "Reactions in North Carolina to Jackson's Banking Policy, 1829-1832," *NCHR*, XXV, No. 2 (April, 1958), 167-178.

Hoyt, W. H. *The Mecklenburg Declaration of Independence.* New York, 1907. 284 pp.

———— (ed.). *The Papers of Archibald D. Murphey.* 2 vols. Raleigh, 1914.

Hoyt, William D., Jr. (ed.). "Letters from Willie Jones to His Son at the University of North Carolina, 1796-1801," *NCHR*, XIX, No. 4 (October, 1942), 375-379.

Hudson, A. P. *Songs of the Carolina Charter Colonists, 1663-1763.* Raleigh, 1962. x, 82 pp.

————. "Songs of the North Carolina Regulators," *WMQ*, Series 3, IV, No. 4 (October, 1947), 470-485.

Hühner, Leon. "The Jews of North Carolina Prior to 1800," *Am. Jew. Hist. Soc.*, XXIX (1925), 137-148.

Huggins, M. A. *A History of the North Carolina Baptists, 1727-1932.* Raleigh, 1967.

Hughson, S. C. *Carolina Pirates and Colonial Commerce, 1670-1740.* Baltimore, 1894. 134 pp.

Hulton, Paul. "John White, Artist," *North Carolina Museum of Art Bulletin,* V (Spring-Summer, 1965), 2-43.

————, and David B. Quinn (eds.). *The American Drawings of John White, 1577-1590.* 2 vols. London and Chapel Hill, 1964. (The first reproduction in color of White's "drawings.")

Hunter, C. L. *Sketches of Western North Carolina, Historical and Biographical.* Raleigh, 1877. 357 pp. reprint. Raleigh, 1930.

Hunter, Dard. *Paper Making in Pioneer America.* Philadelphia, 1952. 178 pp.

Hunter, Floyd. "The Outdoor Historical Drama," *NCHR,* XXX, No. 2 (April, 1953), 218-222.

Hunter, Kermit. *Horn in the West: A Drama of the Southern Appalachian Highlands.* Boone, 1952. 62 pp.

————. *Unto These Hills: A Drama of the Cherokee.* Chapel Hill, 1951. 100 pp.

Hurley, James M. "The Political Status of Roman Catholics in North Carolina," *Am. Cath. Hist. Soc. Rec.,* XXXVIII (September, 1927), 237-296.

Iobst, Richard W., and Louis H. Manarin. *The Bloody Sixth: The Sixth North Carolina Regiment Confederate States of America.* Raleigh, 1965. xv, 493 pp.

Irby, Louise. "An Old-Time North Carolina Election" *N.C. Lit. and Hist. Assoc. Proc.* (1922), 102-111.

Jackson, W. C. " Culture and the New Era in North Carolina," *NCHR,* II, No. 1 (January, 1925), 3-18.

Jacobs, W. R. (ed.). *Indians of the Southern Colonial Frontier: The Edmond Atkin Report and Plan of 1755.* Columbia, S.C., 1954. xxxviii, 108 pp.

James, Fleming H. "Richard Marsden, Wayward Clergyman," *WMQ,* XI, No. 4 (October, 1954), 578-591.

Jameson, J. F. (ed.). "Autobiography of Omar ibn Said, Slave in North Carolina, 1831," *AHR* (July, 1925), 787-795.

————. *Privateering and Piracy in the Colonial Period: Illustrative Documents.* New York, 1923. 619 pp.

Jenkins, J. W. *James B. Duke, Master Builder.* New York, 1927. 302 pp.

Johnson, Clifton H. "Abolitionist Missionary Activities in North Carolina," *NCHR,* XL, No. 3 (July, 1963), 295-320.

Johnson, Elmer D. "James Yadkin Joyner, Educational Statesman," *NCHR,* XXXIII, No. 3 (July, 1956), 359-383.

Johnson, F. Roy. *The Peanut Story.* Murfreesboro, N.C. 1964. 192 pp.
————. *The Tuscaroras: Mythology-Medicine Culture.* Part I. Murfreesboro, N.C., 1967. 2 vols.

Johnson, Guion G. *Ante-Bellum North Carolina: A Social History.* Chapel Hill, 1937. 935 pp.
————. "The Ante-Bellum Town in North Carolina," *NCHR,* V, No. 4 (October, 1928), 372-389.
————. "The Camp Meeting in Ante-Bellum North Carolina," *NCHR,* X, No. 2 (April, 1933), 95-100.
————. "Courtship and Marriage Customs in Ante-Bellum North Carolina," *NCHR,* VIII, No. 4 (October, 1931), 384-402.
————. "Recreational and Cultural Activities in the Ante-Bellum Town of North Carolina," *NCHR,* VI, No. 1 (January, 1929), 17-37.
————. "Revival Movements in Ante-Bellum North Carolina," *NCHR,* X, No. 1 (January, 1933), 21-43.
————. "Social Characteristics of Ante-Bellum North Carolina," *NCHR,* VI, No. 2 (April, 1929), 140-157.

Johnson, Le Roy. *The Evolution Controversy during the 1920's.* Ann Arbor, Mich., 1955. 210 pp.

Johnson, T. S. (comp.). *North Carolina Today and Tomorrow.* Raleigh, 1936. 270 pp.

Johnson, William P. "Migration to and from North Carolina, 1650-1950," *North Carolinian,* I (June, 1955), 35-42.

Johnston, France Benjamin, and Thomas W. Waterman. *The*

*Early Architecture of North Carolina.* Chapel Hill, 1941. xxiii, 290 pp.

Johnston, Frontis. "The Courtship of Zeb Vance," *NCHR,* XXXI, No. 2 (April, 1954), 222-239.

———— (ed.). *The Papers of Zebulon Baird Vance,* Vol. I, 1843-1862, Raleigh, 1963. 475 pp.

———— (ed.). "Zeb Vance: A Personality Sketch," *NCHR,* XXX, No. 2 (April, 1953), 178-190.

Johnston, Hugh B., Jr. "The Confederate Letters of Ruffin Barnes of Wilson County," *NCHR,* XXXI, No. 1 (January, 1954), 75-99.

———— (ed.). "The Journal of Ebenezer Hazard in North Carolina, 1777 and 1778," *NCHR,* XXXVI, No. 3 (July, 1959), 358-381.

———— (ed.). "The Vinson Confederate Letters," *NCHR,* XXV, No. 1 (January, 1948), 101-111.

Jolley, Harley E. "The Labor Movement in North Carolina, 1880-1922," *NCHR,* XXX, No. 3 (July, 1953), 354-375.

Jones, H. G. "Bedford Brown: State Rights Unionist," *NCHR,* XXXII, Nos. 3 and 4 (July and October, 1955), 321-345, 483-511.

————. *For History's Sake: The Preservation and Publication of North Carolina History, 1663-1903.* Chapel Hill, 1966. xvi, 319 pp.

————. "Stephen Beauregard Weeks: North Carolina's First 'Professional Historian,'" *NCHR,* XLII, No. 4 (October, 1965), 410-423.

————, and Julius H. Avant (eds.). *North Carolina Newspapers on Microfilm: A Checklist of Early North Carolina Newspapers Available on Microfilm from the State Department of Archives and History.* Raleigh, 1965.

————, and Julius H. Avant (eds.). *Union List of North Carolina Newspapers, 1751-1900.* Raleigh, 1963.

Jones, Rufus M. *The Quakers in the American Colonies.* London, 1911. xxxii, 603 pp.

Justice, William S., and C. Ritchie Bell. *Wild Flowers of North Carolina*. Chapel Hill, 1968. 217 pp.

Karraker, C. H. *Piracy Was A Business*. Rindge, N.H., 1953. 244 pp.

Keith, Alice B. "John Gray and Thomas Blount, Merchants, 1783-1800," *NCHR*, XXV, No. 2 (April, 1948), 194-205.
———— (ed.). *The John Gray Blount Papers, 1764-1795*. 2 vols. Raleigh, 1952-1959. Vol. III, *1796-1802*, ed. by W. H. Masterson, Raleigh, 1965.
————. "White Relief in North Carolina, 1865-1867," *Social Forces*, XVII, No. 3 (1939), 337-355.
————. "William Blount in North Carolina Politics, 1781-1789," J. C. Sitterson (ed.) *Studies in Southern History*, Chapel Hill, 1957, pp. 47-61.
———— (ed.). "William Maclean's Travel Journal from Lincolnton, North Carolina, to Nashville, Tennessee, May-June, 1811," *NCHR*, XV, No. 4 (October, 1938), 378-388.

Kellam, Ida B., and others. *Wilmington: Historic Colonial City*. Wilmington, 1954. 54 pp.

Kennedy, Fronde. "Fighting Adult Illiteracy in North Carolina," *Sou. Atl. Quar.*, XIX, No. 3 (July, 1920), 189-200.

Kephart, Horace. *The Cherokees of the Smoky Mountains*. . . . Ithaca, N.Y., 1936. 36 pp.
————. *Our Southern Highlanders*. New York, 1913. 395 pp.; new and enlarged ed., New York, 1922. 469 pp.

Ketcham, Earle H. "The Sources of the North Carolina Constitution of 1776," *NCHR*, IV, No. 3 (July, 1929), 215-238.

Kilgo, John C. "William H. Branson," TCHS, *Papers*, IV (1900), 21-30.

King, Clyde L. "Military Organizations of North Carolina during and after the Revolution," *NCB*, VIII, No. 1 (July, 1908), 41-55.

King, Edward. *The Great South: A Record of Journeys in the Southern States*. Hartford, 1875. 802 pp.

King, Emma. "Some Aspects of the Work of the Society of

Friends for Negro Education in North Carolina," *NCHR,* I, No. 4 (October, 1924), 403-411.

King, Spencer B., Jr. *Selective Service in North Carolina in World War II.* Chapel Hill, 1949. 451 pp.

Kinnaird, Lucia B. "The Rock Landing Conference of 1789," *NCHR,* IX, No. 4 (October, 1932), 349-365.

Klain, Zora. *Quaker Contributions to Education in North Carolina.* Philadelphia, 1925. 351 pp.

Klebner, Benjamin J. "Some Aspects of North Carolina Public Poor Relief, 1700-1860," *NCHR,* XXXI, No. 4 (October, 1954), 479-492.

Klees, Frederic. *The Pennsylvania Dutch.* New York, 1950. 451 pp.

Klingberg, Frank W. "Operation Demonstration: A Report on Southern Unionist Planters," *NCHR,* XXV, No. 4 (October, 1948), 466-484.

————. *The Southern Claims Commission.* Berkeley and Los Angeles, 1955. 261 pp.

Knight, E. W. (ed.). *A Documentary History of Education in the South before 1860.* 5 vols. Chapel Hill, 1949-1953.

————. "Braxton Craven: Pioneer in Teacher Education," *School and Society,* LXXVI (July, 1952), 33-37.

————. "An Educational Practice in Colonial North Carolina," *NCB,* XVI (July, 1916), 39-51.

————. "The Influence of the Civil War on Education in North Carolina," *N.C. Lit. and Hist. Assoc. Proc.,* XVIII (1919), 52-60.

————. "Interest in the South in Lancasterian Methods," *NCHR,* XXV, No. 3 (July, 1948), 377-402.

————. "Notes on John Chavis," *NCHR,* VII, No. 3 (July, 1930), 326-345.

————. "The Peabody Fund and Its Early Operation in North Carolina," *Sou. Atl. Quar.,* XIV, No. 2 (April, 1915), 168-180.

————. *Public School Education in North Carolina.* Boston, 1916. 384 pp.

Konkle, B. A. *John Motley Morehead and the Development of North Carolina, 1796-1866.* Philadelphia, 1922. 437 pp.

Kornegay, William G. "The North Carolina Institute of Education, 1831-1834," *NCHR,* XXXVI, No. 1 (January, 1959), 141-152.

Kyte, George W. "Victory in the South: An Appraisal of General Greene's Strategy in the Carolinas," *NCHR,* XXXVII, No. 3 (July, 1960), 321-347.

Lacy, Dan. "Records in the Offices of Registers of Deeds in North Carolina," *NCHR,* XIV, No. 3 (July, 1937), 213-229.

Lambert, Robert S. "The Oconaluftee Valley, 1800-1860," *NCHR,* XXXV, No. 4 (October, 1958), 415-426.

Landon, Charles E. "Recent Developments in the Tobacco Manufacturing Industry," *Sou. Atl. Quar.,* XXXI, No. 1 (January, 1932), 88-97.

Laney, F. B. *The Gold Hill Mining District of North Carolina.* Raleigh, 1910. 137 pp.

Lanman, Charles. *Letters from the Alleghany Mountains.* New York, 1849. 198 pp.

Lanning, John T. *The Diplomatic History of Georgia: A Study of the Epoch of Jenkins Ear.* Chapel Hill, 1936. 275 pp.
————. "Don Miguel Wall and the Spanish Attempt against the Existence of Carolina and Georgia," *NCHR,* X, No. 3 (July, 1933), 186-213.

Lapsley, G. T. *The County Palatine of Durham.* New York, 1900. 380 pp.

Larkins, John R. *Patterns of Leadership among Negroes in North Carolina.* Raleigh, 1959. 60 pp.

Larson, Norman C. "The North Carolina Confederate Centennial Commission," *NCHR,* XXXVIII, No. 2 (April, 1861), 194-198.

Lauber, A. W. *Indian Slavery in Colonial Times within the*

*Present Limits of the United States.* New York, 1913. 352 pp.

Lawrence, Elizabeth. *A Southern Garden: A Handbook for the Middle South.* Chapel Hill, 1942; rev. ed., Chapel Hill, 1967. 241 pp.

Lawrence, Robert C. *Here in Carolina.* Lumberton, 1939. 302 pp.

Lawson, John. *A New Voyage to Carolina.* London, 1709. 258 pp. Edited, annotated, and indexed edition by Hugh T. Lefler. Chapel Hill, 1967. liv, 305 pp.

Lazenby, Mary E. *Herman Husband, A Story of His Life.* Washington, 1940. 180 pp.
———— (comp.). *Catawba Frontier, 1775-1781.* Washington, 1950. 109 pp.

Leary, William J. "The Fisheries of Eastern Carolina," *NCB,* XIV (April, 1915), 173-194.

Lederer, John. *The Discoveries of John Lederer in Three Several Marches from Virginia to the West Coast of Carolina, 1669-1670.* London, 1672. 27 pp.

Lee, E. Lawrence, Jr. "Days of Defiance: Resistance to the Stamp Act in the Lower Cape Fear," *NCHR,* XLIII, No. 2 (April, 1966), 186-202.
————. *Indian Wars in North Carolina, 1663-1763,* Raleigh, 1963. 94 pp.
————. *The Lower Cape Fear in Colonial Days.* Chapel Hill, 1965. ix, 334 pp.
————. "Old Brunswick, The Story of a Colonial Town," *NCHR,* XXIX, No. 2 (April, 1952), 230-245.

Lee, Henry. *Memoirs of the War in the Southern Department of the United States.* ed. by Robert E. Lee. Philadelphia, 1812. 2 vols. A new edition with revisions, and a biography of the author, by Robert E. Lee, New York, 1869. 620 pp.

Lefler, Hugh T. (ed.). "Description of 'Carolana' by a 'Well-Willer,' 1649," *NCHR,* XXXII, No. 1 (January, 1955), 102-105.

————. *Hinton Rowan Helper: Advocate of a 'White America.'* Charlottesville, 1935. 45 pp.

————. *History of North Carolina.* 2 vols. New York, 1956.

———— (ed.). *John Lawson's A New Voyage to Carolina.* Chapel Hill, 1967. liv, 305 pp.

————, and A. R. Newsome. *North Carolina: The History of a Southern State.* Chapel Hill, 1954; rev. ed., Chapel Hill, 1963. 676 pp.

————. "North Carolina History—A Summary of What Has Been Done and What Needs to Be Done," *NCHR,* XXXIII, No. 2 (April, 1961), 216-227.

———— (ed.). *North Carolina History Told by Contemporaries.* Chapel Hill, 1934; fourth ed., Chapel Hill, 1965. 454 pp.

————, and A. L. Brooks. (eds.). *The Papers of Walter Clark.* 2 vols. Chapel Hill, 1948 and 1950.

———— (ed.). *A Plea for Federal Union, 1788.* Charlottesville, 1948. 79 pp.

————, and Paul W. Wager (eds.). *Orange County, 1752-1952.* Chapel Hill, 1953. 389 pp.

————, and L. R. Wilson (eds.). *R. D. W. Connor, A Documentary History of the University of North Carolina, 1784-1800.* 2 vols. Chapel Hill, 1953.

————. "Robert Digges Wimberly Connor," Clifford Lord (ed.). *Keepers of the Past.* Chapel Hill, 1966. pp. 109-123.

———— (ed.). "Selected William E. Dodd—Walter Clark Letters," *NCHR,* XXV, No. 1 (January, 1948), 91-100.

Lemert, B. F. *The Cotton Textile Industry of North Carolina.* Chapel Hill, 1933. 188 pp.

————. "Geographic Influences in the History of North Carolina," *NCHR,* XII, No. 4 (October, 1935), 297-319.

————. *The Tobacco Manufacturing Industry in North Carolina.* Raleigh, 1939. 107 pp.

Lemmon, Sarah M. "Entertainment in Raleigh in 1890," *NCHR,* XL, No. 3 (July, 1963), 321-337.

————. "The Genesis of the Protestant Episcopal Diocese of

North Carolina, 1701-1823," *NCHR*, XXVIII, No. 4 (October, 1951), 426-462.

———. *North Carolina's Role in the First World War*. Raleigh, 1966. 91 pp.

———. *North Carolina's Role in World War II*. Raleigh, 1964. 69 pp.

———. "Raleigh—An Example of the 'New South,'" *NCHR*, XLIII, No. 3 (July, 1966), 261-285.

Leonard, Jacob C. "The Germans in North Carolina," *Pa.-German*, X (June, 1909), 266-272.

———. *History of Catawba College*. Salisbury, 1927. 352 pp.

Leonard, Samuel E. "History of the Eastern Carolina Industrial Training School for Boys, Rocky Mount, North Carolina," *NCHR*, XXII, No. 3 (July, 1945), 276-292.

Lerche, Charles O., Jr. *The Uncertain South: Its Changing Patterns of Politics in Foreign Policy*. Chicago, 1964. 324 pp.

Lester, W. A. *The Transylvania Colony*. Spencer, Indiana. 1935. 288 pp.

Lewis, Henry W. "The Dugger-Dromgoole Duel," *NCHR*, XXXIV, No. 3 (July, 1957), 327-345.

Leyburn, J. G. *The Scotch-Irish: A Social History*. Chapel Hill, 1962. xix, 377 pp.

Linden, Fabian. "Repercussions of Manufacturing in the Ante-Bellum South," *NCHR*, XVII, No. 4 (October, 1940), 313-331.

Linder, S. C. "William Louis Poteat and the Evolution Controversy," *NCHR*, XL, No. 2 (April, 1963), 135-157.

———. *William Louis Poteat: Prophet of Progress*. Chapel Hill, 1966. xiv, 224 pp.

Link, Arthur. "The Progressive Movement in the South," *NCHR*, XXIII, No. 3 (April, 1946), 172-195.

———. "Theodore Roosevelt and the South," *NCHR*, XXIII, No. 3 (July, 1946), 483-494.

————. "The Wilson Movement in North Carolina," *NCHR*, XXIII, No. 4 (October, 1946), 483-494.

Link, Eugene P. "The Democratic Societies of the Carolinas," *NCHR*, XVIII, No. 3 (July, 1943), 259-277.

Litton, Gaston. "Enrollment Records of the Eastern Band of Cherokee Indians," *NCHR*, XVII, No. 3 (July, 1940), 199-231.

Lively, Robert A. *The South in Action: A Sectional Crusade Against Freight Rate Discrimination.* Chapel Hill, 1949. 98 pp.

Lockmiller, David A. *The Consolidation of the University of North Carolina.* Raleigh, 1942. 160 pp.
————. "The Establishment of the North Carolina College of Agriculture and Mechanic Arts," *NCHR*, XVI, No. 3 (July, 1939), 273-295.
————. *History of the North Carolina State College of Agriculture and Engineering of the University of North Carolina*, Raleigh, 1939. 310 pp.

Logan, Frenise A. "The Colored Industrial Association of North Carolina and Its Fair of 1886," *NCHR*, XXXII, No. 1 (January, 1957), 58-67.
————. "The Economic Status of the Town Negro in Post-Reconstruction North Carolina," *NCHR*, XXXV, No. 4 (October, 1958), 448-460.
————. "Legal Status of Public School Education for Negroes in North Carolina, 1877-1894," *NCHR*, XXXII, No. 3 (July, 1955), 346-357.
————. "The Movement of Negroes from North Carolina, 1876-1894," *NCHR*, XXXIII, No. 1 (January, 1956), 45-65.
————. "The Movement in North Carolina to Establish a State-Supported College for Negroes," *NCHR*, XXXV, No. 2 (April, 1958), 45-65.
————. *The Negro in North Carolina, 1876-1894.* Chapel Hill, 1964. ix, 244 pp.

Lohr, L. L. "The Germans in North Carolina West of the Catawba," *Pa.-German*, XII (April, 1911), 206-211.

London, Lawrence F. "George Edmund Badger, and the Compromise of 1850," *NCHR*, XV, No. 2 (April, 1938), 99-118.

———. "George Edmund Badger, His Last Years in the United States Senate, 1851-1855," *NCHR*, XV, No. 3 (July, 1938), 231-250.

———. "George Edmund Badger in the United States Senate, 1846-1849," *NCHR*, XV, No. 1 (January, 1938), 1-22.

———. "George Edmund Badger, Member of the Harrison-Tyler Cabinet, 1841," *Jour. Sou. Hist.*, IV (1938), 307-327.

———. "The Representation Controversy in Colonial North Carolina," *NCHR*, XI, No. 3 (July, 1934), 255-270.

Lonn, Ella. *The Colonial Agents of the Southern Colonies.* Chapel Hill, 1945. 438 pp.

———. *Desertion during the Civil War.* New York, 1928. 251 pp.

Lonsdale, Richard E. (comp. and ed.). *Atlas of North Carolina.* Chapel Hill, 1967. ix, 158 pp.

Loomis, Charles P. "Activities of the North Carolina Farmers' Union," *NCHR*, VII, No. 4 (October, 1930), 443-462.

———. "The Rise and Decline of the North Carolina Farmers' Union," *NCHR*, VII, No. 3 (July, 1930), 305-325.

Lord, Clifford L. (ed.). *Keepers of the Past.* Chapel Hill, 1965. 241 pp. (For article on R. D. W. Connor, see pp. 109-123.)

Lowery, Woodbury. *The Spanish Settlements Within the Present Limits of the United States.* New York, 1901. 515 pp.

Lutz, Paul V. "A State's Concern for the Soldier's Welfare: How North Carolina Provided for Her Troops during the Revolution," *NCHR*, XLII, No. 3 (July, 1965), 315-318.

Luvaas, Jay. "Jonston's Last Stand—Bentonville," *NCHR*, XXXIII, No. 3 (July, 1956), 332-358.

Lycan, Gilbert. "Alexander Hamilton and the North Carolina Federalists," *NCHR*, XXV, No. 4 (October, 1948), 442-465.

Lyon, Ralph M. "Moses Waddell and the Willington Academy," *NCHR*, VIII, No. 3 (July, 1931), 284-299.

Mabry, W. A. "The Negro in North Carolina Politics Since Reconstruction," TCHS, *Papers,* XXIII (1940), 3-87.

————. "Negro Suffrage and Fusion Rule in North Carolina," *NCHR*, XII, No. 2 (April, 1935), 79-102.

————. "White Supremacy and the North Carolina Suffrage Amendment," *NCHR*, XIII, No. 1 (January, 1936), 1-24.

McCain, Paul M. *The County Court in North Carolina before 1750*. Durham, 1954. 163 pp.

McCain, William D. "The Papers of the Food Administration for North Carolina, 1917-1919, in the National Archives," *NCHR*, XV, No. 1 (January, 1938), 34-40.

McCall, W. A. *Cherokees and Pioneers*. Asheville, 1952. 106 pp.

McConnell, Roland C. *The Negro in North Carolina Since Reconstruction*. New York, 1949. 25 pp.

———— (ed.). "Records in the National Archives Pertaining to the History of North Carolina, 1775-1943," *NCHR*, XXV, No. 3 (July, 1948), 318-400.

McCorkle, Donald M. "The Collegium Musicum Salem: Its Music, Musicians, and Importance," *NCHR*, XXXIII, No. 4 (October, 1956), 483-498.

————. "Musical Instruments of the Moravians in North Carolina," *Am.-Ger. Rev.*, XXI, No. 3 (1955), 12-17.

McCorkle, Mrs. Lutie A. *Old Time Stories of the Old North State*. Boston, 1903; 159 pp. Boston, 1921. 163 pp.

————. "Was Alamance the First Battle of the Revolution?" *NCB*, VII (November, 1903), 1-26.

McCoy, George W. "Asheville and Thomas Wolfe," *NCHR*, XXX, No. 2 (April, 1953), 200-217.

McCrady, Edward. *The History of South Carolina under the*

[ 70 ]

*Proprietary Government, 1670-1719.* New York, 1897.
762 pp.

McCulloch, Margaret C. "Founding the North Carolina
Asylum for the Insane," *NCHR*, XIII, No. 3 (July, 1936),
185-201.

McCurry, Allan J. "Joseph Hewes and Independence: A
Suggestion," *NCHR*, XL, No. 4 (October, 1963), 455-464.

McDuffie, Penelope. "Chapters in the Life of Willie Person
Mangum," TCHS, *Annual Publication,* XV (1925), 7-54.

McFarland, Daniel M. "North Carolina Newspapers, Editors,
and Journalistic Politics, 1815-1835," *NCHR*, XXX, No. 3
(July, 1953), 376-414.

McGrew, Ellen Z. *North Carolina Census Records, 1787-1890.*
Raleigh, 1967. 15 pp.

McGuire, Peter S. "The Seaboard Airline," *NCHR*, XI, No. 2
(April, 1934), 94-115.

McIver, George W. "North Carolinians at West Point before
the Civil War," *NCHR*, VII, No. 1 (January, 1930), 15-45.

McKay, Marvin L. "Provincial Taxes in North Carolina
during the Administrations of Dobbs and Tryon," *NCHR*,
XLII, No. 4 (October, 1965), 440-453.

McKelway, A. J. "The Scotch-Irish of North Carolina," *NCB*,
IV, No. 11 (March, 1905), 3-24.

McKinley, A. E. *The Suffrage Franchise in the Thirteen
English Colonies in America.* Philadelphia, 1905. 518 pp.

McKoy, W. B. "Incidents of the Early and Permanent Settlement of the Cape Fear," *NCB*, VII (January, 1908), 210-
235.

McLean, J. P. *An Historical Account of the Settlements of
Scotch Highlanders in America.* Cleveland, 1900. 459 pp.
———. *Flora Macdonald in America, with a Brief Sketch of
Her Life and Adventures.* Lumberton, 1909. 84 pp.

McMahon, John A. "The Local Records Program in North
Carolina," *NCHR*, XXXIX, No. 2 (April, 1962), 165-174.

McMillan, M. B. *The War Governors in the American Revolution.* New York, 1943. 309 pp.

McMurtrie, D. C. "A Bibliography of North Carolina Imprints, 1761-1800." *NCHR,* Nos. 1, 2, 3 (January, April, July, 1936), 47-88, 143-166, 219-254.

————. *Eighteenth Century North Carolina Imprints, 1749-1800.* Chapel Hill, 1938. 198 pp.

————. "The First Twelve Years of Printing in North Carolina, 1749-1760," *NCHR,* X, No. 3 (July, 1933), 214-234.

————. "Pioneer Printers in North Carolina," *Nat. Printer Journalist.* L, No. 11 (1932), 21-27, 84-85.

McNeill, Ben Dixon. *The Hatterasman.* Winston-Salem, 1958. 276 pp.

McNitt, Virgil V. *Chain of Error and the Mecklenburg Declaration of Independence.* Palmer, Mass., 1960. 134 pp.

McPherson, Elizabeth G. "Nathaniel Batts, Landholder on Pasquotank River, 1660," *NCHR,* XLIII, No. 1 (January, 1966), 61-81.

———— (ed.). "Unpublished Letters from North Carolinians to James Madison and James Monroe," *NCHR,* XIV, No. 2 (April, 1937), 156-187.

———— (ed.). "Unpublished Letters from North Carolinians to Jefferson," *NCHR,* XII, No. 3 (July, 1935), 354-380.

———— (ed.). "Unpublished Letters from North Carolinians to Polk," *NCHR,* XVI, Nos. 1, 2, 3, 4 (January, April, July, October, 1939), 54-79, 174-200, 328-457; *NCHR,* XVII, Nos. 1, 2, 3 (January, April, July, 1940), 37-66, 139-166, 249-266.

———— (ed.). "Unpublished Letters from North Carolinians to Van Buren," *NCHR,* XV, Nos. 1 and 2 (January and April, 1938), 53-81, 131-155.

———— (ed.). "Unpublished Letters from North Carolinians to Washington," *NCHR,* XII, No. 2 (April, 1935), 149-172.

———— (ed.). "Unpublished Letters of North Carolinians to Andrew Jackson," *NCHR,* XIV, No. 4 (October, 1937), 361-392.

McPherson, O. M. *Indians of North Carolina*. Washington, 1915. 252 pp.

McRee, G. J. (ed.). *The Life and Correspondence of James Iredell*. 2 vols. New York, 1857-1858; reprint, New York, 1949. See Index (mimeographed), compiled by Helen Dortch, U.N.C. Library, 1955.

McSweeney, Edward F. "Judge William Gaston of North Carolina," *U.S. Catholic Hist. Soc. Rec.*, XVII (1926), 172-188.

Mahon, John K. "The Carolina Brigade Sent against the Creek Indians in 1814," *NCHR*, XXVIII, No. 4 (October, 1951), 421-425.

Malone, Henry T. *Cherokees of the Old South: A People in Transition*. Athens, Ga., 1956. 238 pp.
———. "Cherokee-White Relations on the Southern Frontier in the Early Nineteenth Century," *NCHR*, XXXIV, No. 1 (January, 1957), 1-14.

Manarin, Louis H. (comp.). *A Guide to Military Organizations and Installations, North Carolina, 1861-1865*. Raleigh, 1961. 81 pp.
——— (comp.). *North Carolina Troops, 1861-1865: A Roster. Vol. I: Artillery*. Raleigh, 1966. 613 pp.

Mangum, A. W. "History of the Salisbury, N.C. Confederate Prison," *Pub. South. Hist. Assoc.*, III (1899), 307-336.

Marley, Branson (ed.). "Minutes of the General Court of Albemarle, 1684," *NCHR*, XIX, No. 1 (January, 1942), 48-58.

Marshall, Helen. *Dorothea Dix, Forgotten Samaritan*. Chapel Hill, 1937. 298 pp.

Marshall, Roger P. "A Mythical Mayflower Competition: North Carolina Literature in the Half-Century following the Revolution," *NCHR*, XXVII, No. 2 (April, 1950), 178-192.

Martin, François. *The History of North Carolina from the Earliest Period*. New Orleans, 1829. 2 vols.

Massey, Mary E. "Confederate Refugees in North Carolina," *NCHR*, XL, No. 2 (April, 1963), 158-182.

———. *Ersatz in the Confederacy*. Columbia, S.C. 1952. 233 pp.

———. "The Food and Drink Shortage on the Confederate Homefront," *NCHR*, XXVI, No. 3 (July, 1949), 306-334.

———. "Southern Refugee Life during the Civil War," *NCHR*, XX, Nos. 1 and 2 (January and April, 1943), 1-21, 132-156.

Masterson, W. H. (ed.). *The John Gray Blount Papers*, Vol. III, *1796-1802*. Raleigh, 1965.

———. *William Blount*. Baton Rouge, 1954. 378 pp.

———. "William Byrd in Lubberland," *Am. Lit.*, IX (1937), 153-170.

Matthews, Donald R. (ed.). *North Carolina Votes: General Election Returns, by County for President of the United States, 1868-1960, Governor of North Carolina, 1868-1960, United States Senator from North Carolina, 1914-1960.* Chapel Hill, 1962. 315 pp.

Maurer, Maurer. "Music in Wachovia, 1753-1800," *WMQ*, VIII, No. 2 (April, 1951), 214-227.

Maurice, George H. *On the Trail of Daniel Boone in North Carolina*. Eagle Springs, N.C., 1955. 19 pp.

Maxwell, A. J., and William O. Suiter. "The North Carolina Department of Revenue," *NCHR*, XXI, No. 4 (October, 1944), 265-293.

Mayo, A. D. "The Final Establishment of the American Common School System in North Carolina, South Carolina, and Georgia, 1863-1900," *U.S. Bureau Educ. Rept.* (1904), 999-1090.

Menhold, Lucy L. "The Salem Boarding School between 1802 and 1822," *NCHR*, XXVII, No. 1 (January, 1950), 32-45.

Merrens, Harry R. *Colonial North Carolina in the Eighteenth Century: A Study in Historical Geography*. Chapel Hill, 1964. ix, 293 pp.

Merrill, James M. "The Fort Fisher and Wilmington Campaign: Letters from Rear Admiral David D. Porter," *NCHR*, XXXV, No. 4 (October, 1958), 461-475.

———. "The Hatteras Expedition, August, 1861," *NCHR*, XXIX, No. 2 (April, 1952), 204-219.

Meyer, Duane. *The Highland Scots of North Carolina, 1732-1776*. Chapel Hill, 1961. 218 pp.

Midwinter, Sir Edward. "The Society for the Propagation of the Gospel and the Colonial Church in America," *P. E. Church Hist. Mag.*, IV (1935), 281-299.

Miles, Edwin A. "Benson Lossing and North Carolina Revolutionary History," *NCHR*, XXXV, No. 1 (January, 1955), 11-19.

———. "Joseph Seawell Jones of Shocco—Historian and Humbug," *NCHR*, XXXIV, No. 4 (October, 1957), 483-506.

Miller, Helen H. *The Case for Liberty*. Chapel Hill, 1965. 254 pp. Ch. IX, "Freedom from Extortion," 203-266.

Miller, John C. *Origins of the American Revolution*. Boston, 1943. 519 pp.

———. *The Triumph of Freedom, 1775-1783*. Boston, 1948. 718 pp.

Miller, Zane L. "Senator Nathaniel Macon and the Public Domain, 1815-1828," *NCHR*, XXXVIII, No. 4 (October, 1961), 376-414.

Milling, J. C. *Red Carolinians*. Chapel Hill, 1940. 438 pp.

Milton, George Fort. *The Eve of Conflict: Stephen A. Douglas and the Needless War*. Boston, 1934. 608 pp.

Mims, Edwin. "A Semi-Centennial Survey of North Carolina's Intellectual Progress," *NCHR*, XXIV, No. 2 (April, 1947), 235-257.

"Minutes of the Kentucky Baptist Association, 1769-1778," *Ky. Bapt. Hist. Soc. Publ.*, III (1913), 17-37.

Mitchell, B. S. *The Rise of Cotton Mills in the South*. Baltimore, 1921. 281 pp.

Mitchell, George. *Trade Unionism and the South*. Chapel Hill, 1931. 92 pp.

Mitchell, H. H. "A Forgotten Institution—Private Banks in North Carolina," *NCHR*, XXXV, No. 1 (January, 1958), 34-49.

Mitchell, Memory F. *Legal Aspects of Conscription and Exemption in North Carolina, 1861-1865*. Chapel Hill, 1965. 103 pp.
———— (ed.). *Messages, Addresses, and Public Papers of Terry Sanford, Governor of North Carolina, 1961-1965*. Raleigh, 1966. xxxvii, 792 pp.
————. *North Carolina's Signers: Brief Sketches of the Men Who Signed the Declaration of Independence and the Constitution*. Raleigh, 1964. 61 pp.

Monaghan, Jay. "North Carolinians in Illinois History," *NCHR*, XXII, No. 4 (October, 1945), 418-459.

Monroe, Haskell. "Religious Toleration and Politics in Early North Carolina," *NCHR*, XXXIX, No. 3 (July, 1962), 267-283.
———— (ed.). " 'Road to Gettysburg'—The Diary and Letters of Leonidas Torrence of the Gaston Guards," *NCHR*, XXXVI, No. 4 (October, 1959), 476-517.

Moody, Robert E. (ed.). "Massachusetts Trade with Carolina, 1686-1709," *NCHR*, XX, No. 1 (January, 1943), 43-53.

Mooney, James. *The Aboriginal Population of America North of Mexico*. Washington, 1928. 40 pp.
————. *Myths of the Cherokees*. Washington, 1902. 576 pp.
————. *The Siouan Tribes of the East*. Washington, 101 pp.

Moore, A. B. *Conscription and Conflict in the Confederacy*. New York, 1924. 367 pp.

Moore, John B. "Adolph Nussmann, Pioneer Lutheran Preacher in North Carolina," *Luth. Church Quar.*, XIII (1940), 375-391.

Moore, John H. "Jared Sparks in North Carolina," *NCHR*, XL, No. 3 (July, 1963), 285-294.

Moore, John R. "The Shaping of a Political Leader: Josiah W. Bailey and the Gubernatorial Campaign of 1924," *NCHR,* XLI, No. 2 (April, 1964), 190-213.

Moore, John W. *History of North Carolina; from the Earliest Discoveries to the Present Times.* 2 vols. Raleigh, 1880.

Moore, Louis T. *Stories Old and New of the Cape Fear Region.* Wilmington, 1956. 261 pp.

Moore, M. H. *Sketches of the Pioneers of Methodism in North Carolina and Virginia.* Nashville, 1884. 314 pp.

Moose, John B. "The First Constitution of St. John's Church," *NCHR,* XIII, No. 4 (October, 1936), 335-355.

Morgan, Edmund S., and Helen Morgan. *The Stamp Act Crisis.* Chapel Hill, 1953. 310 pp.

Morgan, L. N. "Land Tenure in Proprietary North Carolina," *JSHP,* XII, No. 1 (1912), 41-63.
———. "State Aid to Transportation in North Carolina: The Pre-Railroad Era," *NCB,* X (1911), 122-154.

Morison, S. E. "The Willie Jones—John Paul Jones Tradition," *WMQ,* XVI, No. 2 (April, 1959), 198-206.

Morrill, James R. "The Presidential Election of 1852: Death Knell of the Whig Party in North Carolina," *NCHR,* XLIV, No. 4 (October, 1967), 342-359.

Morrill, John R., Jr. "North Carolina and the Administration of Brevet Major General Sickles," *NCHR,* XLII, No. 3 (July, 1965), 291-305.

Morris, Frances G., and Phyllis M. Morris. "Economic Conditions in North Carolina about 1780," *NCHR,* Nos. 2 and 3 (April and July, 1939), 107-133, 296-327.

Morris, J. A. *Woolen and Worsted Manufacturing in the Southern Piedmont.* Columbia, S.C., 1952. 197 pp.

Morrison, Alfred J. "Arthur Dobbs of Castle Dobbs and Carolina," *Sou. Atl. Quar.,* XVI, No. 1 (January, 1917), 30-38.
———. "Lord Granville's Line," *Sou. Atl. Quar.,* XIV, No. 1 (January, 1915), 70-75.

Morrison, Joseph L. *Josephus Daniels Says. . .* Chapel Hill, 1962. 339 pp.

————. *Josephus Daniels: The Small-d Democrat.* Chapel Hill, 1966. 316 pp.

————. "The Tar Heel Editor in North Carolina Crisis," *NCHR,* XLIV, No. 3 (July, 1967), 270-282.

Morton, Richard L. (ed.). "A 'Yankee Teacher' in North Carolina by Margaret Newbold Thorpe," *NCHR,* XXX, No. 4 (October, 1953), 564-582.

Moser, Harold D. "Reaction in North Carolina to the Emancipation Proclamation," *NCHR,* XLIV, No. 1 (January, 1967), 53-71.

Murray, Paul. "Thirty Years of the New History: A Study of the North Carolina Historical Review, 1924-1953," *NCHR,* XXXII, No. 2 (April, 1955), 174-193.

————, and Stephen R. Bartlett (eds.). "The Letters of Stephen Chaulker Bartlee Aboard the USS 'Lenapee,' January to August, 1865," *NCHR,* XXXIII, No. 1 (January, 1965), 66-92.

Nash, Francis. "The Borough Towns of North Carolina," *NCB,* VI, No. 2 (1916), 83-102.

————. *Hillsboro, Colonial and Revolutionary.* Raleigh, 1903. 100 pp. reprint, Chapel Hill, 1903. 100 pp.

————. *Historic Hillsboro.* Raleigh, 1903. 18 pp.

————. "Revaluation and Taxation in North Carolina," *Sou. Atl. Quar.,* XIX, No. 4 (October, 1920), 289-301.

Nash, Frank. "An Eighteenth Century Circuit Rider," *N.C. Lit. and Hist. Assoc. Proc.* (1920), 58-71.

————. "Governor Abner Nash," *NCB,* XXII (1923), 3-11.

————. "The Continental Line of South Carolina," *NCB,* XVII (January, 1918), 105-134.

————. "The North Carolina Constitution of 1776 and Its Makers," *JSHP,* XI (1912), 5-23.

Neal, John W. "Life and Public Services of Hugh Williamson, 1735-1819," TCHS, *Papers,* XIII (1919), 62-111.

———. "Unpublished Letters of Hugh Williamson," TCHS, *Papers,* XIII (1919), 112-115.

Nelson, Andrew T. "'Enthusiasm' in Carolina, 1740," *Sou. Atl. Quar.,* XLIV, No. 4 (October, 1945), 397-405.

Nelson, B. H. "Some Aspects of Negro Life in North Carolina during the Civil War," *NCHR,* XXV, No. 2 (April, 1948), 143-166.

Nevins, Allan. *The American States during and after the Revolution, 1775-1789.* New York, 1924. 727 pp.

Newsome, A. R. (ed.). "A British Orderly Book, 1780-1781," *NCHR,* IX, Nos. 1, 2, 3, 4 (January, April, July, October, 1932), 57-78, 163-186, 273-298, 366-392.

——— (ed.). "The A. S. Merrimon Journal, 1853-1854," *NCHR,* VIII, No. 3 (July, 1931), 300-330.

——— (ed.). "Correspondence of John C. Calhoun, George McDuffie, and Charles Fisher, Relating to the Presidential Campaign of 1824," *NCHR,* VII, No. 4 (October, 1930), 477-504; IV, No. 4 (October, 1927), 428-470.

———. "Debate on the Fisher Resolutions," *NCHR,* V, Nos. 1, 2, 3 (January, April, July, 1928), 65-96, 204-223, 310-318.

——— (ed.). "John Brown's Journal of Travel in Western North Carolina in 1795," *NCHR,* XI, No. 4 (October, 1934), 284-313.

——— (ed.). "Letters of Lawrence O'Bryan Branch, 1856-1861," *NCHR,* X, No. 1 (January, 1933), 44-79.

——— (ed.). "Letters of Romulus M. Saunders to Bartlett Yancey, 1821-1828," *NCHR,* VIII, No. 4 (October, 1931), 427-462.

——— (ed.). "A Miscellany from the Thomas Henderson Letter Book, 1810-1811," *NCHR,* VI, No. 4 (October, 1929), 398-410.

——— (ed.). *North Carolina Social Science Maps.* Chicago, 1938. 10 sheets, 37 pp.

———. "North Carolina's Ratification of the Federal Constitution," *NCHR,* XVII (October, 1940), 287-301.

———. *The Presidential Election of 1824 in North Carolina.* Chapel Hill, 1939. 202 pp.

———— (ed.). "Records of Emigrants from England and Scotland to North Carolina, 1774-1775," *NCHR*, XI, Nos. 1 and 2 (January and April, 1934), 39-54, 129-143. Reprinted by State Department of Archives and History, Raleigh. Third printing, 1966.

————. "Simeon Colton's Railroad Report, 1840," *NCHR*, XI, No. 3 (July, 1934), 205-238.

———— (ed.). "Twelve North Carolina Counties in 1810-1811," *NCHR*, V, Nos. 1, 2, 3, 4 (January, April, July, October, 1929), 67-99, 171-189, 281-309, 413-446; V, No. 4 (October, 1928), 413-446 (Ashe, Caswell, Duplin); VI, No. 1 (January, 1929), 67-99 (Edgecombe); VI, No. 2 (April, 1929), 177-189 (Franklin, Greene, Lenoir); VI, No. 3 (July, 1929), 281-309 (Moore, Rockingham, Stokes, Surry, and Wayne).

————. "Udney Maria Blakeley," *NCHR*, IV, No. 2 (April, 1927), 158-171.

Newton, J. G. "Expansion of Negro Suffrage in North Carolina [1900-1957]," *Jour. Negro Educ.*, XXVI, (Spring, 1957), 351-358.

Nichols, Roy F. (ed.). "Fighting in North Carolina Waters," *NCHR*, XL, No. 1 (January, 1963), 75-84.

Nixon, J. R. "The German Settlers in Lincoln County and Western North Carolina," *JSHP*, XI, No. 2 (1912), 29-62.

Noble, Alice. *The School of Pharmacy of the University of North Carolina.* Chapel Hill, 1961. 237 pp.

Noble, M. C. S. *A History of the Public Schools of North Carolina.* Chapel Hill, 1930. 463 pp.

Noblin, Stuart. *Leonidas Lafayette Polk, Agrarian Crusader.* Chapel Hill, 1949. 325 pp.

————. "Leonidas Lafayette Polk and the North Carolina Department of Agriculture," *NCHR*, XX, Nos. 2 and 3 (April and July, 1943), 103-121, 197-218.

————. *The Grange in North Carolina, 1929-1954: A Story of Agricultural Progress.* Greensboro, 1954. 59 pp.

Noël-Hume, Ivor. *Here Lies Virginia: An Archaeologist's*

*View of Colonial Life and History.* New York, 1963. 316 pp. (See Chapters I and II for N.C.)

*North Carolina Authors: A Selective Handbook.* Chapel Hill, 1952. 136 pp.

*North Carolina Bureau of Labor Statistics, Annual Reports,* Raleigh, 1887-1898.

*North Carolina Fiction: 1734-1957: An Annotated Bibliography.* U.N.C. Library, Chapel Hill, 1958. 189 pp.

"The North Carolina Fuel Administration [Documents]," *NCHR,* I, No. 2 (April, 1924), 188-175

*The North Carolina Guide,* ed. by Blackwell P. Robinson. Chapel Hill, 1955. 649 pp.

*North Carolina Manual, 1913.* ed. by R. D. W. Connor. Raleigh, 1913. Other legislative manuals are published biennially in odd-numbered years.

Norton, Clarence C. "Democratic Newspapers and Campaign Literature in North Carolina, 1835-1861," *NCHR,* VI, No. 4 (October, 1929). 345-361.
————. *The Democratic Party in Ante-Bellum North Carolina, 1835-1861.* Chapel Hill, 1930. 276 pp.

Oates, John A. *The Story of Fayetteville and the Upper Cape Fear.* Fayetteville, 1950. 868 pp.

O'Connell, J. J. *Catholicity in the Carolinas and Georgia.* New York, 1879. 647 pp.

Odum, Eugene P. (ed.) *A North Carolina Naturalist: H. H. Brimley: Selections from His Writings.* Chapel Hill, 1949. 205 pp.

Odum, Howard W. *Southern Regions of the United States.* 664 pp.

*The Old North State Fact Book.* (Third Printing, Raleigh, 1965), 92 pp.

Olds, Fred A. "The Celebrated Edenton N.C. Tea Party," *D.A.R. Mag.,* LVI (June, 1922), 327-333.
————. *Guide to the Hall of History.* Raleigh, 1914. 97 pp.

————. "Our North Carolina Indians," *NCB*, XVII (July, 1917) , 39-47.

————. "The Parishes of North Carolina," *NCB*, XXI (1922) , 81-89.

Oliver, D. D. "The Society for the Propagation of the Gospel in the Province of North Carolina," *JSHP*, IX, No. 1 (1910), 23 pp.

Olmsted, Denison. *Report on the Geology of North Carolina.* Raleigh, 1824. 141 pp.

Olmsted, F. L. *A Journey in the Seaboard Slave States in the Years 1853-1854.* New York, 1856. 723 pp.; reprint, New York, 1904. 2 vols.

Olsen, Otto H. "Albion W. Tourgée: Carpetbagger," *NCHR*, XL, No. 4 (October, 1963) , 434-454.

————. *Carpetbagger's Crusade: The Life of Albion Winegar Tourgée.* Baltimore, 1965. 395 pp.

————. "The Ku Klux Klan: A Study in Reconstruction Politics and Propaganda," *NCHR*, XXXIX, No. 4 (October, 1962) , 340-362.

Ormond, Jesse M. *The Country Church in North Carolina.* Durham, 1931. 369 pp.

Orr, Oliver H., Jr. *Charles Brantley Aycock.* Chapel Hill, 1961. 394 pp.

Osborn, George C. "The Influence of Joseph Ruggles Wilson on His Son Woodrow Wilson," *NCHR*, XXXII, No. 4 (October, 1955), 519-543.

Osgood, H. L. *The American Colonies in the Seventeenth Century.* 3 vols. New York, 1904-1907.

————. *The American Colonies in the Eighteenth Century.* 4 vols. New York, 1924-1925.

Owsley Frank L. *Plain Folk of the Old South.* Baton Rouge, 1949. 235 pp.

————. *State Rights in the Confederacy.* Chicago, 1925. 289 pp.

Oxendine, Clifton. "Pembroke State College for Indians: Historical Sketch," *NCHR*, XXII, No. 1 (January, 1945), 22-53.

Padgett, James A. "From Slavery to Prominence in North Carolina," *Jour. Negro Hist.*, XXII (1937), 433-487.

————— (ed.). "Reconstruction Letters from North Carolina," *NCHR*, XVIII, Nos. 2, 3, 4 (April, July, October, 1941), 171-195, 278-300, 373-397; XIX, Nos. 1, 2, 3, 4 (January, April, July, October, 1942), 59-94, 187-208, 280-302, 380-403; XX, Nos. 1, 2, 3, 4 (January, April, July, October, 1943), 54-82, 181-189, 259-282, 341-370; XXI, Nos. 1, 2, 4 (January, April, October, 1944), 46-71, 139-157, 232-247.

————— (ed.). "With Sherman through Georgia and the Carolinas: Letters of a Federal Soldier," *Ga. Hist. Quar.*, XXXIII (March, 1949), 49-81.

Parker, Coralie. *The History of Taxation in North Carolina during the Colonial Period, 1663-1776*. New York, 1928. 178 pp.

Parker, Mattie E. *Money Problems of Early Tar Heels*. Raleigh. 14 pp.

————— (ed.). *North Carolina Charters and Constitutions, 1578-1698*. Raleigh, 1963. xxii, 247 pp.

—————. "Report on the Survey of Federal Archives in North Carolina through June 30, 1937," *NCHR*, XV, No. 4 (October, 1938), 389-399.

—————. *Tar Heel Tales*. Raleigh, 1946. 34 pp.

Parker, Robert J. (ed.). "A Yankee in North Carolina: Observations of Thomas Oliver Larkin, 1821-1826," *NCHR*, XIV, No. 4 (October, 1937), 325-342.

—————, and D. L. Corbitt (eds.). "California's Larkin settles Old Debts: A View of North Carolina, 1847-1856," *NCHR*, XVII, No. 4 (October, 1940), 332-346.

Parramore, Thomas C. "The Burning of Winton in 1861," *NCHR*, XXXIX, No. 1 (January, 1962), 18-31.

—————. *Cradle of the Colony: The History of Chowan County and Edenton, North Carolina*. Edenton, 1967. 92 pp.

—————. "The Ironic Fate of the *Southern Star*," *NCHR*, XLII, No. 3 (July, 1965), 335-344.

————. "The North Carolina Background of Richard Jordan Gatling," *NCHR,* XLI, No. 1 (January, 1964), 54-61.

Paschal, G. W. "Baptist Academies in North Carolina," *NCHR,* XXVIII, No. 1 (January, 1951), 47-62.

————. "The Educational Convention of February, 1873, and the Common Schools," *NCHR,* XXVI, No. 2 (April, 1949), 208-215.

————. "Morgan Edwards' Materials toward a History of the Baptists in the Province of North Carolina," *NCHR,* VII, No. 3 (July, 1930), 365-399.

————. *History of North Carolina Baptists.* 2 vols. Raleigh, 1930-1955.

————. *A History of Printing in North Carolina.* Raleigh, 1946. 313 pp.

————. *History of Wake Forest College.* 3 vols. Wake Forest, 1935-1943.

Paschal, Herbert R., Jr. "Charles Griffin, Schoolmaster to the Southern Frontier," *Essays in Southern Biography.* Greenville, N.C. Vol. II, 1-16.

————. *A History of Colonial Bath.* Raleigh, 1955. 69 pp.

Pascoe, C. F. *Classified Digest of the Records of the Society for the Propagation of the Gospel in Foreign Parts, 1701-1892.* London, 1893. 980 pp.

————. *Two Hundred Years of the S.P.G.* London, 1901. 2 vols.

Patton, J. W. (ed.). *The Addresses and Papers of Governor Luther Hartwell Hodges, 1954-1960.* 3 vols. Raleigh, 1960-1963.

————. "New England Tutors in Granville County, North Carolina, 1845-1850," *NCHR,* XXXVII, No. 4 (October, 1960), 544-567.

————. "Serious Reading in Halifax County, 1861-1865," *NCHR,* XLII, No. 2 (April, 1965), 169-179.

Patton, Sadie (Smathers) *Buncombe to Mecklenburg—Speculation Lands.* Forest City, N.C., 1955. 47 pp.

Paul, Charles L. "Colonial Beaufort," *NCHR*, XLII, No. 2 (April, 1965), 139-152.

———. "Factors in the Economy of Colonial Beaufort," *NCHR*, XLIV, No. 2 (April, 1967), 111-134.

Paulson, John D. "A Jewel of the Greek Revival Style" [N.C. Capitol], *Art and Archael.*, XXXV (1934), 69-74.

Pearce, H. J., Jr. "The Dare Stones," *Brenau College Bulletin*, XXX, No. 3 (March, 1939), 8 pp.

———. "New Light on the Roanoke Colony, *Jour. Sou. Hist.*, IV, No. 2 (April, 1938), 148-163.

Pearson, C. C. "Race Relations in North Carolina: A Field Study of Moderate Opinion," *Sou. Atl. Quar.*, XXIII, No. 1 (January, 1924), 1-9.

Peele, Juliana. "The Founders of Rich Square Meeting," TCHS, *Papers*, VI (1906), 93-98.

Peele, W. J. (ed.). *Lives of Distinguished North Carolinians, with Illustrations and Speeches.* Raleigh, 1898. 605 pp. (Contains fifteen biographical sketches.)

———. "The White Pictures," *NCB* (April, 1907), 243-250.

Pegram, W. H. "A Ku Klux Raid and What Came of It," TCHS, *Papers*, I (1897), 65-70.

Pennington, E. L. *The Church of England and the Reverend Clement Hall in Colonial North Carolina.* Hartford, 1937. 51 pp.

Peterson, Owen M. "W. W. Avery in the Democratic National Convention of 1860," *NCHR*, XXXI, No. 4 (October, 1954), 463-478.

Phifer, Edward W. "Certain Aspects of Medical Practice in Ante-Bellum Burke County," *NCHR*, XXXVI, No. 1 (January, 1959), 28-46.

———. "Champagne at Bridletown: The Story of the Burke County Gold Rush, 1829-1833," *NCHR*, XL, No. 4 (October, 1963), 489-500.

———. "Money, Banking, and Burke County in Ante-Bellum

North Carolina," *NCHR,* XXXVII, No. 1 (January, 1960), 22-37.

――――. "Saga of a Burke County Family," *NCHR,* XXXIX, Nos. 1, 2, 3 (January, April, July, 1962), 1-17, 140-147, 305-339.

Phillips, U. B. *American Negro Slavery.* New York, 1918. 529 pp.

――――. *History of Transportation in the Eastern Cotton Belt to 1860.* New York, 1908. 405 pp.

――――. *Life and Labor in the Old South.* Boston, 1929. 375 pp.

―――― (ed.). *Plantation and Frontier Documents: 1649-1863.* Cleveland, 1909. 2 vols.

Pierson, W. W., Jr. "The Sovereign State of North Carolina, 1787-1789," *N.C. Lit. and Hist. Assoc. Proc.,* XVII (1917), 50-69.

Pinkett, Harold T. "Gifford Pinchot at Biltmore," *NCHR,* XXXIV, No. 3 (July, 1957), 346-357.

Pittman, T. M. "Crime and Punishment in North Carolina," *N.C. Lit. and Hist. Assoc. Proc.,* XVII (1917), 78-85.

――――. "Industrial Life in Colonial North Carolina," *NCB,* VII, No. 11 (1907), 50-58.

――――. "The Revolutionary Congress of North Carolina," *NCB,* No. 6 (1902), 3-18.

Plyler, M. T. "Family Traditions of Early Pioneers in Piedmont North Carolina," *Sou. Atl. Quar.,* XXXV, No. 4 (October, 1936), 420-433.

――――. "Family Traditions of Tidewater North Carolina," *Sou. Atl. Quar.,* XXXVII, No. 4 (October, 1938), 397-409.

――――. "Peter Doub: Itinarant of Heroic Days," TCHS, *Papers,* IX (1912), 33-50.

Poe, Clarence. "Builders of an Agricultural Commonwealth," *Sou. Atl. Quar.,* VIII, No. 1 (January, 1909), 1-11.

――――. "Exploding Agricultural Myths: Comparing Farm Prosperity South and West," *Sou. Atl. Quar.,* XXXIII, No. 2 (April, 1934), 113-127.

————. "L. L. Polk: A Great Agrarian Leader in a Fifty-Year Perspective," *Sou. Atl. Quar.*, XLI, No. 4 (October, 1942), 405-415.

————. "Nathaniel Macon: The Cincinnatus of America," *Sou. Atl. Quar.*, XXXVII, No. 1 (January, 1938), 12-21.

————. "Rural Land Segregation between the Whites and Negroes: A Reply to Mr. Stephenson," *Sou. Atl. Quar.*, XIII, No. 3 (July, 1914), 207-212.

———— (ed.). *True Tales of the South at War: How Soldiers Fought and Families Lived, 1861-1865*. Chapel Hill, 1961. 208 pp.

Polk, William T. *The Fallen Angel and Other Stories*. Chapel Hill, 1956. 180 pp.

————. "The Hated Helper," *Sou. Atl. Quar.*, XXX, No. 2 (April, 1931), 177-190.

————. *Southern Accent: From Uncle Remus to Oak Ridge*. New York, 1953. 264 pp.

Pomeroy, Kenneth B., and James G. Yoho. *North Carolina Lands: Ownership, Use, and Management of Forest and Related Lands*. Washington, 1964. 372 pp.

Pool, Bettie F. *Literature in the Albemarle*. Baltimore, 1915. 335 pp.

Pool, William C. "An Economic Interpretation of the Ratification of the Federal Constitution in North Carolina," *NCHR*, Nos. 2, 3, 4 (April, July, October, 1950), 119-141, 289-313, 437-461.

Porter, Charles W., III. "Fort Raleigh National Historic Site, North Carolina: Part of the Settlement Sites of Sir Walter Raleigh's Colonies of 1585-1586 and 1587," *NCHR*, XX, No. 1 (January, 1943), 22-42.

Pound, Merritt B. "Colonel Benjamin Hawkins—North Carolinian—Benefactor of the Southern Indians," *NCHR*, XIX, Nos. 1 and 2 (January and April, 1942), 1-21, 168-186.

Powell, William S. "The Bicentennial of Printing in North Carolina," *NCHR*, XXVII, No. 2 (April, 1950),193-199.

————. *The Carolina Charter of 1663: How it Came to*

*North Carolina and Its Place in History, with Biographical Sketches of the Proprietors.* Raleigh, 1954. 79 pp.

———— (ed.). "Carolina in the Seventeenth Century: An Annotated Bibliography of Contemporary Publications," *NCHR,* XLI, No. 1 (January, 1964), 74-104.

———— (ed.). *Clement Hall: A Collection of Many Christian Experiences, Sentences, and Several Places of Scripture Improved; A Facsimile of a North Carolina Literary Landmark.* Raleigh, 1961. 25 [51] pp.

———— (ed.). *Ye Countie of Albemarle in Carolina: A Collection of Documents, 1664-1675.* Raleigh, 1958. 101 pp.

———— (ed.). "The Diary of Joseph Gales, 1794-1795," *NCHR,* XXVI, No. 3 (July, 1949), 335-347.

————. "Eighteenth Century North Carolina Imprints: A Revision and Supplement to McMurtrie," *NCHR,* XXXV, No. 1 (January, 1958), 50-73.

————. *Higher Education in North Carolina.* Raleigh, 1964. 71 pp.

———— (ed.). *The Journal of the House of Burgesses of the Province of North Carolina, 1749.* Raleigh, 1949. xvii, [14] pp.; second printing, 1958.

————. *The North Carolina Gazetteer.* Chapel Hill. 1968. 580 pp.

————. *Paradise Preserved: A History of the Roanoke Island Historical Association.* Chapel Hill, 1965. 259 pp.

————. "Patrons of the Press: Subscription Book Purchases in North Carolina, 1733-1850," *NCHR,* XXXIX, No. 4 (October, 1962), 423-499.

————. "Roanoke Colonists and Explorers: An Attempt at Identification," *NCHR,* XXXIV, No. 2 (April, 1957), 202-226.

————. "Tryon's 'Book' on North Carolina," *NCHR,* XXXIV, No. 3 (July, 1957), 406-415.

————. *The War of the Regulation and the Battle of Alamance, May 16, 1771.* Raleigh, 1949. 32 pp. Fourth printing, 1965.

Pratt, Fletcher. "Johnston Blakeley, the Carolina Sea Raider," *U.S. Naval 1st. Proc.,* LXXVI (September, 1950), 996-1007.

Pratt, J. W. *Expansionists of 1812.* New York, 1925. 309 pp.

Prince, William Meade. *The Southern Part of Heaven.* [Chapel Hill]. New York, 1950. 314 pp.

Pruett, James, and Lee Rigsby. *A Selective Music Bibliography from the Period 1663-1763.* Raleigh, 1962. 53 pp.

Pugh, Robert C. "The Revolutionary Militia in the Southern Campaign, 1780-1781," *WMQ,* XIV, No. 2 (April, 1957), 154-175.

Purcell, James S. "A Book Pedlar's [Mason Weems] Progress in North Carolina," *NCHR,* XXIX, No. 1 (January, 1952), 8-23.

Purefoy, George W. *A History of the Sandy Creek Baptist Association.* New York, 1859. 329 pp.

Puryear, Elmer L. *Democratic Party Dissension in North Carolina, 1928-1936.* Chapel Hill, 1962. 251 pp.

Quarles, Benjamin. *The Negro in the American Revolution.* Chapel Hill, 1961. 231 pp.

———. *The Negro in the Civil War.* Boston, 1953. 379 pp.

Quattlebaum, Paul. *The Land Called Chicora: The Carolinas under Spanish Rule with French Intrusions, 1520-1670.* Gainesville, Florida, 1956. 153 pp.

Quinn, David B. *The New Found Land: The English Contributions to the Discovery of North America.* Providence, 1965. 45 pp.

———. "Preparations for the 1585 Virginia Voyage," *WMQ,* VI, No. 2 (April, 1949), 208-236.

———. *Raleigh and the British Empire.* New York, 1949. 284 pp.

——— (ed.). *The Roanoke Voyages, 1584-1590.* London, 1955. 2 vols.

Quyn, Dorothy M. "Flora Macdonald in History," *NCHR,* XVIII, No. 3 (July, 1941), 236-258.

Ramsey, Annie S. "Utility Regulation in North Carolina, 1891-1941: Fifty Years of History and Progress," *NCHR,* XXII, No 2 (April, 1945), 125-151.

Ramsey, Robert W. *Carolina Cradle: Settlement of the Northwest Carolina Frontier, 1747-1762.* Chapel Hill, 1964. xiii, 251 pp.

———. "James Carter, Founder of Salisbury," *NCHR,* XXXIX, No. 2 (April, 1962), 131-139.

Rand, J. H. "The Indians of North Carolina and Their Relations with the Settlers," *JSHP,* XII, No. 2 (1938), 1-41.

Randall, J. G. *The Civil War and Reconstruction.* Boston, 1937. 959 pp.

Randolph, Bessie C. "Foreign Bondholders and the Repudiated Debts of the Southern States," *Am. Jour. Int. Law,* XXV (1931), 63-82.

Rankin, Hugh F. "Cowpens: Prelude to Yorktown," *NCHR,* XXXI, No. 3 (July, 1954), 333-369.

———. "The Moore's Creek Bridge Campaign, 1776," *NCHR,* XXX, No. 1 (January, 1953), 23-60.

———. *North Carolina in the American Revolution.* Raleigh, 1959. Third printing, 1965. 75 pp.

———. *The Pirates of Colonial North Carolina.* Raleigh, 1960. 72 pp. Third printing, 1965.

———. *Upheaval in Albemarle, 1675-1689: The Story of Culpeper's Rebellion.* Raleigh, 1962. 87 pp.

Rankin, Robert S. *The Government and Adminstration of North Carolina.* New York, 1955. 429 pp.

Raper, C. L. *The Church and Private Schools in North Carolina: A Historical Study.* Greensboro, 1898. 247 pp.

———. "The Finances of the North Carolina Colonists," *NCB,* VII (1907), 84-104.

———. *North Carolina: A Study in English Colonial Government.* New York, 1904. 260 pp.

———. "North Carolina's Taxation and Its Solution," *Sou. Atl. Quar.,* XIV, No. 1 (January, 1915), 1-14.

———. "Social Life in Colonial North Carolina," *NCB,* III, No. 5 (September, 1905), 5-21.

———. "The Use of Credit by the North Carolina Farmers," *Sou. Atl. Quar.,* XIII, No. 2 (April, 1914), 118-128.

———. "Why North Carolina at First Refused to Ratify the Federal Constitution," *AHA Annual Report,* I (1895), 99-108.

Raper, Horace W. "William W. Holden and the Peace Movement in North Carolina," *NCHR,* XXXI, No. 4 (October, 1954), 493-516.

Ratchford, B. U. "The Adjustment of the North Carolina Public Debt, 1879-1883," *NCHR,* X, No. 3 (July, 1933), 156-167.

———. "The Conversion of the North Carolina Public Debt After 1879," *NCHR,* X, No. 4 (October, 1933), 251-272.

———. "The Financial Crisis of North Carolina," *Sou. Atl. Quar.,* XXXII, No. 1 (January, 1933), 43-62.

———. "An International Debt Settlement: The North Carolina Debt to France," *AHR,* XL (1934), 163-169.

———. "The North Carolina Public Debt, 1870-1878," *NCHR,* X, No. 1 (January, 1933), 291-305.

———. "The Public Finances of North Carolina Since 1920," *Sou. Atl. Quar.,* XXVII, No. 1 (January, 1928), 1-15.

Ravenscroft, John Stark. "Manuscript Journal of John Stark Ravenscroft, First Bishop of North Carolina," *P. E. Church Hist. Mag.,* V (1936), 42-46.

Reid, Paul A. "Gubernatorial Campaigns and Administrations of David S. Reid, 1848-1854," *Bulletin Western Carolina College: Faculty Studies,* XXX, No. 3 (July, 1953), Cullowhee, 1953. 119 pp.

Rice, Philip M. "The Early Development of the Roanoke Waterway—A Study in Interstate Relations," *NCHR,* XXXI, No. 1 (January, 1954), 50-74.

Richard, Leonard L. "John Adams and the Moderate Federalists: The Cape Fear Valley as a Test Case," *NCHR,* XLIII, No. 1 (January, 1966), 14-30.

Rights, Douglas L. "Adelaide Lisetta Fries," *NCHR,* XXIX, No. 1 (January, 1952), 1-7.

———. *The American Indian in North Carolina.* Durham, 1947. 296 pp.

————. "The Buffalo in North Carolina," *NCHR*, XX, No. 3 (July, 1932) , 242-249.

————. "The Horse Society," *NCHR*, XVII, No. 4 (October, 1940) , 347-355.

————. "Salem in the War Between the States," *NCHR*, XXVII, No. 3 (July, 1950), 277-288.

————. "Traces of the Indians in Piedmont North Carolina," *NCHR*, I, No. 3 (July, 1924), 279-288.

————. "The Trading Path of the Indians," *NCHR*, VIII, No. 4 (October, 1931) , 403-426.

Rippy, J. Fred (ed.) . *F. M. Simmons, Statesman of the New South, Memoirs and Addresses.* Durham, 1936. 535 pp.

————. "A View of the Carolinas in 1783," *NCHR*, VI, No. 4 (October, 1929) , 362-370.

Ritcheson, Charles R. "The Preparation of the Stamp Act," *WMQ*, X, No. 4 (October, 1953), 543-559.

Rives, Ralph H. "Littleton Female College," *NCHR*, XXXIX, No. 3 (July, 1962) , 363-377.

————. "Panacea Springs: Fashionable Spa," *NCHR*, XLII, No. 4 (October, 1965) , 430-439.

Robert, Joseph C. "The Tobacco Industry in Ante-Bellum North Carolina," *NCHR*, IV, No. 2 (April, 1938) , 119-130.

————. *The Tobacco Kingdom, Plantation, Market and Factory in Virginia and North Carolina, 1800-1860.* Durham, 1938. 286 pp.

Roberts, A. Sellew. "The Peace Movement in North Carolina," *MVHR*, XI, (September, 1924), 190-199.

Roberts, Bruce, and Frances Griffin. *Old Salem in Pictures.* Charlotte, 1966. 59 pp.

Roberts, W. C. "Cockfighting: An Early Entertainment in North Carolina," *NCHR*, XLII, No. 3 (July, 1965) , 306-314.

Robinson, Blackwell P. *Battles and Engagements of the American Revolution in North Carolina.* Raleigh. 1961. 23 pp.

————. *The Five Royal Governors of North Carolina.* Raleigh, 1963. 74 pp.

————. *The History of Escheats.* Chapel Hill, 1955. 62 pp.

———— (ed.). *The North Carolina Guide.* Chapel Hill, 1955. xxi, 649 pp.

————. *William R. Davie.* Chapel Hill, 1954. 495 pp.

————. "Willie Jones of Halifax," *NCHR,* XVIII, Nos. 1 and 2 (January and April, 1941), 1-26, 133-170.

Robinson, Melvin. *Riddle of the Lost Colony.* New Bern, 1946. 64 pp.

Robinson, William M., Jr. "Admiralty in 1861: The Confederate States District Court for the Division of the Pamlico of the District of North Carolina," *NCHR,* XVII, No. 2 (April, 1940), 132-138.

Rodman, Lida T. "Pamptico and Bath, North Carolina," *N.C. Hist. Com. Publ.,* I (1907), 174-200.

————. "Patriotic Women of North Carolina in the Revolution," *D.A.R. Mag.,* XLV (August, 1914), 145-152.

Rogers, Adolph. "North Carolina and Indiana: A Tie that Binds," *Ind. Mag. Hist.,* V (September, 1909), 49-56.

Roller, David C. "Republican Factionalism in North Carolina, 1904-1906," *NCHR,* XLI, No. 1 (January, 1964), 62-73.

Rondthaler, Edward. *The Memorabilia of Fifty Years, 1877 to 1927, by Rt. Rev. Edward Rondthaler, Pastor of Salem Congregation of the Moravian Church at Winston-Salem.* Raleigh, 1928. 520 pp.

————. "New Plans against an Old Background: Salem College, 1866-1884," *NCHR,* XXVII, No. 4 (October, 1950), 430-436.

Ross, Charles (ed.). *Correspondence of Charles, First Marquis Cornwallis.* 3 vols. London, 1859.

Ross, Malcolm. *The Cape Fear.* New York, 1965. 340 pp.

————. "North Carolina, Dixie Dynamo," *Nat. Geog.,* Vol. 121, No. 2 (February, 1962), 141-183.

Ross, M. H. "Court Decisions Involving Trade Unions in North Carolina," *NCHR,* XXX, No. 4 (October, 1953), 467-482.

Rouse, William H. "The Romance of a Boundary Line," *Va. State Bar Assoc. Proc.* (1931), 258-273.

Rowe, Nellie. *Discovering North Carolina.* Chapel Hill, 1933. 363 pp. Elementary textbook.

Royce, C. C. *The Cherokee Nation of Indians.* Washington, 1887. 378 pp.

————. *Indian Land Cessions in the United States.* Washington, 1899. 521-997.

Ruark, Bryant W. "Some Phases of Reconstruction in Wilmington and New Hanover County," TCHS, *Papers,* XI (1915), 79-112.

Ruffin, Edmund. *Agricultural, Geological, and Descriptive Sketches of Lower North Carolina.* Raleigh, 1861. 296 pp.

Rulfs, Donald J. "The Ante-Bellum Professional Theater in Fayetteville," *NCHR,* XXXI, No. 2 (April, 1954), 125-133.

————. "The Ante-Bellum Professional Theater in Raleigh," *NCHR,* XXIX, No. 3 (July, 1952), 344-358.

————. "The Era of the Opera House in Piedmont North Carolina," *NCHR,* XXXV, No. 3 (July, 1958), 328-346.

————. "The Professional Theater in Wilmington, 1858-1870," *NCHR,* Nos. 2, 3, 4 (April, July, and October, 1951), 119-136, 316-331, 463-485.

————. "The Theater in Asheville 1879 to 1931," *NCHR,* XXXVI, No. 4 (October, 1959), 429-441.

Russ, William A., Jr. "Radical Disfranchisement in North Carolina, 1867-1868," *NCHR,* XI, No. 4 (October, 1934), 271-283.

Russell, Phillips. *North Carolina in the Revolutionary War.* Charlotte, 1965. 323 pp.

————. *The Woman Who Rang the Bell: The Story of Cornelia Phillips Spencer.* Chapel Hill, 1949. 293 pp.

St. Clair, Kenneth E. "Debtor Relief in North Carolina during Reconstruction," *NCHR,* XVIII, No. 3 (July, 1941), 215-235.

———. "Judicial Machinery in North Carolina in 1865," *NCHR*, XXXI, No. 4 (October, 1954), 493-516.

Salley, A. S. *The Boundary Line between North Carolina and South Carolina*. Columbia, S.C., 1929. 38 pp.

——— (ed.). *Narratives of Early Carolina, 1650-1708*. New York, 1911. 388 pp.

Salls, Helen H. "Pamela Savage of Champlain, Health Seeker in Oxford," *NCHR*, XXIX, No. 4 (October, 1952), 540-568.

Sams, C. W. *The Conquest of Virginia: The First Attempt*. Norfolk, 1924. 547 pp.

Sanders, Jennings B. "Thomas Burke in the Continental Congress," *NCHR*, IX, No. 1 (January, 1932), 22-37.

Sanders, John B. (ed.). "The Journal of Ruffin Wirt Tomlinson, The University of North Carolina, 1841-1842," *NCHR*, Nos. 1 and 2 (January and April, 1953), 86-114, 233-260.

Sanford, Terry. *Storm over the States*. New York, 1967. 218 pp.

Savage, Henry, Jr. *River of the Carolinas: The Santee*. New York, 1956. 435 pp. reprint, Chapel Hill, 1968.

Schauinger, Joseph H. *William Gaston, Carolinian*. New York, 1949. 242 pp.

———. "William Gaston: Southern Statesman," *NCHR*, XVIII, No. 2 (April, 1941), 99-132.

———. "William Gaston and the Supreme Court of North Carolina," *NCHR*, XXI, No. 2 (April, 1944), 97-117.

Scheer, Julian. "Tweetsie," *NCHR*, XXXVI, No. 1 (January, 1959), 168-172.

Schenck, David. *North Carolina, 1780-1781*. Raleigh, 1889. 498 pp.

Schöpf, J. D. *Travels in the Confederation, 1783-84*. Philadelphia, 1911. 2 vols.

Schütz, Géza. "Additions to the History of the Swiss Colonization Projects in Carolina," *NCHR*, X, No. 2 (April, 1933), 133-141.

Schuyler, Montgomery. *Notes on the Patroonships, Manors, and Seigneuries in Colonial Times.* New York, 1953. 430 pp.

Scott, Kenneth. "Counterfeiting in Colonial North Carolina," *NCHR*, XXIV, No. 4 (October, 1957), 467-482.

Scotus Americanus (pseud.). *Information Concerning the Province of North Carolina.* Glasgow, 1773; reprinted *NCHR*, III, No. 4 (October, 1926), 591-621.

Sellers, Charles G., Jr. "Colonel Ezekiel Polk: Pioneer and Patriarch," *WMQ*, X, No. 1 (January, 1953), 80-93.

———. *James K. Polk, Jacksonian, 1795-1843.* Princeton, 1957. 526 pp.

———. "Jim Polk Goes to Chapel Hill," *NCHR*, XXIX, No. 2 (April, 1952), 189-203.

———. "Making a Revolution: The North Carolina Whigs, 1765-1775," J. C. Sitterson (ed.). *Studies in Southern History*, Chapel Hill, 1957, 23-46.

———. "Private Profits and British Colonial Policy: The Speculations of Henry McCulloh," *WMQ*, VIII, No. 4 (October, 1951), 535-557.

———. "Walter Hines Page and the Spirit of the New South," *NCHR*, XXIX, No. 4 (October, 1952), 481-499.

Shackford, James A. "David Crockett and North Carolina," *NCHR*, XXVIII, No. 3 (July, 1951), 298-315.

Shanks, Henry T. (ed.). *The Papers of Willie P. Mangum.* 5 vols. Raleigh, 1950-1956.

Sharpe, John A. "Diary of a Confederate Refugee," TCHS, *Papers*, III (1899), 81-95.

Sharpe, William P. (Bill). *A New Geography of North Carolina.* 5 vols. Raleigh, 1954-1967.

Shaw, Albert. "Walter Hines Page—Memorial Address," *NCHR*, I, No. 1 (January, 1924), 3-25.

Shaw, Cornelia. *Davidson College.* New York, 1923. 307 pp.

Shaw, G. C. *John Chavis, 1763-1838: A Remarkable Negro Who Conducted a School in North Carolina for White Boys and Girls.* Binghamton, N.Y., 1931. 60 pp.

Sherrill, Paul M. "The Quakers and the North Carolina Manumission Society," TCHS, *Papers,* X (1914), 32-51.

Shinn, James F. "Edward Moseley: A North Carolina Patriot and Statesman," *South. Hist. Publ.,* III (1899), 15-34.

Shryock, Richard. "Medical Practice in the Old South," *Sou. Atl. Quar.,* XXIX, No. 2 (1930), 160-178.

Shuford, August. *Colonial North Carolina.* Cincinnati, 1927. 33 pp.

Sikes, E. W. "Social and Economic Legislation in North Carolina during the Civil War," *N.C. Lit. and Hist. Assoc. Proc.,* XVI (1916), 42-49.
———. *The Transition of North Carolina from Colony to Commonwealth.* Baltimore, 1898. 84 pp.

Silver, James W. "The Confederate Preacher Goes to War," *NCHR,* XXXIII, No. 4 (October, 1956), 499-509.
———. "North Carolinians in Mississippi History," *NCHR,* XXII, No. 1 (January, 1945), 43-57.

Simkins, Francis B. *A History of the South.* [2nd ed. rev.] New York, 1953. 655 pp.

Simpson, William H. "Credit Unions in North Carolina," *NCHR,* XXIX, No. 4 (October, 1962), 541-548.

Sitterson, J. C. "Business Leaders in Post-Civil War North Carolina, 1865-1900," J. C. Sitterson (ed.). *Studies in Southern History.* Chapel Hill, 1957. pp. 111-121.
———. "Economic Sectionalism in Ante-Bellum North Carolina," *NCHR,* XVI, No. 2 (April, 1939), 134-146.
———. *The Secession Movement in North Carolina.* Chapel Hill, 1939. 285 pp.

Skaggs, M. L. "The First Boundary Survey between the Carolinas," *NCHR,* XII, No. 3 (July, 1935), 213-232.
———. *North Carolina Boundary Disputes Involving Her Southern Line.* Chapel Hill, 1941. 250 pp.

———. "Progress in the North Carolina–South Carolina Boundary Dispute," *NCHR*, XV, No. 4 (October, 1938), 341-353.

Smathers, George H. *The History of Land Titles in Western North Carolina.* Asheville, 1938. 148 pp.

Smiley, David L. "Educational Attitudes of North Carolina Baptists," *NCHR*, XXXV, No. 3 (July, 1958), 316-327.

Smith, A. E. *Colonists in Bondage: White Servitude and Convict Labor in America, 1607-1776.* Chapel Hill, 1947. 435 pp.

Smith, C. Alphonso. "John Motley Morehead," *Sou. Atl. Quar.,* V, No. 1 (January, 1906), 35-43.

Smith, Charles D. "The Appalachian National Park Movement, 1885-1901," *NCHR,* XXXVII, No. 1 (January, 1960), 38-65.

Smith, Helen Burr, and Elizabeth V. Moore. "John Mare: A Composite Portrait," *NCHR,* XLIV, No. 1 (January, 1967), 18-52.

Smith, L. L. "Methodism in the Albemarle Section," TCHS, *Papers,* VIII (1908-1909), 51-65.

Smith, Mary P. "Borough Representation in North Carolina," *NCHR,* VII, No. 2 (April, 1930), 177-191.

Smith, Mary S. *Union Sentiment in North Carolina during the Civil War.* Raleigh, 1915. 21 pp.

Smith, Minnie J. (ed.). *Records of the Moravians in North Carolina.* Vol. IX, *1838-1847.* Raleigh, 1967. 4371-5056.

Smith, Samuel D. *The Negro in Congress, 1870-1901.* Chapel Hill, 1940. 160 pp.

Smith, Willis. "James Robert Rent Hathaway—A Gleaner in North Carolina History," TCHS, *Papers,* VII (1907), 32-38.

Smyth, J. F. D. *A Tour in the United States.* London, 1784. 2 vols.

Sondley, F. A. *Samuel Davidson* [first settler of western N.C.]. Asheville, 1913. 22 pp.

South, Stanley A. *Indians in North Carolina.* Raleigh, 1959. (Fourth printing, 1965), 69 pp.

——. "Russellborough: Two Royal Governors' Mansions at Brunswick Town," *NCHR*, XLIV, No. 4 (October, 1967) , 360-372.

——. "Searching for Clues to History through Historic Site Archeology," *NCHR*, XLIII, No. 2 (April, 1966), 166-173.

Sowle, Patrick. "The North Carolina Manumission Society, 1816-1834," *NCHR*, XLII, No. 1 (January, 1965) , 47-69.

Sparkes, Boyden. "Writ on Rocke," *Saturday Evening Post*, April 26, 1941, 9-11, 118-128.

Speck, Frank G. "The Catawba Nation and Its Neighbors," *NCHR*, XVI, No. 4 (October, 1939), 404-417.

——. "Remnants of the Machapunga Indians of North Carolina," *Am. Anthrop.*, Vol. 18 (April-June, 1916) , 271-276.

——. "Siouan Tribes of the Carolinas," *Am. Anthrop.*, XXXVII (1935) , 201-225.

Spencer, Cornelia P. *The Last Ninety Days of the War in North Carolina.* New York, 1866. 287 pp.

Spraggins, Tinsley L. "Mobilization of Negro Labor for the Department of Virginia and North Carolina, 1861-1865," *NCHR*, XXIV, No. 2 (April, 1947) , 160-197.

Spruill, Julia C. "Southern Housewives before the Revolution," *NCHR*, XIII, No. 1 (January, 1936), 25-46.

——. "Virginia and Carolina Homes before the Revolution," *NCHR*, XII, No. 4 (October, 1935) , 320-340.

——. "Women in the Founding of the Southern Colonies," *NCHR*, XIII, No. 3 (July, 1936) , 202-218.

——. *Women's Life and Work in the Southern Colonies.* Chapel Hill, 1938. 426 pp.

Sprunt, James. *Chronicles of the Cape Fear River, 1660-1916.* 2nd ed. Raleigh, 1914. 732 pp.

————. *Derelicts: An Account of Ships Lost at Sea . . . along the North Carolina Coast.* Wilmington, 1920. 304 pp.

————. *Tales and Traditions of the Lower Cape Fear, 1661-1896.* Wilmington, 1896. 215 pp.

Stampp, Kenneth M. *The Peculiar Institution: Slavery in the Ante-Bellum South.* New York, 1956. 435 pp.

————. "The Southern Refutation of the Pro-Slavery Argument," *NCHR,* XXI, No. 1 (January, 1941), 35-45.

Stanard, Diffie W., and Richard W. Griffin. "The Cotton Textile Industry in Ante-Bellum North Carolina," *NCHR,* Nos. 1 and 2 (January and April, 1957), 15-35, 131-164.

Starling, Robert B. "The Plank Road Movement in North Carolina," *NCHR,* XVI, Nos. 1 and 2 (January and April, 1939), 1-22, 147-173.

Stephens, George M. "The Beginnings of the Historical Drama: 'Unto These Hills,'" *NCHR,* XXVIII, No. 2 (April, 1951), 212-218.

Stephenson, Gilbert T. "The Segregation of the White and Negro Races in Rural Communities in North Carolina," *Sou. Atl. Quar.,* XIII, No. 2 (April, 1914), 107-117.

————. "The War Savings Campaign of 1918," *NCHR,* I, No. 1 (January, 1924), 26-34.

Stephenson, Wendell H. "John Spencer Bassett As a Historian of the South," *NCHR,* XXV, No. 3 (July, 1918), 289-317.

————. "The Negro in the Thinking and Writing of John Spencer Bassett," *NCHR,* XXV, No. 4 (October, 1948), 427-441.

Stewart, Joseph (ed.). "Extract from a Letter by Pastor Storch in North Carolina, dated Salisbury, January 30—February 25, 1796," *NCHR,* XX, No. 4 (October, 1943), 336-340.

Stewart, S. A. "Court System of North Carolina before the Revolution," TCHS, *Papers,* IV (1900), 12-20.

Steelman, Joseph F. "Richmond Pearson, Roosevelt Republicans, and the Campaign of 1912 in North Carolina," *NCHR*, No. 2 (April, 1966), 122-139.

⸻. "Republicanism in North Carolina: John Motley Morehead's Campaign to Revive a Moribund Party," *NCHR*, XLII, No. 2 (April, 1965), 153-168.

⸻. "The Trials of a Republican State Chairman: John Motley Morehead and North Carolina Politics, 1910-1912," *NCHR*, XLIII, No. 1 (January, 1966), 31-42.

⸻. "Vicissitudes of Republican Party Politics: The Campaign of 1892 in North Carolina," *NCHR*, XLIII, No. 4 (October, 1966), 430-442.

Stick, David. *Fabulous Dare: The Story of Dare County, Past and Present.* Kitty Hawk, N.C. 71 pp.

⸻. *Graveyard of the Atlantic: Shipwrecks of the Carolina Coast.* Chapel Hill, 1952. 276 pp.

⸻. *The Outer Banks of North Carolina, 1584-1958.* Chapel Hill, 1958. 352 pp.

Still, William. "The Career of the Confederate Ironclad 'Neuse,'" *NCHR*, XLIII, No. 1 (January, 1966), 1-13.

Stokes, Durward T. "Henry Pattillo in North Carolina," *NCHR*, XLIV, No. 4 (October, 1967), 373-391.

⸻. "Nathaniel Rochester in North Carolina," *NCHR*, XXXVIII, No. 4 (October, 1961), 467-481.

⸻. "North Carolina and the Great Revival of 1800," *NCHR*, XLIII, No. 4 (October, 1966), 401-412.

⸻. "Thomas Hart in North Carolina," *NCHR*, XLI, No. 3 (July, 1964), 324-337.

Stover, John F. *The Railroads of the South, 1865-1900: A Study in Finance and Control.* Chapel Hill, 1955. 310 pp.

Stowell, Grance (comp.). *Index to the North Carolina Booklet* (Vols. 1-20), *May 1901-April, 1921.* Greensboro, 1922.

Strasburger, R. B., and W. J. Hinke (eds.). *Pennsylvania German Pioneers: A Publication of the Original List of Arrivals in the Port of Philadelphia from 1727 to 1808.* Morristown, Pa., 1934. 3 vols.

Strong, Robert C. "North Carolina's Attitude to the Revolution," *NCB*, VI (April, 1907), 217-226.

Stroupe, Henry S. "The Beginnings of Religious Journalism in North Carolina, 1823-1865," *NCHR*, XXX, No. 1 (January, 1953), 1-22.

———. "North Carolina Baptist Convention History," *Quar. Rev.* (Bapt.), XVI (January-March, 1957), 60-76.

———. "The North Carolina Department of Archives and History—the First Half Century," *NCHR*, XXXI, No. 2 (April, 1954), 184-200.

———. (comp.). *The Religious Press in the South Atlantic States, 1802-1865: An Annotated Bibliography.* Durham, 1956. 172 pp.

Stuckey, Jasper L., and Warren G. Steel. *Geology and Mineral Resources of North Carolina.* Raleigh, 1953. 34 pp.

———. *North Carolina: Its Geology and Mineral Resources.* Raleigh, 1965. xviii, 550 pp.

Sutherland, Stella H. *Population Distribution in Colonial America.* New York, 1936. 353 pp.

Swanton, John R. *The Indians of the Southeastern United States.* Washington, 1946. 943 pp.

Taliaferro, H. E. *Fisher's River* [North Carolina] *Scenes and Characters.* New York, 1859. 269 pp.

Tarlton, W. S. *Guide to North Carolina Historical Highway Markers* (sixth edition) Raleigh, 1964. 123 pp.

Tatum, Georgia Lee. *Disloyalty in the Confederacy.* Chapel Hill, 1934. 176 pp.

Taylor, A. Elizabeth. "The Woman Suffrage Movement in North Carolina," *NCHR*, XXXVIII, Nos. 1 and 2 (January and April, 1961), 46-62, 173-189.

Taylor, George V. "Scholarship and Legend: William Henry Hoyt's Research on the Ney Controversy," *Sou. Atl. Quar.,* LIX, No. 4 (October, 1966), 360-396.

Taylor, Joseph H. "The Great Migration from North Carolina in 1789," *NCHR,* XXXI, No. 1 (January, 1954), 18-33.

Taylor, Rosser H. *Carolina Crossroads: A Study of Rural Life at the End of the Horse and Buggy Era.* Murfreesboro, N.C., 1966. 172 pp.

——. "Fertilizers and Farming in the Southeast, 1840-1950," *NCHR*, XXX, Nos. 3 and 4 (July and October, 1953), 305-328, 483-523.

——. "The Free Negro in North Carolina," *JSHP*, XVII, No. 1 (1920), 5-26.

——. "Humanizing the Slave Code of North Carolina," *NCHR*, II, No. 3 (July, 1925), 323-331.

——. "Slave Conspiracies in North Carolina," *NCHR*, V, No. 1 (January, 1928), 20-34.

——. "Slaveholding in North Carolina: An Economic View," *JSHP*, Nos. 1 and 2 (1926), 8-98.

Thomas, David N. "Getting Started in High Point," *Forest History*, II, No. 3 (July, 1967) 23-32.

Thompson, Holland. *From the Cotton Field to the Cotton Mill: A Study of the Industrial Transition in North Carolina.* New York, 1906. 284 pp.

——. *The New South.* New Haven, 1919. 250 pp.

——. "Some Effects of Industrialism in an Agricultural State," *Sou. Atl. Quar.*, IV, No. 1 (January, 1905), 71-77.

——. "The Southern Textile Situation," *Sou. Atl. Quar.*, XXIX, No. 2 (April, 1930), 113-125.

Thompson, Lawrence S. "Foreigners in North Carolina, 1900-1950," *NCHR*, XXXI, No. 1 (January, 1954), 34-40.

Thorne, Dorothy G. "North Carolina Friends and the Revolution," *NCHR*, XXXVIII, No. 3 (July, 1961), 323-340.

Thornton, Mary (comp.). *A Bibliography of North Carolina, 1589-1956.* Chapel Hill, 1958. 597 pp.

—— (comp.). *Official Publications of the Colony and State of North Carolina, 1749-1939: A Bibliography.* Chapel Hill, 1954. 347 pp.

—— (ed.). "Prison Diary of Adjutant Atherton Boyle, C.S.A.," *NCHR*, XXXIX, No. 1 (January, 1962), 58-84.

——. "Public Printing in North Carolina, 1749-1815," *NCHR*, XXI, No. 3 (July, 1944), 181-202.

Thorpe, F. N. (ed.). *Charters and Constitutions.* Washington, 1909. 5 vols. See Vol. V for North Carolina.

Tilley, Nannie May. "Agitation against the American Tobacco Company in North Carolina, 1890-1911," *NCHR*, XXIV, No. 3 (April, 1947), 207-223.

——. *The Bright-Tobacco Industry, 1860-1929.* Chapel Hill, 1948. 754 pp.

——. "Industries of Colonial Granville County," *NCHR*, XIII, No. 4 (October, 1936), 273-289.

—— (ed.). "Journal of the Surry County (N.C.) Agricultural Society," *NCHR*, XXIV, No. 4 (October, 1947), 495-531.

——. "Political Disturbances in Colonial Granville County," *NCHR*, XVIII, No. 4 (October, 1941), 339-359.

——. "The Settlement of Granville County," *NCHR*, XI, No. 1 (January, 1934), 1-19.

——. *The Trinity College Historical Society, 1892-1941.* Durham, 1941. 133 pp.

Tindall, George B. "Business Progressivism: Southern Politics in the Twenties," *Sou. Atl. Quar.*, XXII, No 1 (January, 1963), 92-106.

——. *The Emergence of the New South, 1913-1945.* Baton Rouge, 1967. 807 pp.

Tingley, Ralph R. "Postal Service in Colonial North Carolina," *Am. Philatelist*, LXII (January, 1919), 310-312.

Tischendorf, Alfred P. "North Carolina and the British Investor, 1880-1910," *NCHR*, XXXII, No. 4 (October, 1955), 512-518.

Todd, Richard C. "The Produce Loans: A Means of Financing the Confederacy," *NCHR*, XXVII, No. 1 (January, 1950), 46-74.

Todd, V. H. *Baron Christoph Von Graffenried's New Bern Adventure.* Urbana, Ill., 1913. 124 pp.

—— (ed.). *Christoph Von Graffenried's Account of the Founding of New Bern.* Raleigh, 1920. 434 pp.

Todd, Willie G. "North Carolina Baptists and Slavery," *NCHR*, XXIV, No. 2 (April, 1947), 135-159.

Tolbert, Noble J. "Daniel Worth: Tar Heel Abolitionist," *NCHR*, XXXIX, No. 3 (July, 1962), 284-302.

———— (ed.). *The Papers of John W. Ellis.* Raleigh, 1964. 2 vols.

Tourgée, Albion W. *A Fool's Errand.* New York, 1880. 521 pp. Novel.

Treacy, M. F. *Prelude to Yorktown: The Southern Campaign of Nathanael Greene, 1780-1781.* Chapel Hill, 1963. 261 pp.

Trenholme, Louis Irby. *The Ratification of the Federal Constitution in North Carolina.* New York, 1932. 282 pp.

Troxler, George. "Eli Caruthers: A Silent Dissenter in the Old South," *Jour. of Presb. Hist.*, Vol. 45, No. 2 (June, 1967), 95-111.

Truett, R. B. *Trade and Travel Around the Southern Appalachians before 1830.* Chapel Hill, 1935. 192 pp.

Tucker, Glenn. "For the Want of a Scribe," *NCHR*, XLIII, No. 2 (April, 1966), 174-185.

————. *Front Rank: A Story of North Carolina in the Civil War.* Raleigh, 1962. 83 pp.

————. "Some Aspects of North Carolina's Participation in the Gettysburg Campaign," *NCHR*, XXXV, No. 2 (April, 1958), 191-212.

————. *Zeb Vance: Champion of Personal Freedom.* Indianapolis, 1965. 564 pp.

Turner, Charles W. (ed.). "Reuben Knox Letters, 1848-1851," *NCHR*, XXXVII, Nos. 1 and 3 (January and July, 1960), 66-93, 397-418.

Turner, Herbert S. *Church in the Old Fields: Hawfields Presbyterian Church and Community in North Carolina.* Chapel Hill, 1962. 297 pp.

Turner, Joseph K. "Slavery in Edgecombe County," TCHS, *Papers*, XII, (1916), 5-36.

Ubbelohde, Carl W., Jr. "The Vice-Admiralty Court of Royal North Carolina, 1729-1759," *NCHR*, XXXI, No. 4 (October, 1954), 517-528.

*United States Census Reports,* 1790-1960. Washington.

Vance, David, and Robert Henry. "King's Mountain Expedition," TCHS, *Papers,* III (1898), 24-35.

Vance, Rupert B. *All These People. The Nation's Human Resources in the South.* Chapel Hill, 1945. 503 pp.

——. "Aycock of North Carolina," *Southern Rev.,* XVIII (1933), 288-306.

——. *Human Factors in Cotton Culture.* Chapel Hill, 1929. 346 pp.

——. *Human Geography of the South.* Chapel Hill, 1932. 596 pp.

Vandiveer, Frank E. "The Capture of a Confederate Blockade Runner: Extracts from the Journal of a Confederate Naval Officer," *NCHR,* XXI, No. 2 (April, 1944), 136-138.

Van Noppen, Ina W. "The Significance of Stoneman's Last Raid," *NCHR,* Nos. 1, 2, 3, 4 (January, April, July, October, 1961), 19-44, 149-172, 341-361, 500-526.

Van Oesen, Elaine. "Public Library Extension in North Carolina and the WPA," *NCHR,* XXIX, No. 3 (July, 1952), 379-399.

Vinson, John C. "Electioneering in North Carolina, 1800-1815," *NCHR,* XXIX, No. 2 (April, 1952), 171-188.

Waddell, A. M. *A Colonial Officer and His Times, 1754-1773. A Biographical Sketch of Gen. Hugh Waddell of North Carolina.* Raleigh, 1890. 242 pp.

——. *Some Memories of My Life.* Raleigh, 1908. 249 pp.

Wager, Paul W. (ed.). *County Government Across the Nation.* Chapel Hill, 1950. 817 pp.

——. *County Government and Administration in North Carolina.* Chapel Hill, 1928. 447 pp.

Wagstaff, H. M. "Federalism in North Carolina," *JSHP,* IX, No. 2 (1910), 3-44.

—————. "A Footnote to Social History," *NCHR*, XXIII, No. 1 (January, 1946), 32-46.

—————. *Impressions of Men and Movements at the University of North Carolina* [1789-1914], ed. by L. R. Wilson. Chapel Hill, 1950. 110 pp.

————— (ed.). "Letters of Thomas Jefferson Strayhorn," *NCHR*, XIII, No. 4 (October, 1936), 311-334.

————— (ed.). "Letters of William Barry Grove [to James Hogg]," *JSHP*, IX (1910), 45-88.

————— (ed.). "Minutes of the North Carolina Manumission Society, 1816-1834," Chapel Hill, 1934. 230 pp.

————— (ed.). *The Papers of John Steele.* Raleigh, 1924. 2 vols.

—————. *State Rights and Political Parties in North Carolina, 1776-1861.* Baltimore, 1906. 155 pp.

—————. "State Rights in North Carolina through Half a Century," *NCB*, IX (October, 1909), 79-97.

—————. "William Richardson Davie and Federalism," *N.C. Lit. and Hist. Assoc. Proc.*, XX-XXI (1922), 46-71.

Wall, Bennett H. "Charles Pettigrew, First Bishop-Elect of the North Carolina Episcopal Church," *NCHR*, XXVIII, No. 1 (January, 1951), 15-46.

—————. "The Founding of the Pettigrew Plantations," *NCHR*, XXVII, No. 4 (October, 1950), 395-408.

—————. "The Medical Care of Ebenezer Pettigrew's Slaves," *MVHR*, XXXVII, No. 4 (December, 1950), 451-470.

Wallace, Lee A. "Raising a Volunteer Regiment for Mexico, 1846-1847," *NCHR*, XXXV, No. 1 (January, 1958), 20-33.

Wallace, Wesley H. "Cultural and Social Advertising in Early North Carolina Newspapers," *NCHR*, XXXIII, No. 3 (July, 1956), 281-309.

—————. "North Carolina's Agricultural Journals, 1835-1861, A Crusading Press," *NCHR*, XXXVI, No. 3 (July, 1959), 275-306.

—————. "Property and Trade: Main Themes of Early North Carolina Newspapers," *NCHR*, XXXII, No. 4 (October, 1955), 451-482.

Wallace, Willard M. *Appeal to Arms: A Military History of the American Revolution.* New York, 1951. 308 pp.

Wallis, P. J. " A Further Note on Joseph Gales of Newark, Sheffield, and Raleigh," *NCHR,* XXX, No. 4 (October, 1953), 561-563.

Walser, Richard. "Culture in North Carolina Today," *NCHR,* XXXVII, No. 2 (April, 1960), 229-237.
———. "Dare County Belles-Lettres," *NCHR,* XXXIV, No. 2 (April, 1957), 180-201.
———. *Inglish Fletcher of Bandon Plantation.* Chapel Hill, 1952. 79 pp.
——— (ed.). "Letters of a Young Novelist: Calvin Henderson Wiley," *NCHR,* XXXI, Nos. 3 and 4 (July and October, 1954), 410-421, 550-575.
———. "The Mysterious Case of George Higby Throop (1818-1896) ; or, The Search for the Author of the Novels *Nag's Head, Bertie,* and *Lynde Weiss,*" *NCHR,* XXXIII, No. 1 (January, 1956), 12-44.
——— (ed.). *The North Carolina Miscellany.* Chapel Hill, 1962. 275 pp.
——— (ed.). *North Carolina Poetry.* Richmond, 1941. 196 pp.
———. "North Carolina Short Stories," *NCHR,* XXV, No. 2 (April, 1948), 206-211.
———. "The North Carolina Sojourn of the First American Novelist," *NCHR,* XXVIII, No. 2 (April, 1951), 138-155.
——— (ed.). *Picturebook of Tar Heel Authors.* 2nd, ed. enl. Raleigh, 1960. 46 pp.
——— (ed.). *The Poems of Governor Thomas Burke of North Carolina.* Raleigh, 1961. 69 pp.
———. *Poets of North Carolina.* Richmond, 1963. 142 pp.
———. "Senator Strange's Indian Novel," *NCHR,* XXVI, No. 1 (January, 1949), 1-27.
———. *Short Stories from the Old North State.* Chapel Hill, 1959. 288 pp.
———. *Young Reader's Picturebook of Tar Heel Authors.* 3rd ed. Raleigh, 1966. 70 pp.

Ward, Christopher. *The War of the Revolution.* 2 vols. New York, 1952.

Ware, Charles C. *North Carolina Disciples of Christ.* St. Louis, 1927. 372 pp.

Washburn, George C. "Cornwallis in the Carolinas, 1780, from a Contemporary British Account." *Jour. Am. Hist.,* XXIV, No. 2 (April, 1960), 107-113.
———. "Our Victory at King's Mountain, October 7, 1780; Narrated from the British Point of View in 1781," *Jour. Am. Hist.,* XXIV, No. 4 (October, 1930), 216-219.

Watson, Alan D. "Ordinaries in Colonial Eastern North Carolina," *NCHR,* XLV, No. 1 (January, 1968), 67-83.

Watson, Richard L. "The Defeat of Judge Parker: A Study in Pressure Groups and Politics," *MVHR,* L, No. 2 (September, 1963), 213-234.
———. "Furnifold M. Simmons: Jehovah of the Tar Heels," *NCHR,* XLIV, No. 2 (April, 1967), 166-187.
———. "A Political Leader Bolts—F. M. Simmons in the Presidential Election of 1928," *NCHR,* XXXVII, No. 4 (October, 1960), 517-543.
———. "A Southern Democratic Primary: Simmons vs. Bailey in 1930," *NCHR,* XLII, No. 1 (January, 1965), 21-46.

Waugh, Edward, and Elizabeth Waugh. *The South Builds: New Architecture in the Old South.* Chapel Hill, 1960. 173 pp.

Waugh, Elizabeth. *North Carolina's Capital: Raleigh.* Raleigh, 1967. 216 pp.

Waynick, Capus. *North Carolina Roads and Their Builders.* Raleigh, 1952. 308 pp.

Waynick, Capus, John C. Brooks, and Elsie W. Pitts. *North Carolina and the Negro.* Raleigh, 1964. 309 pp.

Weaver, C. C. *Internal Improvements in North Carolina Previous to 1860.* Baltimore, 1903. 94 pp.

———. "The North Carolina Manumission Society," *TCHS, Papers,* I (1897), 71-76.

Webb, Elizabeth Yates. "Cotton Manufacturing and State Regulation in North Carolina, 1861-1865," *NCHR,* IX, No. 2 (April, 1932), 117-137.

Weeks, Stephen B. *Calvin Henderson Wiley and the Organization of the Common Schools of North Carolina.* Washington, 1898. Ch. XXIX, *Report of the Commissioner of Education for 1896/97.* pp. 1379-1474.

———. *Church and State in North Carolina.* Baltimore, 1893. 65 pp.

———. *Historical Review of the Colonial and State Records of North Carolina.* Raleigh, 1914. 169 pp.

———. "John Lawson and John Brickell, Early Historians of North Carolina," *Trinity Archive,* V (September, 1892), 1-8.

———. "Libraries and Literature in North Carolina in the Eighteenth Century," *AHA, Ann. Rept. 1895.* Washington, 1896. pp. 169-207.

———. "The Lost Colony: Its Fate and Survival," *AHA, Papers,* V (1891), 439-480.

———. "Pre-Revolutionary Printers in North Carolina: Davis, Steuart, and Boyd," *NCB,* XV, No. 2 (1915), 104-122.

———. *The Press of North Carolina in the Eighteenth Century.* Brooklyn, 1891. 80 pp.

———. *The Religious Development in the Province of North Carolina.* Baltimore, 1892. 68 pp.

———. *Southern Quakers and Slavery.* Baltimore, 1896. 400 pp.

Weir, Robert M. "North Carolina's Reaction to the Currency Act of 1764," *NCHR,* XL, No. 2 (April, 1963), 183-199.

Weis, Frederick L. *The Colonial Clergy of Virginia, North Carolina, and South Carolina.* Boston, 1955. 100 pp.

Wellman, Manly Wade. *The Life and Times of Sir Archie: The Story of America's Greatest Thoroughbred, 1805-1833.* Chapel Hill, 1958. 232 pp.

Wells, B. W. *The Natural Gardens of North Carolina.* Chapel Hill, 1932. 458 pp.; reprint 1967.

Wenhold, Lucy L. "Salem Boarding School Between 1802 and 1822," *NCHR,* XXVII, No. 1 (January, 1950), 32-45.

Wertenbaker, T. J. *The Old South: The Founding of American Civilization.* New York, 1942. 364 pp.

Weslager, C. A. (ed.). "Letter Concerning a Visit to Ocracoke," *NCHR,* XXXV, No. 3 (July, 1958), 347-352.
———. "Place Names on Ocracoke Island," *NCHR,* XXXI, No. 1 (January, 1954), 41-49.

Wheeler, E. Milton. "Development and Organization of the North Carolina Militia," *NCHR,* XLI, No. 4 (October, 1964), 307-323.

Wheeler, John H. *Historical Sketches of North Carolina from 1584 to 1851.* Philadelphia, 1851. 2 vols. in one. 138, 480 pp.
———. *Reminiscences and Memoirs of North Carolina and Eminent North Carolinians.* Columbus, Ohio, 1884. 478 pp.

Whitaker, Arthur P. "Spain and the Cherokee Indians, 1738-98," *NCHR,* IV, No. 3 (July, 1927), 252-269.

Whitaker, Bessie L. "The Provincial Council and Committees of Safety," *JSHP,* VIII (1908), 1-49.

White, Julia S. "A Church Quarrel and What Resulted," *Friend's Hist. Soc. Bull.,* V (May, 1914), 90-98.
———. "The Quakers of Perquimans," *NCB,* VII, No. 4 (1908), 278-279.
———. "The Peace Testimony of North Carolina Friends Prior to 1860," *Friend's Hist. Soc. Bull.,* XVI, No. 2 (1927), 60-67.

Whitener, D. J. "The Dispensary Movement in North Carolina," *Sou. Atl. Quar.,* XXXVI, No. 1 (January, 1937), 33-48.
———. "Education for the People," *NCHR,* XXXVI, No. 2 (April, 1959), 187-196.

———. "North Carolina Prohibition Election of 1881 and Its Aftermath," *NCHR*, XI, No. 1 (January, 1934), 71-73.

———. *Prohibition in North Carolina, 1715-1945.* Chapel Hill, 1946. 268 pp.

———. "Public Education in North Carolina during Reconstruction, 1865-1876," *Essays in Southern History Presented to J. G. de R. Hamilton*, Chapel Hill, 1949, pp. 67-91.

———. "The Republican Party and Public Education in North Carolina, 1867-1900," *NCHR*, XXXVIII, No. 3 (July, 1960), 382-396.

———. "The Temperance Movement in North Carolina," *Sou. Atl. Quar.*, XXXIV, No. 3 (July, 1935), 305-313.

Wilborn, Elizabeth W. (comp.). *North Carolina Historical Almanack.* (Fourth printing, Raleigh, 1964), 48 pp.

Wiley, Bell I. "Camp Newspapers of the Confederacy," *NCHR*, XX, No. 4 (October, 1943), 327-335.

Wiley, Mary C. "Childhood Recollections of My Father," *NCHR*, XXIV, No. 4 (October, 1957), 517-529.

——— (ed.). "Unpublished Letters of Calvin Henderson Wiley," *NCHR*, XXIX, No. 1 (January, 1952), 91-103.

Williams, Charles B. *History of the Baptists in North Carolina.* Raleigh, 1901. 214 pp.

Williams, Justin. "English Mercantilism and Carolina Naval Stores, 1705-1776," *Jour. Sou. Hist.*, I (1935), 168-185.

Williams, Max R. "The Education of William A. Graham," *NCHR*, XL, No. 1 (January, 1963), 1-14.

———. "William A. Graham and the Election of 1844: A Study in North Carolina Politics," *NCHR*, XLV, No. 1 (January, 1968), 23-46.

Williams, S. C. *History of the Lost State of Franklin.* Johnson City, Tenn., 1924. 371 pp.

———. "The North Carolina-Tennessee Boundary Line Survey (1799)," *Tenn. Hist. Mag.*, VI (July, 1920), 46-57.

Williamson, Hugh. *History of North Carolina.* Philadelphia, 1812. 2 vols.

Willis, F. T. "Historic Points on the Cape Fear," TCHS, *Papers,* III (1899), 36-39.

Wilson, E. M. "The Congressional Career of Nathaniel Macon," *JSHP,* No. 2 (1900), 1-115.

Wilson, L. R. "The Acquisition of the Stephen B. Weeks Collection of Caroliniana," *NCHR,* XLII, No. 4 (October, 1966), 424-429.
———— (ed.). *Selected Papers of Cornelia Phillips Spencer, 1865-1900.* Chapel Hill, 1953. 753 pp.
————. *The University of North Carolina, 1900-1930: The Making of a Modern University.* Chapel Hill, 1957. 633 pp.

Wilson, N. H. D. "The Reids: Eminent Itinerants through Three Generations," TCHS, *Papers,* IX (1912), 5-21.

Wilson, W. S. "Suffrage in North Carolina," *N.C. Lit. and Hist. Assoc. Proc.,* XVII (1917), 70-77.

Winston, George T. *A Builder of the New South, Being the Story of the Life Work of Daniel Augustus Tompkins.* New York, 1920. 403 pp.

Winston, Robert W. "North Carolina: A Militant Mediocracy," *Nation,* CXVI (February 21, 1923), 209-212.

Winston, R. W. *Andrew Johnson: Plebeian and Patriot.* New York, 1928. 549 pp.
————. "The Passenger Rate War in North Carolina," *Sou. Atl. Quar.,* VI, No. 4 (October, 1907), 342-347.
————. "Robert Potter: Tar Heel and Texas Daredevil," *Sou. Atl. Quar.,* XXIX, No. 2 (April, 1930), 140-159.

Winston, Sanford. "Indian Slavery in the Carolina Region," *Jour. Negro Hist.,* XIX (1934), 431-440.

Wittke, Carl. *We Who Built America.* New York, 1939. 547 pp.

Woodward, C. Vann. *Origins of the New South, 1877-1913.* Baton Rouge, 1951. 542 pp.

————. *The Strange Career of Jim Crow.* New York, 1955. 155 pp.

Wooten, Hugh Hill. "A Fourth Creek Farm from 1800 to 1830," *NCHR,* XXX, No. 2 (April, 1953), 167-175.
————. "The Land Valuations of Iredell County in 1800," *NCHR,* XXIX, No. 4 (October, 1952), 523-539.
————. "Westward Migration from Iredell County, 1800-1850," *NCHR,* XXX, No. 1 (January, 1953), 61-71.

Wootten, Bayard, and Archibald Henderson. *Old Homes and Gardens of North Carolina.* Chapel Hill, 1939. xxii, 134 pp.

Wright, Louis B. "Elizabethan Politics and Colonial Enterprise," *NCHR,* XXXII, No. 2 (April, 1955), 254-270.
———— (ed.). *The Prose Works of William Byrd of Westover: Narratives of a Colonial Virginian.* Cambridge, Mass., 1966. 438 pp.

Yamuck, Julius. "Thomas Ruffin and North Carolina Slave Law," *Jour. Sou. Hist.,* XXI (November, 1955), 447-475.

Yates, Richard E. *The Confederacy and Zeb Vance.* Tuscaloosa, Ala., 1958. 132 pp.
————. "Governor Vance and the End of the War in North Carolina," *NCHR,* No. 4 (October, 1941), 315-338.
————. "Governor Vance and the Peace Movement," Part I, *NCHR,* XXIX, No. 1 (January, 1940), 1-25. Part II, *NCHR,* XVII, No. 2 (April, 1940), 89-113.
————. *Zebulon B. Vance As War Governor of North Carolina, 1862-1865.* Nashville, Tenn., 1937. 33 pp.

Yearns, W. B., Jr. "François X. Martin and His History of North Carolina," *NCHR,* XXXVI, No. 1 (January, 1959), 17-27.
————. "North Carolina in the Confederate Congress," *NCHR,* XXIX, No. 3 (July, 1951), 359-378.

Zimmerman, Jane. "The Formative Years of the North Carolina Board of Health, 1877-1893," *NCHR,* XXI, No. 1 (January, 1944), 1-34.

Zornow, William F. "North Carolina Tariff Policies, 1775-1789," *NCHR*, XXXI, No. 2 (April, 1955), 151-164.

Zuber, Richard L. *Jonathan Worth: A Biography of a Southern Unionist*. Chapel Hill, 1965. 351 pp.

## III. / ROSTERS OF
## NORTH CAROLINA SOLDIERS
## IN VARIOUS WARS

Clark, Walter (ed.). *Histories of the Several Regiments and Battalions from North Carolina in the Great War 1861-1865.* 5 vols., Raleigh, 1901.

Manarin, Louis H. (comp.). *North Carolina Troops, 1861-1865: A Roster. Vol. I. Artillery.* Raleigh, 1966.

*Muster Rolls of the Soldiers of the War of 1812: Detached from the Militia of North Carolina, in 1812 and 1814.* Raleigh, 1851; reprinted, Winston-Salem, 1926.

*Roster of North Carolina Troops in the War between the States,* ed. by John W. Moore. 4 vols., Raleigh, 1882.

*Roster of North Carolina Troops in the War with Mexico.* Raleigh, 1887.

*Roster of the North Carolina Volunteers in the Spanish-American War, 1898-1899.* Raleigh, 1900.

*Roster of Soldiers from North Carolina in the American Revolution* (published by the North Carolina Daughters of the American Revolution). Durham, 1932.

(No rosters of North Carolina soldiers in World War I and World War II have been published.)

## IV. / SELECT LIST OF NOVELS,
## SHORT STORIES,
## AND PAGEANTS—CHIEFLY HISTORICAL

Blythe, W. LeGette. *Alexandriana*. Harrisburg, Pa., 1940. 445 pp. The American Revolution in the South.

Boyd, James. *Drums*. New York, 1940. 490 pp. The American Revolution, chiefly in the Albemarle Sound region.

————. *Marching On*. New York, 1927. 426 pp. The same region during the Civil War era.

————. *Old Pines and Other Stories*. Chapel Hill, 1952. 165 pp. Ten short stories, chiefly about the Sandhills region.

Burt, Katherine Newlin. *Captain Millet's Island*. Philadelphia, 1944. 256 pp. The coastal area.

Byrd, Sam. *The Duplin Story, an Historical Play with Music*. Wilmington, 1949. 46 pp.

————. *Small Town South*. Boston, 1942. 237 pp. Portrayal of life in a twentieth century North Carolina town [Goldsboro]. Sociological.

Chesnutt, Charles Waddell. *The Conjure Woman*. Boston, 1899. 229 pp. Seven tales depicting the life and struggles of the Negro "along the Wilmington Road."

Cotten, Sallie S. *The White Doe, the Fate of Virginia Dare, an Indian Legend*. Philadelphia, 1901. 89 pp. Romance.

Dargan, Olive Tilford (pen name "Fielding Burke"). *Call Home the Heart*. New York, 1932. 432 pp.

———. *From My Highest Hill* (revision of *Highland Annals*). Philadelphia, 1941. 221 pp.

———. *Highland Annals.* New York, 1925. 286 pp.

———. *Sons of the Stranger.* New York, 1947. 405 pp.

———. *A Stone Came Rolling.* New York, 1935. 412 pp.

Davidson, Chalmers. *Cloud over Catawba.* Charlotte, 1949. 210 pp. Catawba Valley about the 1840's.

Davis, Burke. *The Ragged Ones.* New York, 1951. 336 pp. Revolutionary campaign of 1781 through the Carolinas.

Dixon, Thomas. *The Clansman, an Historical Romance of the Ku Klux Klan.* New York, 1905. 382 pp. From this novel was made the motion picture *The Birth of a Nation.*

———. *The Leopard's Spots. A Romance of the White Man's Burden—1865-1900.* New York, 1902. 469 pp.

Dugger, Shepherd Monroe. *The Balsam Groves of the Grandfather Mountain: A Tale of the Western North Carolina Mountains.* Philadelphia, 1892. 300 pp. "Romance combined with a mountain guide book and reflects conditions of the times and habits of the people."

Ehle, John. *The Land Breakers.* New York, 1964. 401 pp. Settlement of the North Carolina mountain region.

———. *The Road.* New York, 1967. 401 pp. The story of the building of the Western North Carolina Railroad into Asheville.

Fletcher, Inglis. The Carolina Series (Bobbs-Merrill, Indianapolis), all dealing with colonial or Revolutionary North Carolina.

*Bennett's Welcome* (1950). 451 pp.

*Cormorant's Brood* (1959). 345 pp.

*Lusty Wind for Carolina* (1944). 509 pp.

*Men of Albemarle* (1942). 566 pp.

*Queen's Gift* (1952). 448 pp.

*Raleigh's Eden* (1940). 662 pp.

*Roanoke Hundred* (1948). 492 pp.

*Rogue's Harbor* (1964). 242 pp.

*The Scotswoman* (1955). 480 pp.

*Toil of the Brave* (1946). 547 pp.

*Wicked Lady* (1962). 256 pp.

*The Wind in the Forest* (1957). 448 pp.

Gray, Elizabeth Janet (Vining). *Jane Hope.* New York, 1933. 276 pp. Chapel Hill in the pre-Civil War era.

――――. *Meggy MacIntosh.* New York, 1930. 274 pp. Flora MacDonald and events leading to the Battle of Moore's Creek Bridge (1776).

Green, Paul. *Dog on the Sun.* Chapel Hill, 1949. 280 pp. Collection of twelve short stories.

――――. *The Highland Call.* Fayetteville, 1941. 178 pp. Pageant about early Highland Scottish settlement of the Upper Cape Fear Valley.

――――. *The Lost Colony.* Chapel Hill, 1937. 138 pp. Later editions, 1939, 1946, 1954, and 1961. Symphonic drama about Roanoke Island colony, presented annually at Roanoke Island.

――――. *This Body the Earth.* New York, 1935. Sociological novel about share-croppers.

Harris, Bernice Kelly. *Hearthstone: A Novel of the Roanoke River Country in North Carolina.* Garden City, N.Y., 1948. 273 pp.

――――. *Janey Jeems.* Garden City, N.Y., 1946. 306 pp.

――――. *Portulacca.* Garden City, N.Y., 1939. 335 pp.

――――. *Purslane.* Chapel Hill, 1939. 316 pp. The first novel ever published by a university press.

――――. *Sage Quarter.* Garden City, N.Y., 1945. 264 pp.

――――. *Southern Savory.* Chapel Hill, 1964. 256 pp.

――――. *Sweet Beulah Land.* Garden City, N.Y., 1943. 389 pp.

――――. *Wild Cherry Tree Road.* Garden City, N.Y., 1951. 282 pp.

Though the numerous volumes written by Mrs. Harris are not historical novels, they throw much light on the ordinary life of ordinary people. The title of Richard Walser's *Bernice Kelly Harris: Storyteller of Eastern Carolina* (Chapel Hill, 1955), 52 pp., is most appropriate.

Hunter, Kermit. *Horn in the West.* Boone, N.C., 1952. 62 pp. Drama of Appalachian region staged annually at Boone.

————. *Unto These Hills.* Chapel Hill, 1951. 100 pp. Pageant about Cherokee Indians, chiefly 1830-1840, staged annually at Cherokee.

Kennedy, John P. *Horse-Shoe Robinson.* New York, 1883. 554 pp. The Revolution in the Carolina backcountry.

Knox, Rose B. *Gray Caps.* Garden City, N.Y., 1932. 304 pp. Story of women and children of the Confederacy.

————. *Marty and Company on a Carolina Farm.* Garden City, N.Y., 1933. 280 pp. About "eastern Carolina where farmers still live upon land granted to their ancestors in Colonial days."

McCorkle, Sarah "Lutie." *Old Time Stories of the Old North State.* Boston, 1903. 159 pp. Stories for children—historical and legendary.

*North Carolina Fiction, 1734-1947: An Annotated Bibliography.* U.N.C. Library, Chapel Hill, 1958. 189 pp.

Page, Walter Hines. *The Southerner, a Novel, Being the Autobiography of Nicholas Worth.* New York, 1909. 424 pp. A study of the problems of the youth in the late nineteenth century—historical and sociological.

Pierce, Ovid Williams. *On a Lonesome Porch.* Garden City, N.Y., 1960. 237 pp. Novel about eastern North Carolina.

————. *The Plantation.* Garden City, N.Y., 1953. 217 pp. Scene is early nineteenth-century plantation in Halifax County.

Polk, William T. *The Fallen Angel and Other Stories.* Chapel Hill, 1956. 180 pp.

Pridgen, Tim. *Tory Oath.* Garden City, N.Y., 1941. 371 pp. Cape Fear section during Revolution.

Prince, William Meade. *The Southern Part of Heaven.* New York, 1950. 314 pp. Chapel Hill in early twentieth century; Mr. Prince's boyhood experiences.

"Reid, Christian" (Frances Christine Fisher Tiernan). North Carolina's most prolific novelist of the last quarter of the nineteenth century.

*His Victory.* Notre Dame, Ind., 1887. 82 pp. A short novel of the Linville region.

*The Land of the Sky.* New York, 1876. 130 pp. Gave that part of the state its picturesque name.

*The Wargave Trust.* New York, 1912. 384 pp. Setting at Cooleemee Plantation, Davie County.

Sawyer, Lemuel. *Blackbeard; A Comedy* . . . Washington, 1824. 66 pp. Currituck county politicians, treasure-hunters, and over-credulous backwoodsmen—not about the notorious pirate of that name.

Sims, Marian. *The City on the Hill.* Philadelphia, 1940. 356 pp. Charlotte—sociological.

Strange, Robert. *Eoneguski, or, The Cherokee Chief, a Tale of Past Wars, by an American.* 2 vols. in one. Washington. 1839. First novel by a resident North Carolinian with a North Carolina setting.

Throop, George H. *Bertie; or Life in the Old Field.* Philadelphia. 1851. 242 pp.

———. *Nag's Head; or, Two Month's among "the Bankers."* Philadelphia, 1850. 180 pp. The story of a summer's vacation at Nag's Head. These two novels were published anonymously, but it seems almost certain that Throop wrote them.

Tourgée, Albion W. *The C Letters Published in the North State.* Greensboro, 1878. 54 pp. North Carolina politics during Reconstruction—by the state's leading carpetbagger.

———. *A Fool's Errand.* New York, 1880. 361 pp. Problems of Reconstruction.

Tracy, Don. *Carolina Corsair.* New York, 1955. 375 pp. Ribald tale of pirate Blackbeard.

———. *Roanoke Renegade.* New York, 1954. 367 pp. Racy novel of Roanoke Island, 1584-1590.

Walser, Richard (ed.). *North Carolina in the Short Story.*

Chapel Hill, 1948. 309 pp. Fifteen selected short stories by as many different authors, including O. Henry, Thomas Wolfe, Paul Green, and William T. Polk.

———. *Short Stories from the Old North State.* Chapel Hill, 1959. 288 pp.

Wellman, Manly Wade. *Battle for King's Mountain.* New York, 1962. 170 pp.

———. *Clash on the Catawba.* New York, 1962. 177 pp.

———. *Dead and Gone: Classic Crimes of North Carolina.* Chapel Hill, 1953. 190 pp. Ten noted murders in the state, 1808-1914.

———. *Settlement on Shocco: Adventures in Colonial Carolina.* Winston-Salem, 1964. 184 pp.

Wiley, Calvin H. *Alamance.* New York, 1847. 151 pp. Revolutionary events, especially in Alamance-Guilford area, and centering around the Rev. David Caldwell.

———. *Roanoke, or Where is Utopia?* Philadelphia, 1866. 156 pp. Revolutionary days in eastern North Carolina, culminating in Battle of Moore's Creek Bridge (1776).

Wolfe, Thomas. *Look Homeward Angel.* New York, 1929. 626 pp. The "passionate story of a boy's beginnings in a North Carolina hill-town" [Asheville].

———. *Of Time and the River.* New York, 1935. 912 pp. Story of Wolfe's early years of maturity.

———. *The Webb and the Rock.* New York, 1939. 695 pp. A transitional work.

———. *You Can't Go Home Again.* New York, 1940. 743 pp. Emphasis on Wolfe's faith in democracy. "I believe we are lost here in America, but I believe we shall be found." On this note, Wolfe died at the age of 37.

## V. / SELECT BIBLIOGRAPHY
## OF NORTH CAROLINA FOLKLORE

Brown, Frank C. "Ballad Literature in North Carolina." *N.C. Lit. and Hist. Assoc. Proc.* (1915), pp. 92-102.

Chase, Richard. *The Jack Tales.* Boston, 1943. 201 pp.
———. *Grandfather Tales. American-English Folk Tales,* Boston, 1948. 239 pp.

*The Frank C. Brown Collection of North Carolina Folklore.* 5 vols., Durham, 1952-1962. ". . . surely the most imposing monument ever erected in this country to the common memory of the people of any single State." This great collection includes: (1) games and rhymes, beliefs and customs, riddles, proverbs, folk speech, tales and legends; (2) ballads; (3) folksongs; (4) the music of the ballads and songs; (5) superstitions.

Harden, John. *The Devil's Tramping Ground and Other North Carolina Mystery Stories.* Chapel Hill, 1949. 178 pp. Tales and legends.
———. *Tar Heel Ghosts.* Chapel Hill, 1954. 178 pp.

Hendricks, W. C. *Bundle of Troubles and Other Tar Heel Tales.* Durham, 1943. 206 pp.

Jackson, George Pullen. *White and Negro Spirituals.* New York, 1943. 349 pp.

Koch, Frederick H. (ed.). *American Folk-Plays.* New York, 1939. 592 pp.
——— (ed.). *Carolina Folk-Plays.* New York, 1931. 311 pp.

Odum, Howard, and Guy B. Johnson. *The Negro and His Songs*. Chapel Hill, 1925. 306 pp.

————. *Negro Workaday Songs*. Chapel Hill, 1926. 278 pp.

Sharp, Cecil J. *English Folk Songs from the Southern Appalachians*, ed. by Maud Karpeles. 2 vols. New York, 1932. (273 songs and ballads, with 968 tunes.)

Stringfield, Lamar. *Cripple Creek Suite*. New York, 1930. 20 pp. This won the Pulitzer Prize in Music in 1930.

Taliaferro, H. E. *Fisher's River (North Carolina) Scenes and Characters*. New York, 1859. 269 pp.

White, Newman I. *American Negro Folk-Songs*. Cambridge, Mass., 1928. 501 pp.

Scholarly study of folklore has been pursued on the campuses of The University of North Carolina and Duke University for over forty years. Besides Frank C. Brown and Newman I. White at Duke, a succession of scholars at Chapel Hill, Greensboro, and Raleigh, including C. Alphonso Smith, Howard W. Odum, Guy B. Johnson, Ralph S. Boggs, A. P. Hudson, J. P. Schinhan, J. D. Clark, George P. Wilson, and John E. Keller, have collected, studied, and published folklore. Many of their books, bearing the imprint of The University of North Carolina Press, have appeared from time to time, and their articles have appeared in such periodicals as *Journal of American Folklore, Southern Folklore Quarterly,* and *South Atlantic Quarterly.* The North Carolina Folklore Society (founded in 1912) and the North Carolina Folklore Council (founded in 1937) have fostered the organized study of folklore. *North Carolina Folklore,* a journal founded in 1948, is published at Chapel Hill under the joint auspices of the two organizations.

# VI. / TOPICAL SUMMARIES
## AND CHAPTER BIBLIOGRAPHIES

## 1. THE LAND AND ITS RESOURCES

SUMMARY—*Boundaries and area of North Carolina:* (1) in colonial era; 1629, 1663, 1665 charters; (2) boundary disputes with Virginia, South Carolina, Georgia, and Tennessee; (3) present boundaries.—*Physical divisions of North Carolina:* Coastal Plain, Piedmont, Mountains; characteristics of different regions, their soils, climate, rainfall.—*Influence of geographic factors on North Carolina:* coast line, capes, inlets, and sounds; the river systems and their relation to state's history.—*Natural resources:* land; various soil types and their effects on agriculture; forest resources, forest divisions, and types of trees; minerals and building stones; game and fish; relation of natural resources to economic development.

TEXT—Lefler-Newsome, *North Carolina,* 17-23.

BASIC READING—

Connor, R. D. W. *Rebuilding an Ancient Commonwealth,* I, 1-39.

Crittenden, C. C. *The Commerce of North Carolina,* 1763-1789, Chs. 1 and 2.

Hobbs, S. H., Jr. *North Carolina, Economic and Social,* 13-25.

———. *North Carolina: An Economic and Social Profile,* 3-34.

*North Carolina Guide,* 26-49.

SUGGESTED READING—

Avery, Myron H., and Kenneth S. Boardman. "Arnold Guyot's Notes on the Geography of the Mountain District of Western North Carolina," *NCHR*, XV, No. 3 (July, 1938), 251-318.

Barringer, Paul B. "The Influence of Peculiar Conditions in the Early History of North Carolina," *N.C. Lit. and Hist. Assoc. Proc.*, XVIII (1919), 13-25.

Bassett, J. S. "The Influence of Coast Line and Rivers on North Carolina," *AHA Annual Report*, 1908, I, 58-61.

Broadhurst, S. D. *An Introduction to the Topography, Geology, and Mineral Resources of North Carolina*, 1-17.

Bryson, Herman. *Gold Deposits in North Carolina*, 1-157.

————. *The Story of the Geologic Making of North Carolina*, 1-42.

Camp, Cordelia. *The Influence of Geography upon Early North Carolina*, 1-31.

Cumming, William P. *North Carolina in Maps*, 1-36.

————. *The Southeast in Early Maps*, 1-62. (Use index for individual maps.)

Deyton, Jason B. "The Toe River Valley to 1865," *NCHR*, XXIV, No. 4 (October, 1947), 423-466.

Dunbar, Gary S. *Geographical History of the North Carolina Outer Banks*, 1-249.

Emmons, Ebenezer. *The Swamp Lands of North Carolina*, 1-95.

Hamnett, W. L., and D. C. Thornton. *Tar Heel Wildlife*, 1-98.

Holmes, J. S. *Common Forest Trees of North Carolina: A Pocket Manual*, 1-76.

Lemert, B. F. "Geographic Influences in the History of North Carolina," *NCHR*, XII, No. 4 (October, 1935), 297-319.

Lonsdale, Richard E. (comp.). *Atlas of North Carolina*, 2-32.

Merrens, Harry Roy. *Colonial North Carolina in the Eighteenth Century: A Study in Historical Geography*, 1-293.

Ross, Malcolm. *The Cape Fear*, 1-340.

Rowland, Buford. "Some Observations on the Low Parts of

North Carolina," *NCHR*, XV, No. 2 (April, 1938), 156-158.

Stick, David. *Graveyard of the Atlantic*, 1-276.

——. *The Outer Banks of North Carolina, 1584-1958*, 1-352.

Stuckey, Jasper L., and W. G. Steel. *Geology and Mineral Resources of North Carolina*, 1-34.

——. *North Carolina: Its Geology and Mineral Resources*, 1-550.

Thoenen, J. R., and Jasper L. Stuckey. *The Mineral Industry of North Carolina*, 1-20.

Wells, B. W. *The Natural Gardens of North Carolina*, 1-458.

Weslager, C. A. "Place Names on Ocracoke Island," *NCHR*, XXXI, No. 1 (January, 1954), 41-49.


## 2. *THE INDIANS OF NORTH CAROLINA*

SUMMARY—*Origin of the North American Indians:* dates and circumstances of migration; how Indian population spread. —*Linguistic groups and tribes in early North Carolina:* population estimates at various periods; regional distribution.— *How the Indians lived:* characteristics, culture, religion, government, agriculture, trade.—*Contributions to agriculture:* land, methods of clearing land, hill cultivation, fertilization, native dishes.—*Effects of white settlement upon Indians:* trade, warfare, disease, slavery.—*Gradual "removal" of Indians:* methods, treaties, population figures at various times; the "vanishing American."—*"Trading paths":* most famous ones; use by whites.—*Place names and other permanent Indian contributions:* excavations of Indian villages, mounds, and burial grounds; types of artifacts found.

TEXT—Lefler-Newsome, *North Carolina*, 23-28.

BASIC READING—

Brickell, John. *The Natural History of North Carolina*, 277-408.

Connor, R. D. W. *Rebuilding an Ancient Commonwealth*, I, Ch. 3.

Lefler, Hugh T. (ed.). *John Lawson's A New Voyage to Carolina*, 13-67, 120-246.

Rights, Douglas L. *The American Indian in North Carolina*, 28-61, 113-210.

SUGGESTED READING—

Barton, Lew. *The Most Ironic Story in American History: An Authoritative Documented History of the Lumbee Indians of North Carolina*, 1-142.

Bleeker, Sonia. *The Cherokee Indians of the Mountains*, 1-159.

Bloom, Leonard. "The Acculturation of the Eastern Cherokee: Historical Aspects," *NCHR*, XIX, No. 4 (October, 1942), 322-357.

Brown, D. S. *The Catawba Indians: The People of the River*, 1-400.

Carrier, Lyman. *The Beginnings of Agriculture in America*, 1-323.

Corkran, David H. "Cherokee Pre-History," *NCHR*, XXXIV, No. 4 (October, 1957), 455-466.

Crane, V. W. *The Southern Frontier*, 1-46.

Dillard, Richard. "The Indian Tribes of Eastern North Carolina," *NCB*, VI (July, 1906), 3-26.

Dirket, A. L. "The Noble Savage Convention As Epitomized in Lawson's *A New Voyage to Carolina*," *NCHR*, XLIII, No. 4 (October, 1966), 413-429.

Gulick, John. *Cherokees at the Cross Roads*, 1-24.

Harper, Roland M. "A Statistical Study of the Croatans," *Rural Sociology*, II (1937), 444-456.

Herndon, Melvin G. "Indian Agriculture in the Southern Colonies," *NCHR*, XLIV, No. 3 (July, 1967), 283-297.

Hodge, F. W. *Handbook of the American Indians North of Mexico*, 841-853.

Hunter, Kermit. *Unto These Hills*, 1-100. Symphonic drama.

Johnson, F. Roy. *The Tuscaroras: Mythology-Medicine Culture*. 2 vols.

Lee, E. Lawrence, Jr. *The Indian Wars in North Carolina, 1663-1763*, 1-94.

Litton, Gaston. "Enrollment Records of the Eastern Band of

Cherokee Indians," *NCHR,* XVII, No. 3 (July, 1940), 199-231.

Lonsdale, Richard E. (comp.). *Atlas of North Carolina,* 33-34.

McCall, W. A. *Cherokees and Pioneers,* 1 106.

McPherson, O. M. *Indians of North Carolina,* 1-252.

Milling, J. C. *Red Carolinians,* 3-34, 266-285.

Mooney, James. *Myths of the Cherokees,* 11-29.

Olds, F. A. "Our North Carolina Indians," *NCB,* XVII (July, 1917), 39-47.

Quattlebaum, Paul. *The Land Called Chicora: The Carolinas under Spanish Rule with French Intrusions, 1520-1670,* 1-153.

Rights, Douglas L. "The Buffalo in North Carolina," *NCHR,* IX, No. 3 (July, 1932), 242-249.

———. "Traces of the Indian in Piedmont North Carolina," *NCHR,* I, No. 3 (July, 1924), 277-288.

———. "The Trading Path of the Indians," *NCHR,* VIII, No. 4 (October, 1931), 403-426.

Royce, C. C. *The Cherokee Nation of Indians,* 129-144.

———. *Indian Land Cessions in the United States,* 545-562, 624-630.

South, Stanley A. *Indians in North Carolina,* 1-67.

Speck, Frank. "The Catawba Nation and Its Neighbors," *NCHR,* XVI, No. 4 (October, 1939), 404-417.

———. "Remnants of the Machapunga Indians of North Carolina," *Am. Anthrop.,* Vol. 18 (April-June, 1916), 271-276.


## 3. EXPLORATIONS AND ATTEMPTS AT SETTLEMENT

SUMMARY—*Early explorations:* French (Verrazzano) in 1524; Spanish (Ayllón) in 1526; De Soto and other Spanish explorers; why France and Spain did not colonize the Carolina region.—*English interest in colonization:* Anglo-Spanish rivalry; Queen Elizabeth's interest in colonies; Richard Hakluyt and other publicists; Elizabethan "Sea Dogs"; Humphrey

Gilbert fails to plant a colony in New World; Raleigh's patent of 1584. —*The Roanoke Island Colonies:* expedition of Amadas and Barlowe (1584) ; the Ralph Lane colony (1585-1586) ; the Grenville expedition (1586) ; the John White or "Lost Colony" (1587-1590).—*The fate of the "Lost Colony":* various theories—*Permanent colony at Jamestown, Virginia (1607):* John Pory's report about Albemarle Sound region (1622).— *Carolina granted to Sir Robert Heath* (1629) : failure to plant a colony; patent assigned to others.—*Explorations of North Carolina area from Virginia:* Edward Bland (1650) ; grant of land to Roger Green (1653); Francis Yeardley's report (1654) ; land purchases from Indians by 1662 or earlier.

TEXT—Lefler-Newsome, *North Carolina,* Ch. 1.

BASIC READING—

Lefler, Hugh T. (ed.). *North Carolina History Told by Contemporaries,* 1-15.

Ashe, S. A. *History of North Carolina,* I, 1-49.

Connor, R. D. W. *North Carolina: Rebuilding an Ancient Commonwealth,* I, 63-72. Hereafter cited as *Rebuilding.*

———. *History of North Carolina: The Colonial and Revolutionary Periods,* I, 1-31. Hereafter cited as *History of North Carolina,* I.

SUGGESTED READING—

Adams, Randolph. "An Effort to Identify John White," *AHR,* XLI (1935) , 87-91.

Betts, Robert E. "The Lost Colony," *Cornhill Mag.,* CLVII (1938) , 50-67.

Brown, Alexander. *Genesis of the United States,* I, 1-22.

Cheshire, Joseph B. "Baptism of Virginia Dare." *NCB,* X (April, 1911) , 167-175.

Connor, R. D. W. "The Voyage of Verrazzano: The First Exploration of the North Carolina Coast by Europeans," *NCB,* XVI (April, 1917), 209-218.

Corbitt, D. L. (ed.). *Explorations, Descriptions, and Attempted Settlements of Carolina, 1584-1590.* 1-154.

Craven, W. F. *The Southern Colonies in the Seventeenth Century,* 27-59.

Cumming, W. P. "The Identity of John White Governor of Roanoke Island and John White the Artist," *NCHR*, XV, No. 3 (July, 1938), 197-203.

Daves, Edward G. "Raleigh's New Fort in Virginia, 1585," TCHS, *Papers*, I (1897), 27-52.

Doran, Joseph I. "Sir Walter Raleigh, Chief Governor of Virginia, and Founder of Roanoke Colony, 1585," *Pa. Soc. Coll.: Governors Publ.*, I (1916), 52-72.

Epler, Blanche N. "A Part of Elizabethan England in America," *Nat. Geog. Mag.*, LXIV (1933), 695-730.

Fiske, John. *Old Virginia and Her Neighbors*, I, 30-40.

Fitch, W. E. *The First Founders in America . . .* , 1-40.

Fletcher, Inglis. *Roanoke Hundred*. Novel.

Glasgow, Tom. "H. M. S. Tiger," *NCHR*, XLIII, No. 2 (April, 1966), 115-121.

Green, Paul. *The Lost Colony*, 1-138. Symphonic drama.

Harrington, J. C. "Archeological Explorations at Fort Raleigh National Historic Site," *NCHR*, XXVI, No. 2 (April, 1949), 127-149.

————. "The Finding of Fort Raleigh," *Southern Indian Studies*, I (April, 1949), 18-19.

————. "The Manufacture and Use of Brick at the Raleigh Settlement on Roanoke Island," *NCHR*, XLIV, No. 1 (January, 1967), 1-17.

————. *Search for the Cittie of Raleigh*. 1-63.

————. *An Outwork at Fort Raleigh: Further Archeological Excavations at Fort Raleigh National Historic Site*. Philadelphia, 1966. 66 pp.

Hawks, F. L. *History of North Carolina*, I, 69-254.

Hulton, Paul. "John White Artist," *North Carolina Museum of Art Bulletin*, V (Spring-Summer, 1965), 2-43.

————, and David B. Quinn (eds.). *The American Drawings of John White, 1577-1590*. 2 vols.

Lonsdale, Richard E. (comp.). *Atlas of North Carolina*, 35-36.

Lowery, Woodbury. *The Spanish Settlements within the Present Limits of the United States*. 168, 230, 355, 449.

Pearce, H. J., Jr. "The Dare Stones," *Brenau College Bulletin*, XXX (March, 1939), 1-8.

————. "New Light on the Roanoke Colony," *Jour. Sou. Hist.*, IV (May, 1938), 148-163.

Peek, W. J. "The White Pictures," *NCB*, VI (April, 1907), 243-250.

Quinn, David B. *The New Found Land: The English Contributions to the Discovery of North America*, 1-45.

————. "Preparations for the 1585 Virginia Voyage," *WMQ*, VI, No. 2 (April, 1949), 208-236.

————. *Raleigh and the British Empire*, 47-129.

———— (ed.). *The Roanoke Voyages, 1584-1590*. 2 vols.

Rights, Douglas L. *The American Indian in North Carolina*, 6-27.

Robinson, Melvin. *Riddle of the Lost Colony*, 1-64.

Sams, C. W. *The Conquest of Virginia: The First Attempt*, 1-367.

Sparkes, Boyden. "Writ on Rocke," *Saturday Evening Post* (April 26, 1941), 9-11, 118-128.

Wallace, D. D. *South Carolina: A Short History*, 15-22.

Weeks, S. B. "The Lost Colony: Its Fate and Survival," *AHA Papers*, V (1891), 439-480.

Wright, Louis B. "Elizabethan Politics and Colonial Enterprise," *NCHR*, XXXII, No. 2 (April, 1955), 254-270.

## 4. THE CAROLINA PROPRIETARY: ALBEMARLE COUNTY

SUMMARY—*The "Restoration" of Charles II (1660):* characteristics of this era; Carolina one of several proprietary grants. —*The Charter of 1663:* County of Durham, the English prototype; the eight Lords Proprietors; reasons for their grant.— *Provisions of charter:* boundaries, crown royalty, government, religion, rights of settlers.—*The 1665 Charter:* extension of boundaries northward and southward; effects of this change. —*Changes in Proprietors, 1663-1729—Perpetuation of their names in the two Carolinas.—Proprietary plans for three counties:* Albemarle, Clarendon (Cape Fear area), Craven (South Carolina area).—*Problems of the Proprietors:* Heath claimants, advertising the colony—nature of offers, procuring settlers, establishment of government.—*William Drummond, first governor of Albemarle County* (1664).—*The short-lived County of Clarendon (1664-1667):* reasons for its failure. —*The Fundamental Constitutions of Carolina* (1669 and later revisions): difficulties of enforcement.—*Governmental structure of Albemarle County:* governor, council, assembly, courts, local (precinct) government; executive-legislative conflicts— causes and results.—*Problems of Albemarle:* geographic handicaps, land problem (Great Deed of Grant, 1668); unstable and inefficient government; Virginia animosity; Indian hostility; British Navigation Acts and other trade laws, especially the Plantation Duty Act (1673).—*Culpeper's Rebellion:* causes, leaders, results.—*The end of Albemarle County:* Seth Sothel, the last governor, banished in 1689.

TEXT—Lefler-Newsome, *North Carolina,* Ch. 3.

BASIC READING—

Lefler, Hugh T. (ed.). *North Carolina History Told by Contemporaries,* 15-31.

Ashe, S. A. *History of North Carolina,* I, 55-140.

Connor, R. D. W. *North Carolina, Rebuilding,* I, 73-107.

———. *History of North Carolina,* I, 32-63.

SUGGESTED READING—

Albertson, Catherine. "Enfield Farm where the Culpeper Rebellion Began," *NCB,* XII (April, 1913), 224-231.

———. "The First Albemarle Assembly [1665]-Hall's Creek, near Nixonton," *NCB,* XII (January, 1913), 202-207.

———. *In Ancient Albemarle,* 1-53.

Andrews, C. M. "Captain Henry Wilkinson," *Sou. Atl. Quar.,* XV (July, 1916), 177-202.

———. *The Colonial Period of American History,* III, 182-267.

——— (ed.). *Narratives of the Insurrections,* 1675-1690, 145-164.

Barner, A. M. "Locke's Grand Model: Historical Review of the First Form of Government of the Carolina Colonies," *Lawyer and Banker,* XIII (July, 1920), 210-215.

Bassett, J. S. *The Constitutional Beginnings of North Carolina,* 9-73.

————. "The County of Clarendon," *NCB,* II, No. 9 (February, 1903) , 1-20.

————. "The Naming of the Carolinas," *Sewanee Review,* II, No. 3 (1894) , 343-352.

Cheshire, Joseph B. "The Fundamental Constitutions of Carolina, and Religious Liberty in the Province of North Carolina," *P.E. Church Hist. Mag.,* I (1921), 204-221.

Corbitt, D. L. *The Formation of North Carolina Counties, 1663-1943,* 11, 18, 25, 206, 227.

Craven, W. F. *The Southern Colonies in the Seventeenth Century, 1607-1689,* 408-410.

Cumming, W. P. "Naming Carolina," *NCHR,* XXII, No. 1 (January, 1945), 34-42.

Dodd, W. E. *The Old South: Struggles for Democracy,* 208-234, 276-293.

Fiske, John. *Old Virginia and Her Neighbors,* II, 270-289.

Goodpasture, A. V. "Pepys and the Proprietors of Carolina," *Tenn. Hist. Mag.,* VI (October, 1920) , 166-176.

Guess, W. C. "County Government in Colonial North Carolina," *JSHP,* XI, No. 1 (1911) , 7-39.

Hamilton, P. J. *The Colonization of the South,* 133-147.

Hawks, F. L. *History of North Carolina,* II, 15-212.

Lapsley, G. T. *The County Palatine of Durham,* 1-310.

Lefler, Hugh T. "Promotional Literature of the Southern Colonies," *Jour. Sou. Hist.,* XXXIII, No. 1 (February, 1967), 3-5, 15-20.

McCain, Paul M. *The County Court in North Carolina before 1750,* 3-148.

McPherson, Elizabeth G. "Nathaniel Bats, Landholder on Pasquotank River, 1660," *NCHR,* XLIII, No. 1 (January, 1966) , 66-81.

Marley, Branson (ed.). "Minutes of the General Court of Albemarle, 1684," *NCHR,* XIX, No. 1 (January, 1942) , 48-58.

Osgood, H. L. *The American Colonies in the Seventeenth Century,* II, 200-241.

Parker, Coralie. *The History of Taxation in North Carolina during the Colonial Period,* 68-96.

Parker, Mattie E. (ed.). *North Carolina Charters and Constitutions, 1578-1698,* 3-240.

Powell, William S. *The Carolina Charter of 1663: How It Came to North Carolina and Its Place in History. With Biographical Sketches of the Proprietors,* 1-79.

———— (ed.). Carolina in the Seventeenth Century: An Annotated Bibliography of Contemporary Publications, *NCHR,* XLI, No. 1 (January, 1964), 74-104.

———— (ed.). *Ye Countie of Albemarle in Carolina: A Collection of Documents, 1664-1675.* xiii-xxxii, 1-90.

Rankin, Hugh F. *Upheaval in Albemarle, 1675-1689: The Story of Culpeper's Rebellion,* 1-87.

Raper, C. L. *North Carolina: A Study in English Colonial Government,* 1-26.

Rights, Douglas L. *The American Indian in North Carolina,* 62-70.

Salley, A. S. (ed.). *Narratives of Early Carolina, 1650-1708,* 65-73, 137-176.

Schuyler, Montgomery. *Notes on the Patroonships, Manors, and Seigneuries in Colonial Times,* 1-43.

Wager, Paul W. *County Government and Administration in North Carolina,* 1-16.

Wertenbaker, T. J. *The Old South: The Founding of American Civilization,* 1-21.


## 5. THE EMERGENCE OF NORTH CAROLINA, 1689-1729

SUMMARY—*Reorganization of the government:* deputy governors—Jarvis, Harvey, and Walker.—*Expansion of settlement:* French Huguenots from Virginia; town of Bath founded; New Bern settled (1710) under leadership of Von Graffenried and Lawson.—*The Problem of the Established Church and Cary's Rebellion:* influence of Quakers; Vestry Act of 1703.—*Edward Hyde, first governor of "North Caro-*

*lina":* Cary's armed forces defy Hyde; defeat and aftermath.—
*The Tuscarora War* (1711-1713): causes—encroachment on
Indian lands, "sharp practices" of white traders, enslavement
of Indians, founding of New Bern; Governor Hyde calls on
Virginia and South Carolina for aid; expedition of John
Barnwell (1711) and James Moore (1712-1713) from South
Carolina; defeat and expulsion of Tuscarora; Tom Blunt and
"friendly Tuscarora" rewarded with large land grant.—*Revision of laws* (1715) : beneficial results.—*The "Golden Age
of Piracy":* reasons for piracy; Blackbeard, Bonnet, and other
pirates; execution of many pirates at Charleston, S.C., in 1718.
*Immigration and expansion:* new areas settled, especially
Lower Cape Fear Valley; founding of Brunswick and Wilmington.—*Settlement of Virginia-North Carolina boundary*
(1728): North Carolina wins disputed area.—*Crown purchases
seven of eight proprietary shares* (1729) : reasons for royali-
zation; unsold share (Carteret) eventually becomes Granville
District.

TEXT—Lefler-Newsome, *North Carolina,* Ch. 4.

BASIC READING—

Lefler, Hugh T. (ed.). *North Carolina History Told by Con-
    temporaries,* 30-51.
Ashe, S. A. *History of North Carolina,* I, 141-223.
Connor, R. D. W. *North Carolina: Rebuilding,* I, 108-148.
———. *History of North Carolina,* I, 64-142.

SUGGESTED READING—

Adams, Percy G. "John Lawson's Alter Ego—Dr. John
    Brickell," *NCHR,* XXIV, No. 3 (July, 1957), 313-326.
Allred, Fred J., and Alonzo T. Dill (eds.). "The Founding
    of New Bern: A Footnote," *NCHR,* XL, No. 3 (July,
    1963), 361-374.
Ashe, S. A. "Our Own Pirates: Blackbeard and Bonnet,"
    *NCB,* II, No. 2 (1902), 3-23.
Barnwell, John. "The Tuscarora Expedition," *S.C. Hist.
    Mag.,* XI (January, 1908), 28-58.
Channing, Edward. *History of the United States,* II, 354-362.

Clark, Walter. "Indian Massacre and the Tuscarora War," *NCB*, II, No. 3 (1902), 3-16.

Dill, Alonzo T. "Eighteenth Century New Bern," *NCHR*, XXII, Nos. 1, 2, 3, 4 (January, April, July, October, 1945), 1-21, 152-175, 292-313, 460-489; XXIII, Nos. 1, 2, 3, 4 (January, April, July, October, 1946), 47-78, 142-171, 325-359, 495-535.

Faust, A. B. *The German Element in the United States*, I, 212-216.

Fiske, John. *Old Virginia and Her Neighbors*, II, 289-322.

Fletcher, Inglis. *Lusty Wind for Carolina*, 1-509. Novel about North Carolina pirates.

Haywood, M. de L. "Governor Charles Eden," *NCB*, III, No. 8 (1903), 1-24.

Hendren, Linville L. "De Graffenried and the Swiss Palatine Settlement of New Berne, N.C." TCHS, *Papers*, IV (1910), 64-71.

Hodge, F. W. *Handbook of American Indians North of Mexico*, Part II, 841-853.

Howell, A. J. *The Book of Wilmington*, 1-31.

Hughson, S. C. *Carolina Pirates and Colonial Commerce*, 535-548.

Jameson, J. F. *Privateering and Piracy in the Colonial Period*, 535-548.

Karraker, Cyrus. *Piracy Was a Business*. (Use index for N.C. pirates).

Lee, E. Lawrence, Jr. *The Indian Wars in North Carolina, 1663-1763*, 1-94.

―――. *The Lower Cape Fear in Colonial Days*, 1-334.

―――. "Old Brunswick, The Story of a Colonial Town," *NCHR*, XXIX, No. 3 (July, 1952), 230-245.

Lonsdale, R. E. (comp.). *Atlas of North Carolina*, 41-43.

McCrady, Edward. *South Carolina under the Proprietary Government*, 506-596.

McPherson, O. M. *Indians of North Carolina*, 180-196.

Masterson, William H. "William Byrd in Lubberland," *Am. Lit.*, IX (1937), 153-170.

Milling, J. C. *Red Carolinians*, 113-135.

Oliver, David D. "The Society for the Propagation of the

Gospel in the Province of North Carolina," *JSHP*, IX, No. 1 (1910) , 1-23.

Paschal, Herbert R., Jr. *A History of Colonial Bath,* 1-69.

Pascoe, C. F. *Two Hundred Years of the S.P.G.,* 20-25.

Rankin, Hugh F. *The Pirates of Colonial North Carolina,* 1-72.

Rodman, Lida T. "Pampticoe and Bath, North Carolina," *N.C. Hist. Com. Publ.* I (1907), 174-200.

Shinn, James F. "Edward Moseley: A North Carolina Patriot and Statesman," *Publ. of Sou. Hist. Assoc.,* III (1899) , 15-34.

Sprunt, James. *Chronicles of the Cape Fear River,* 1660-1916, 1-40.

Todd, V. H., and J. Goebel (eds.) . *Christoph Von Graffenried's Account of the Founding of New Bern,* 35-76.

Weeks, S. B. *Church and State in North Carolina,* 1-25.

———. *The Religious Development in the Province of Carolina,* 1-65.

Wright, Louis B. (ed.) *The Prose Works of William Byrd of Westover.* (Use index for N.C. references.)

## 6. *THE "NEW IMMIGRATION": HIGHLAND SCOTS, SCOTCH-IRISH, GERMANS*

SUMMARY—*More efficient government*: royal governors, George Burrington, Gabriel Johnston, Arthur Dobbs, William Tryon, Josiah Martin.—*Population growth and expansion:* natural increase, high birth rate but also high mortality; immigration: result of conditions in Europe, quest for economic betterment and religious freedom, activities of land companies, encouragement by governors and legislatures.—*Highland Scots settle Upper Cape Fear Valley:* reasons for first settlements; aftermath of battle of Culloden (1746); areas settled; contributions to agriculture, industry, trade, education, and religion; attitude toward England.—*Scotch-Irish settle in the Piedmont:* reasons for migrating to Pennsylvania; reasons why many moved from Pennsylvania to North Carolina; the "Great Wagon Road"; places settled; characteristics; contributions to agriculture, industry, trade, education, and religion.—*Germans also settle in the Piedmont:* reasons for immigration, Moravian settlement of Wachovia Tract (1753-1766 and following); Lutheran and Reformed sects; areas settled; German contributions to agriculture, industry, trade, education, medicine, and religion.—*How North Carolina was changed by the "new immigration."*

TEXT—Lefler-Newsome, *North Carolina*, Ch. 5.

BASIC READING—

Connor, R. D. W. *North Carolina: Rebuilding*, I, 149-163.
———. *History of North Carolina*, I, 162-179.
———. *Race Elements in the White Population of North Carolina*, 7-112.
Hammer, Carl, Jr. *Rhinelanders on the Yadkin*, 11-63.
Leyburn, J. G. *The Scotch-Irish*, 172-186, 210-218, 252-254, 301-303.
Meyer, Duane. *The Highland Scots of North Carolina, 1732-1776*, 3-165.
Ramsey, Robert W. *Carolina Cradle: Settlement of the Northwest Carolina Frontier*, 3-216.

SUGGESTED READING—

Adam, Margaret. "The Highland Emigration of 1770," *Scot. Hist. Rev.*, XVI (1920), 280-293.
Ashe, S. A. "Early Times on the Cape Fear," *NCB*, XIII (January, 1914), 152-174.
Baker, Howard F. "National Stocks in the Population of the United States As Indicated by Their Surnames in the Census of 1790," *AHA Annual Report* (1931), 126-134.
Battle, K. P. (ed.). "Letters and Documents Relating to the Early History of the Lower Cape Fear," *JSHP*, No. 4 (1903), 1-135.
Bolton, C. K. *Scotch-Irish Pioneers in Ulster and America*, 285-295.
Campbell, Mildred. "English Emigration on the Eve of the American Revolution," *AHR*, LXI (1953), 1-20.
Clewell, J. H. *History of Wachovia in North Carolina*, 1-120.
Connor, R. D. W. "The Settlement of the Cape Fear." *Sou. Atl. Quar.*, VI (July, 1907), 272-287.
Dunaway, W. F. *The Scotch-Irish of Colonial Pennsylvania*. 28-49. 102-117.
Eller, Ernest M. *"The House of Peace," being a Historical*

*Legendary and Contemporary Account of the Moravians and their Settlement of Salem in North Carolina.* 1-287.

Faust, A. B. *The German Element in the United States,* I, 212-233.

Fries, Adelaide L. (ed.) . *Records of the Moravians in North Carolina,* Vols. I and II.

———. *The Road to Salem,* 3-215.

Gehrke, William H. "The Beginnings of the Pennsylvania German Element in Rowan and Cabarrus Counties," *Pa. Mag. Hist.,* LVIII (1934) , 342-369.

———. "The Transition from the German to the English Language in North Carolina," *NCHR,* XII, No. 1 (January, 1935) , 1-19.

Glenn, Thomas A. *Welsh Founders of Pennsylvania,* 2 vols. (Use index for N.C.).

Golden, Harry L. "The Jewish People of North Carolina," *NCHR,* XXXII, No. 2 (April, 1955) , 194-216.

Graham, Ian C. C. *Colonists from Scotland, 1707-1783.* (Use index for N.C. references) .

Green, Paul. *The Highland Call,* 2-203. Symphonic drama.

Greene, E. B., and Virginia D. Harrington. *American Population before the Census of 1790,* 156-171.

Henderson, Archibald. "North Carolina and the Ulster Scot," *NCB,* XXIII (1926) , 51-56.

Hühner, Leon. "The Jews of North Carolina Prior to 1800," *Am. Jew. Hist. Soc.,* XXIX (1925), 137-148.

Klees, Frederic. *The Pennsylvania Dutch,* 72-121.

Leonard, J. C. "The Germans in North Carolina." *Pa.-German,* X (June, 1909) , 266-272.

Lohr, L. L. "The Germans in North Carolina West of the Catawba," *Pa.-German,* XII (April, 1911) , 206-211.

Lonsdale, R. E. (comp.) . *Atlas of North Carolina,* 37-38.

McCorkle, Donald M. "Musical Instruments of the Moravians in North Carolina," *Am. Ger. Rev.,* XXI (1955), 12-17.

McKelway, A. J. "The Scotch-Irish of North Carolina," *NCB,* IV, No. 1 (March, 1905) , 3-24.

McKoy, W. B. "Incidents of the Early and Permanent Settlement of the Cape Fear," *NCB,* VII (January, 1908), 210-235.

McLean, J. P. *The Scotch Highlanders in America,* 100-145.

Maurer, Maurer. "Music in Wachovia, 1753-1800," *WMQ,* VIII, No. 2 (April, 1951), 214-227.

Newsome, A. R. (ed.). "Records of Emigrants from England and Scotland to North Carolina, 1774-1775," *NCHR,* XI, Nos. 1 and 2 (January and April, 1934), 39-54, 129-143.

Nixon, J. R. "The German Settlers in Lincoln County and Western North Carolina," *JSHP,* XI, No. 2 (1912), 29-62.

Schütz, Géza. "Additions to the History of Swiss Colonization Projects in Carolina," *NCHR,* X, No. 2 (April, 1933), 133-141.

Sellers, Charles G., Jr. "Colonel Ezekiel Polk: Pioneer and Patriarch," *WMQ,* X, No. 1 (January, 1953), 80-98.

Spruill, Julia C. "Women in the Founding of the Southern Colonies," *NCHR,* XIII, No. 3 (July, 1936), 202-218.

Tilley, Nannie May. "The Settlement of Granville County," *NCHR,* XI, No. 1 (January, 1934), 1-19.

## 7. *AGRICULTURE AND INDUSTRY*

SUMMARY—*Importance of agriculture:* self-sufficiency, need for agricultural exports.—*The land system:* size of grants, terms of land tenure, head right system, quit rents, fees for surveys, confusion in land titles; inheritance laws.—*Crops:* corn, tobacco, wheat, oats, peas and beans, rice and others; fruits and vegetables.—*Agricultural policy of government:* laws designed to encourage agriculture—bounties, "commodity money," inspection laws, and other legislation.—*Methods of farming:* unscientific practices, problems of soil exhaustion, lack of adequate implements.—*"Vermin" and other problems:* falling prices of tobacco.—*Livestock and cattle:* "Scrub" milk cows and "razor-back" hogs; large number of beef cattle.—*Household industries:* food, clothing, beverages, and others.—*Commerical industries:* naval stores (tar, pitch, rosin, turpentine); lumber, potash, shipbuilding, and others.—*How North Carolina ranked with other colonies in manufactures.*

TEXT—Lefler-Newsome, *North Carolina,* Ch. 6.

BASIC READING—

Lefler, Hugh T. (ed.). *North Carolina History Told by Contemporaries,* 62-82.

Connor, R. D. W. *North Carolina: Rebuilding,* I (use index).

Crittenden, C. C. *The Commerce of North Carolina, 1763-1789,* 53-68.

Hawks, F. L. *History of North Carolina,* II, 216-334.

Merrens, Harry R. *Colonial North Carolina in the Eighteenth Century,* 85-141.

SUGGESTED READING—

Bassett, J. S. "Landholding in Colonial North Carolina," TCHS, *Papers,* II (1898), 44-61.

Bond, B. W. *The Quit Rent System in the American Colonies,* 61-82, 113-118, 286, 318.

Boyd, W. K. "Landholding in Colonial North Carolina," TCHS, *Papers,* II (1898), 44-61.

Carrier, Lyman. *The Beginnings of Agriculture in America,* 195-199.

Cathey C. O. *Agricultural Developments in North Carolina, 1783-1860,* 3-29.

Crane, V. W. *The Southern Frontier, 1670-1732,* 139-148.

Franklin, W. N. "Agriculture in Colonial North Carolina," *NCHR,* III, No. 4 (October, 1926), 539-574.

Gray, L. C. *History of Agriculture in the Southern United States to 1860,* I (Use index for North Carolina).

Leary, William J. "The Fisheries of Eastern Carolina," *NCB* XIV (April, 1915), 173-194.

Lefler, Hugh T. (ed.). *John Lawson's A New Voyage to Carolina,* 81-120.

Lonsdale, R. E. (comp.). *Atlas of North Carolina,* 39-40.

Morgan, Lawrence N. "Land Tenure in Proprietary North Carolina," *JSHP,* XII, No. 1 (1912), 41-63.

Pittman, T. M. "Industrial Life in Colonial North Carolina," *NCB,* VII, No. 1 (July, 1907), 50-58.

Smith, A. E. *Colonists in Bondage: White Servitude and Con-*

*vict Labor in America, 1607-1776.* (Use index for N.C. references.)

Tilley, Nannie May. "Industries of Colonial Granville County," *NCHR*, XIII, No. 4 (October, 1936), 273-289.

## 8. TRANSPORTATION, TRADE, AND COMMUNICATION TO 1775

SUMMARY—*Geographic factors:* influence of coast, sounds, and rivers; nature of ships trading in North Carolina waters; efforts to overcome natural handicaps; inland waterways and types of craft used on them.—*Overland trade and travel:* poor roads and "trading paths"; road laws and efforts for better roads; most important roads.—*Bridges and ferries:* laws regulating them.—*Use of horses and oxen:* wagon, carts, and "pleasure vehicles."—*Lodging:* private homes and inns (ordinaries).—*Commercial regulations:* British and colonial; ports of entry; inspection laws.—*Exports:* naval stores, lumber products, "provisions," tobacco, and others.—*Imports:* manufactured goods from England; imports from West Indies and from other Continental colonies, chiefly New England.— *Trade of "back country":* largely with Virginia, South Carolina, and Pennsylvania; nature of exports and imports.—*North Carolina merchants:* leading firms, character of business transactions, scarcity of specie, price of goods.—*Evolution of a postal system.*

TEXT—Lefler-Newsome, *North Carolina,* Ch. 7.

BASIC READING—

Crittenden, C. C. *The Commerce of North Carolina, 1763-1789,* 1-52, 69-115.

Connor, R. D. W. *North Carolina: Rebuilding,* I (use index).

SUGGESTED READING—

Andrews, Evangeline W., and C. M. Andrews (eds.). *The Journal of a Lady of Quality,* 144-179.

Bassett, J. S. "The Influence of Coast Line and Rivers on North Carolina," *AHA Annual Report,* 1908, I, 58-61.

Clonts, F. W. "Travel and Transportation in Colonial North Carolina," *NCHR,* III, No. 1 (January, 1926), 16-35.

Crittenden, C. C. "Inland Navigation in North Carolina, 1763-1789," *NCHR,* VIII, No. 2 (April, 1931), 145-154.

——. "Means of Communication in North Carolina, 1763-1789," *NCHR,* VIII, No. 4 (October, 1931), 373-383.

——. "Overland Travel and Transportation in North Carolina, 1763-1789," *NCHR,* VIII, No. 3 (July, 1931), 239-257.

——. "Ships and Shipping in North Carolina, 1763-1789," *NCHR,* VIII, No. 1 (January, 1931), 1-13.

Lonsdale, R. E. (comp.). *Atlas of North Carolina,* 39-40.

Merrens, Roy H. *Colonial North Carolina in the Eighteenth Century,* 142-172.

Moody, Robert E. "Massachusetts Trade with Carolina, 1686-1709," *NCHR,* XX, No. 1 (January, 1943), 43-53.

Paul, Charles L. "Factors in the Economy of Colonial Beaufort," *NCHR,* XLIV, No. 2 (April, 1967), 111-134.

Phillips, U. B. *History of Transportation in the Eastern Cotton Belt to 1860,* 191-192, 340-342, 353.

Scott, Kenneth. "Counterfeiting in Colonial North Carolina," *NCHR,* XXXIV, No. 4 (October, 1957), 467-482.

Sprunt, James. *Chronicles of the Cape Fear River, 1660-1916,* 1-732.

——. *Derelicts: An Account of Ships Lost at Sea,* 1-304.

Stick, David. *Graveyard of the Atlantic,* 1-276.

Tingley, Ralph R. "Postal Service in Colonial North Carolina," *Am. Philatelist,* LXII (January, 1919), 310-312.

Wallace, Wesley H. "Property and Trade: Main Themes of Early North Carolina Newspaper Advertisements," *NCHR,* XXXII, No. 4 (October, 1955), 451-482.


## 9. THE SOCIAL ORDER

SUMMARY—*Social classes:* gentry or plantation aristocracy, small farmers, indentured ("Christian") servants, free Negroes, slaves.—*Influence of law and custom on social stratification:*

illustrations.—*The planter aristocracy:* homes and outbuildings, furniture and furnishings, dress, food and drink, hospitality, sports and recreation—dancing, horse racing, cockfighting, gambling.—*Life of the small farmer:* subsistence farming; homes, house furnishings, food and drink, social life.—*Indentured servants:* voluntary and involuntary servants, legal provisions concerning "indentures," "freedom dues," problem of runaways; advantages and disadvantages of indentured servitude.—*Apprentices.—Free Negroes:* origin, number, location, economic activities, laws relating to them.—*Slaves:* some Indian slaves at first; majority of slaves were Negroes and majority of Negroes were slaves; number, prices, and treatment of slaves; religious opposition to slavery; advantages of slavery over indentured servitude.

TEXT—Lefler-Newsome, *North Carolina,* Ch. 8.

BASIC READING—

Lefler, Hugh T. (ed.). *North Carolina History Told by Contemporaries,* 35-38, 48-81.

Ashe, S. A. *History of North Carolina,* I, 277-395.

Connor, R. D. W. *North Carolina: Rebuilding,* I, 164-218.

———. *History of North Carolina,* I, 180-209.

Johnson, Guion G. *Ante-Bellum North Carolina: A Social History,* 52-114.

SUGGESTED READING—

Allcott, John V. *Colonial Homes in North Carolina,* 1-100.

Andrews, Evangeline, and Charles M. Andrews. (eds.). *The Journal of a Lady of Quality,* 148-204.

Bailyn, Bernard. "The Blount Papers: Notes on the Merchant 'Class' in the Revolutionary Period," *WMQ,* XI, No. 1 (January, 1954), 98-104.

Bassett, J. S. *Slavery and Servitude in the Colony of North Carolina,* 11-86.

Berkeley, Edmund, and Dorothy S. (eds.). "The Manner of Living of the North Carolinians, December 19, 1730, by Francis Veale," *NCHR,* XLI, No. 2 (April, 1964), 239-245.

Boyd, W. K. (ed.). *William Byrd's Dividing Line Histories,* 17-131, 145-336.

Bridenbaugh, Carl. *Myths and Realities: Societies of the Colonial South,* 119-196.

Bryan, W. A. "Some Social Traits of the Quakers of Rich Square," TCHS, *Papers,* VII (1907), 64-70.

————. "Some Social Traits of the Rich Square Quakers, with New Garden Document, II," TCHS, *Papers,* VIII (1908-1909), 6-14.

Carpenter, B. F. "The Legal Regulation of Public Morals in Colonial North Carolina," TCHS, *Papers,* II (1898), 68-75.

Chappell, Mack. "The Cupola House and Its Associations," *NCB,* XV (April, 1916), 203-217.

Dillard, Richard. "Some Early Physicians of the Albemarle," *NCB,* XI, No. 1 (July, 1911), 17-25.

Franklin, John Hope. *The Free Negro in North Carolina,* 1-13.

Gehrke, W. H. "Negro Slavery among the Germans in North Carolina," *NCHR,* XIV, No. 4 (October, 1937), 307-324.

Grimes, J. Bryan. "Some Notes on Colonial North Carolina, 1700-1750," *NCB,* III, No. 5 (February, 1904), 90-149.

Holladay, J. H. "Social Conditions in Colonial North Carolina," *NCB,* III, No. 10 (February, 1904), 5-30.

Johnston, Frances, and Thomas J. Waterman. *The Early Architecture of North Carolina,* 1-290.

Lauber, A. W. *American Indian Slavery.* (Use index for N.C. references).

Padgett, J. A. "The Status of Slaves in Colonial North Carolina," *Jour. Negro Hist.,* XIV, No. 3 (July, 1929), 300-327.

Pittman, Thomas M. "Crime and Punishment in North Carolina," *N.C. Lit. and Hist. Assoc. Proc.,* XVI (1917), 78-85.

Plyler, M. T. "Family Traditions of Early Pioneers in Piedmont North Carolina," *Sou. Atl. Quar.,* XXXV, No. 4 (October, 1936), 420-433.

————. "Family Traditions of Tidewater North Carolina," *Sou. Atl. Quar.,* XXXVII, No. 4 (October, 1938), 397-409.

Raper, Charles L. "Social Life in Colonial North Carolina," *NCB,* III, No. 5 (September, 1905), 5-21.

Rouse, William H. "The Romance of a Boundary Line," *Va. State Bar Assoc. Proc.* (1931), 258-273.

Rights, Douglas L. "The Horse Society," *NCHR,* XVII, No. 4 (October, 1940), 347-355.

Smith, A. E. *Colonists in Bondage,* 226-306.

Spruill, Julia C. "Southern Housewives before the Revolution," *NCHR,* XIII, No. 1 (January, 1936), 25-46.

———. *Women's Life and Work in the Southern Colonies,* 1-366

Taylor, Rosser H. "The Free Negro in North Carolina," *JSHP,* XVII, No. 1 (1920), 5-26.

———. "Slaveholding in North Carolina: An Economic View," *JSHP,* XVIII (1926), 9-29.

Wall, Bennett H. "The Founding of the Pettigrew Plantations," *NCHR,* XXVII, No. 4 (October, 1950), 395-408.

Wallace, Wesley H. "Cultural and Social Advertising in Early North Carolina Newspapers," *NCHR,* XXXIII, No. 3 (July, 1956), 281-309.

Watson, Alan D. "Ordinaries in Colonial Eastern North Carolina," *NCHR,* XLV, No. 1 (January, 1968), 67-83.

Winston, Sanford. "Indian Slavery in the Carolina Region," *Jour. Negro Hist.,* XIX (1934), 431-440.

Wootten, Bayard, and Archibald Henderson (eds.). *Old Homes and Gardens of North Carolina,* 3-34; Plates 1-12, 17, 19, 23-26, 29, 46-47, 58-59, 65-68, 95.

Wright, Louis B. *The Prose Works of William Byrd of Westover.* (Use index for N.C. references).

## 10. *RELIGION AND EDUCATION, 1729-1776*

SUMMARY—*The Established (Anglican) Church:* Vestry Acts, early parishes and churches, S.P.G. missionaries; reasons for weakness and unpopularity of the Anglican Church.—*Quakers (Society of Friends):* migrations from New England and from Pennsylvania and New Jersey; settlements in Albemarle Sound region and in Guilford County area; early "meeting houses"; Quakers in politics.—*Presbyterians:* growth as a result of Highland and Scotch-Irish migrations; North Carolina as a mission field for Philadelphia and New York Synods; early churches and preachers; Orange Presbytery (1770) ; contributions to education.—*Baptists:* early preachers and churches; reasons for rapid growth; the Kehukee Association; Separate Baptists and the Sandy Creek Association.—*Religious sects among German settlers:* Moravian, Lutheran, Reformed; early churches and ministers. *Methodist "societies":* early preachers, societies, and circuits; no formal Methodist Church in the United States until 1784.—*Education:* close connection with the church; early teachers; interest of planters in education; education of poorer classes—apprenticeship system; early academies.—*The colonial government and education:* movement for schools; Queen's College, the first in North Carolina.—*The state constitution and education* (Section 41) . —*Books and libraries.—Printing and newspapers.*

TEXT—Lefler-Newsome, *North Carolina,* Ch. 9.

BASIC READING—
Lefler, Hugh T. (ed.) . *North Carolina History Told by Contemporaries,* 41-62, 118-122.
Connor, R. D. W. *North Carolina, Rebuilding,* I, 177-184.
———. *History of North Carolina,* I, 180-209.

SUGGESTED READING—
Bernheim, G. D. *Historical Sketch of the Evangelical Lutheran Synod and Ministerium of North Carolina,* 9-27.
———. *History of the German Settlements and the Lutheran Church in North and South Carolina,* 67-148, 175-185, 239-262.
Biggs, Joseph. *A Concise History of the Kehukee Baptist Association.* 1-300.
Boyd, W. K., and Charles A. Krummel (eds.). "German Tracts concerning the Lutheran Church in North Carolina during the Eighteenth Century," *NCHR,* VII, Nos. 1 and 2 (January and April, 1930), 79-147, 225-282.

Brooks, A. L. "David Caldwell and His Log College," *NCHR*, XXVIII, No. 4 (October, 1951), 399-407.

Caruthers, Eli W. *A Sketch of the Life and Character of the Rev. David Caldwell,* 1-109.

Cheshire, J. B. *Sketches of Church History in North Carolina,* 43-90.

Clapp, J. C., and J. C. Leonard. *Historic Sketches of the Reformed Church in North Carolina,* 11-29.

Clewell, J. H. *History of Wachovia in North Carolina,* 1-120.

Conkin, Paul. "The Church Establishment in North Carolina, 1765-1776," *NCHR*, XXXI, No. 1 (January, 1955), 1-30.

Connor, R. D. W. "The Genesis of Higher Education in North Carolina," *NCHR*, XXVIII, No. 1 (January, 1951), 1-14.

Coon, Charles L. (ed.). *The Beginnings of Public Education in North Carolina: A Documentary History, 1790-1840.* I, 1-9.

Corbitt, D. L. "The North Carolina Gazette," *NCHR*, XII, No. 1 (January, 1936), 45-61.

Crittenden, C. C. "North Carolina Newspapers before 1790," *JSHP*, XX, No. 1 (1928), 1-83.

Cross, A. L. *The Anglican Episcopate and the American Colonies.* (Use index for N.C. references).

Davidson, Elizabeth H. "The Establishment of the English Church in the Continental American Colonies," TCHS, *Papers,* XX (1936), 9-94.

Elliott, Robert N., Jr. "James Davis and the Beginnings of the Newspaper in North Carolina," *NCHR*, XLII, No. 1 (January, 1965), 1-20.

Foote, W. H. *Sketches of North Carolina,* 77-83, 125-136, 158-243.

Fries, Adelaide L. "The Moravian Contribution to North Carolina," *NCHR*, VII, No. 1 (January, 1930), 1-14.

Garber, Paul N. *The Romance of American Methodism,* 1-20.

Grissom, W. L. *History of Methodism in North Carolina.*

———. "Some First Things in North Carolina Methodism," TCHS, *Papers,* IX (1912), 22-32.

Hamilton, Kenneth G. "The Moravians and Wachovia," *NCHR*, XLIV, No. 2 (April, 1967), 144-153.

Hamilton, J. G. de R. "Southern Members of the Inns of Court," *NCHR*, X, No. 4 (October, 1933), 273-286.

Haywood, M. de L. *The Beginnings of Freemasonry in North Carolina and Tennessee,* 1-66.

———. *Lives of the Bishops of North Carolina,* 1-40.

———. "Story of Queen's College or Liberty Hall," *NCB*, XI, No. 3 (January, 1912), 169-175.

———. "Thomas and Henry John Burgess, Church of England Missionaries in the Provinces of Virginia and North Carolina during the Eighteenth Century," *NCB*, XXIII (1926), 63-73.

Hirsch, Charles B. *The Experiences of the S. P. G. in Eighteenth Century North Carolina,* 384 pp.

Hooker, Richard J. (ed.). *The Carolina Backcountry on the Eve of the Revolution: The Journal and Other Writings of Charles Woodmason, Anglican Itinerant,* 15, 69, 76-81.

Huggins, M. A. *A History of the North Carolina Baptists, 1727-1932,* 32-37.

James, Fleming H. "Richard Marsden, Wayward Clergyman," *WMQ*, XI, No. 4 (October, 1954), 578-591.

Jones, Rufus. *The Quakers in the American Colonies,* 265-353.

Klain, Zora. *Quaker Contributions to Education in North Carolina,* 17-57.

Knight, E. W. (ed.). *A Documentary History of Education in the South before 1860,* I, 36, 51, 55-57, 369-370, 661-664, 703-726.

———. "An Educational Practice in Colonial North Carolina," *NCB*, XVI (January, 1916), 39-51.

———. *Public Education in North Carolina,* 1-41.

Lemmon, Sarah M. "Genesis of the Protestant Episcopal Church in North Carolina, 1701-1823," *NCHR*, XXVIII, No. 4 (October, 1951), 426-462.

McCorkle, Donald M. "The Collegium Musicum Salem: Its Music, Musicians, and Importance," *NCHR*, XXXIII, No. 4 (October, 1956), 483-498.

McMurtrie, D. C. *Bibliography of Early North Carolina Imprints*, 1-188.

————. "A Bibliography of North Carolina Imprints, 1761-1800," *NCHR*, XIII, Nos. 1, 2, 3 (January, April, July, 1936), 47-88, 143-166, 219-254.

————. "The First Twelve Years of Printing in North Carolina, 1749-1760," *NCHR*, X, No. 3 (July, 1933), 214-234.

Midwinter, Sir Edward. "The Society for the Propagation of The Gospel and the Colonial Church in America," *P.E. Church Hist. Mag.*, IV (1935), 281-299.

"Minutes of the Kentucky Baptist Association, 1769-1778," *Ky. Bapt. Hist. Soc. Publ.*, III (1913), 17-37.

Monroe, Haskell. "Religious Toleration and Politics in Early North Carolina," *NCHR*, XXXIX, No. 3 (July, 1962), 267-283.

Moore, John B. "Adolph Nussmann, Pioneer Lutheran Preacher in North Carolina," *Luth. Church Quar.*, XIII (1940), 375-391.

Moose, John B. "The First Constitution of St. John's Church," *NCHR*, XIII, No. 4 (October, 1936), 335-355.

Nelson, Andrew T. "'Enthusiasm' in Carolina, 1740," *Sou. Atl. Quar.*, XLIV, No. 4 (October, 1945), 397-405.

Noble, M. C. S. *A History of the Public Schools of North Carolina*, 3-24.

O'Connell, J. J. *Catholicity in the Carolinas and Georgia*, 395-499.

Olds, Fred A. "The Parishes of North Carolina," *NCB*, XXI (1922), 81-89.

Oliver, D. D. "The Society for the Propagation of the Gospel in the Province of North Carolina," *JSHP*, IX (1910), 9-23.

Parramore, Thomas C. "John Alexander, Anglican Missionary," *NCHR*, XLIII, No. 3 (July, 1966), 305-315.

Paschal, G. W. *History of the Baptists in North Carolina, I: 1663-1805*, 1-445.

————. *A History of Printing in North Carolina*, 1-27.

Pascoe, C. F. *Two Hundred Years of the S. P. G.* I, 20-25.

Peele, Juliana. "The Founders of Rich Square Meeting," TCHS, *Papers,* VI (1906), 93-98.

Pennington, Edgar L. *The Church of England and the Reverend Clement Hall in Colonial North Carolina,* 1-51.

Powell, William S. "The Bicentennial of Printing in North Carolina," *NCHR,* XXVII, No. 2 (April, 1950), 193-199.

————— (ed.). *Clement Hall: A Collection of Many Christian Experiences.* 1-51.

—————. "Eighteenth Century North Carolina Imprints: A Revision and Supplement to McMurtrie," *NCHR,* XXXV, No. 1 (January, 1955), 50-73.

————— (ed.). *The Journal of the House of Burgesses of North Carolina, 1749,* i-xvii, 14.

Purefoy, George W. *History of the Sandy Creek Baptist Association,* 42-47.

Raper, Charles L. *The Church and Private Schools in North Carolina: A Historical Study,* 1-70.

Smith, L. L. "Methodism in the Albemarle Section," TCHS, *Papers,* IX (1912), 57-65.

Stokes, Durward. "Henry Pattillo in North Carolina," *NCHR,* XLIV, No. 4 (October, 1967), 373-391.

Thornton, Mary L. "Public Printing in North Carolina, 1749-1815," *NCHR,* XXI, No. 3 (July, 1944), 181-202.

Weeks, S. B. "Libraries and Literature in North Carolina in the Eighteenth Century," *AHA Annual Report* (1895), 169-267.

—————. "Pre-Revolutionary Printers in North Carolina—Davis, Steuart, and Boyd," *NCB,* XV, No. 2 (October, 1915), 104-122.

Weis, Frederick L. *The Colonial Clergy of Virginia, North Carolina, and South Carolina,* 1-100.

White, Julia S. "The Peace Testimony of North Carolina Friends Prior to 1860," *Friend's Hist. Soc. Bull.,* XVI (1927), 60-67.

—————. "The Quakers of Perquimans," *NCB,* VII, No. 4 (April, 1908), 278-289.

Williams, Charles B. *History of the Baptists in North Carolina,* 1-50.

## 11. ROYAL GOVERNORS AND THEIR PROBLEMS, 1730-1775

SUMMARY—*Closer relationship to King and Privy Council:* N.C. as part of the "imperial system"; opposition to some British policies, acceptance of others.—*The royal governor's powers:* executive, legislative, judicial, administrative; powers in relation to land, military matters, church, and local government—*The Council:* method of selection; powers and duties. —*The Assembly:* county representation; freehold suffrage; powers and duties; jealousy of its powers.—*The "Popular Party" versus the Prerogative (Governor's) Party:* governor's instructions versus "charter rights."—*Controversies between governors and legislatures:* governor's salary; paper currency; land system, quit rents, and "blank patents"; tenure of judges; legislative quorum; location of capital; representation; taxation, especially poll taxes.—*The problem of the Granville District:* when and where created; problem of law enforcement, rent and tax collection; riots.—*The North Carolina–South Carolina boundary dispute:* the 1735 survey of the line; later surveys; confusion and disorders in the disputed area; effects of disputes on trade; surveys of 1764 and 1772; N.C. opposes the "Compromise Line."—*The Colony's role in the wars "for empire";* French and Spanish attacks on shipping and coastal towns; contributions of men and money; North Carolina in the "Great War for Empire" (1754-1763) —men and money furnished; home defense; Indian war and ultimate British (and N.C.) victory.

TEXT—Lefler-Newsome, *North Carolina,* Ch. 10.

BASIC READING—

Lefler, Hugh T. (ed.). *North Carolina History Told by Contemporaries,* 31-36, 70-77.
Connor, R. D. W. *North Carolina: Rebuilding an Ancient Commonwealth,* I, 219-242.
———. *History of North Carolina,* I, 210-238.

SUGGESTED READING—

Alden, John R. *John Stuart and the Southern Colonial Frontier*, 48, 75, 86, 115-133.

Boyd, W. K. (ed.). *Some Eighteenth Century Tracts concerning North Carolina*, 57-100.

Bullock, C. J. *Essays in the Monetary History of the United States*, 125-155.

Clark, Rosamond. "A Sketch of Fort Dobbs," *NCB*, XIX (April, 1920), 133-138.

Cook, Florence. "Procedure in the North Carolina Colonial Assembly, 1731-1770," *NCHR*, VIII, No. 3 (July, 1931), 258-283.

Cooke, Charles S. "The Governor, Council, and Assembly in Royal North Carolina," *JSHP*, XII, No. 1 (1912), 7-40.

Corbitt, D. L. *Formation of North Carolina Counties, 1663-1943*.

———. "Judicial Districts of North Carolina, 1746-1934," *NCHR*, XII, No. 1 (January, 1935), 45-61.

Coulter, E. M. "The Granville District," *JSHP*, XIII, No. 1 (1913), 35-56.

Eliason, Mrs. Minnie H. *Fort Dobbs: Historical Sketch*, 1-19.

Ervin, Sam J., Jr. "The Provincial Agents of North Carolina," *JSHP*, XVI, No. 2 (1919), 63-67.

Greene, Jack P. "The North Carolina Lower House and the Power to Appoint Public Treasurers, 1711-1775," *NCHR*, XL, No. 1 (January, 1963), 37-53.

———. *The Quest for Power: The Lower Houses of Assembly in the Southern Royal Colonies, 1689-1776.* (Use index for N.C. references.)

Guess, W. C. "County Government in Colonial North Carolina," *JSHP*, XI, No. 1 (1911), 5-39.

Hamer, P. M. "Anglo-French Rivalry in the Cherokee County, 1754-1767," *NCHR*, II. No. 3 (July, 1925), 303-322.

———. "Fort Loudoun in the Cherokee War, 1758-1761," *NCHR*, II, No. 4 (October, 1925), 442-458.

Harmon, George D. "The North Carolina Cherokee and the New Echota Treaty of 1835," *NCHR*, VI, No. 3 (July, 1929), 239-253.

Haywood, M. de L. *Governor William Tryon and His Administration in the Province of North Carolina, 1765-1771,* 9-103.

Hinton, Mary H. "Old Fort Dobbs," *D.A.R. Mag.,* XLV (December, 1914), 299-303.

Lanning, John T. *The Diplomatic History of Georgia: A Study of the Epoch of Jenkins' Ear,* 186-206.

————. "Don Miguel Wall and the Spanish Attempt against the Existence of Carolina and Georgia," *NCHR,* X, No. 3 (July, 1933), 186-213.

London, Laurence F. "The Representation Controversy in Colonial North Carolina," *NCHR,* XI, No. 4 (October, 1934), 255-270.

McCain, Paul M. *The County Court in North Carolina before 1750,* 3-148.

McKay, Marvin L. "Provincial Taxes in North Carolina during the Administrations of Dobbs and Tryon, *NCHR,* XLII, No. 4 (October, 1965), 440-453.

McKinley, A. E. *The Suffrage Franchise in the Thirteen English Colonies in America,* 79-121.

Morrison, Alfred J. "Lord Granville's Line," *Sou. Atl. Quar.,* XIV, No. 1 (January, 1915), 1-14.

Nash, Francis. "The Borough Towns of North Carolina, *NCB,* VI, No. 2 (October, 1906), 83-102.

*North Carolina Manual, 1913,* 320-413.

Parker, Coralie. *History of Taxation in North Carolina during the Colonial Period, 1663-1776,* 36-97.

Powell, William S., and Eva J. Lawrence. *A Bibliography of North Carolina Counties,* 1-13.

Raper, Charles L. *North Carolina: A Study in English Colonial Government,* 27-100.

Robinson, B. P. *The Five Royal Governors of North Carolina.* 1-74.

Sellers, Charles G., Jr. "Private Profits and British Colonial Policy: The Speculations of Henry McCulloh," *WMQ,* VIII, No. 4 (October, 1951), 535-551.

Skaggs, M. L. "North Carolina Boundary Disputes Involving Her Southern Line," *JSHP,* XXV, No. 1 (1941), 1-166.

South, Stanley A. " 'Russellborough: Two Royal Governors' Mansions at Brunswick," *NCHR,* XLIV, No. 4 (October, 1967), 360-372.

Stewart, S. A. "The Court System of North Carolina before the Revolution," TCHS, *Papers,* IV (1900), 12-20.

Waddell, A. M. *A Colonial Officer* [Hugh Waddell] *and his Times, 1754-1773,* 1-242.

Wager, Paul W. *County Government and Administration in North Carolina,* 1-16.

## 12. SECTIONALISM AND SECTIONAL CONTROVERSIES

SUMMARY—*The representation controversy; Sound versus Cape Fear:* origin of dispute—representation and rent questions; Governor Johnston's "management" fails to solve problem; Albemarle counties denounce "Rump Assembly"; the colony's "Long Parliament"; disorder, confusion, and "fist law" in Albemarle region; gradual easing of tension.—*East-West sectionalism:* causes—representation problem, location of capital at New Bern and building of governor's "Palace"; increase in poll taxes; undemocratic character of local government, "courthouse rings," multiple officeholding, and colonial "carpetbaggers"; quit rents, excessive fees, and other grievances.— *The Regulators organize:* leaders, grievances and demands, counties involved; the literature of the Regulators—Rednap Howell, Regulator "advertisements," the "Nutbush Address," and other writings; Herman Husband's *Impartial Relation.— The Regulators fail to solve problems by peaceful means:* the trials at Hillsborough; Regulator grievances before the legislature; the Johnston "Riot Act."—*Governor Tryon's expedition against Regulators (1771) and their defeat at Alamance—Aftermath:* executions, pardons, migration; also exit of Tryon and Fanning.

TEXT—Lefler-Newsome, *North Carolina,* Ch. 11.

BASIC READING—

Lefler, Hugh T. (ed.). *North Carolina History Told by Contemporaries,* 67-73, 87-93.

Connor, R. D. W. *North Carolina: Rebuilding an Ancient Commonwealth,* I, 264-288.

———. *History of North Carolina,* I, 287-320.

Ashe, S. A. *History of North Carolina,* I, 247-279, 326-376.

SUGGESTED READING—

Bassett, J. S. "The Regulators of North Carolina," *AHA Annual Report,* 1894, 141-212.

Best, J. A. "North Carolina in the French and Indian War," *Trinity Archive,* XV (1902), 382-388.

Boyd, Julian P. "The Sheriff in Colonial North Carolina," *NCHR,* V, No. 2 (April, 1928), 151-180.

Boyd, W. K. "Early Relations of North Carolina and the West," *NCB,* VII, No. 3 (1908), 193-209.

——— (ed.). *Some Eighteenth Century Tracts concerning North Carolina,* 175-413.

Bridenbaugh, Carl. *Myths and Realities: Societies of the Colonial South,* 159-163.

Dill, Alonzo T. *Governor Tryon and His Palace,* 103-154.

———. "Public Buildings in Craven County, 1722-1835," *NCHR,* XX, No. 4 (October, 1943), 301-326.

———. "Tryon's Palace—A Neglected Niche of North Carolina History," *NCHR,* XIX, No. 2 (April, 1942), 119-167.

Franklin, W. Neil. "Some Aspects of Representation in the American Colonies," *NCHR,* VI, No. 1 (January, 1949), 57-62.

Haywood, M. de L. *Governor William Tryon and His Administration in the Province of North Carolina, 1765-1771,* 9-194.

Henderson, Archibald. "Herman Husband's Continuation of the 'Impartial Relation,'" *NCHR,* XVIII, No. 1 (January, 1941), 48-81.

———. "Origin of the Regulation in North Carolina," *AHR,* XXI, No. 2 (January, 1916), 320-332.

Hudson, A. P. "Songs of the Regulators," *WMQ*, IV, No. 4 (October, 1947), 470-485.

Lazenby, Mary E. *Herman Husband: A Story of His Life*, 25-123.

Lefler, Hugh T. "Orange County and the War of the Regulation." Lefler, Hugh T., and Paul W. Wager (eds.). *Orange County, 1752-1952*, 24-40.

London, Lawrence F. "The Representation Controversy in Colonial North Carolina," *NCHR*, XI, No. 4 (October, 1934), 255-278.

McCorkle, Lutie A. "Was Alamance the First Battle of the Revolution?" *NCB*, No. 7 (November, 1903), 1-26.

Miller, Helen H. *The Case for Liberty;* Chapter IX, "Freedom from Extortion," 203-226.

Patton, Sadie (Smathers). *Buncombe to Mecklenburg—Speculation Lands*, 1-47.

Powell, William S. "Tryon's 'Book' on North Carolina," *NCHR*, XXXIV, No. 3 (July, 1957), 406-415.

―――. *The War of the Regulation and the Battle of Alamance, May 16, 1771.* 1-32.

Skaggs, Marvin L. "The First Boundary Survey between the Carolinas" *NCHR*, XII, No. 3 (July, 1935), 213-232.

―――. *North Carolina Boundary Disputes Involving Her Southern Line*, 1-250.

―――. "Progress in the North Carolina–South Carolina Boundary Dispute," *NCHR*, XV, No. 4 (October, 1938), 341-353.

Tilley, Nannie May. "Political Disturbances in Colonial Granville County," *NCHR*, XVIII, No. 4 (October, 1941), 339-359.


## 13. *APPROACH OF THE AMERICAN REVOLUTION, 1763-1775*

SUMMARY—*North Carolina as a part of the British empire:* merchantilism as applied to the colony; England's "New Colonial Policy" after 1763 and its application to North Carolina;

the *Proclamation of 1763;* the *Sugar Act,* the *Currency Act,* the *Quartering Act.—The Stamp Act* (1765): reasons for passage, provisions of law; North Carolina opposition—literary attacks, armed demonstrations at Wilmington and Brunswick; repeal of Stamp Act, 1766; why North Carolina was not represented at the Stamp Act Congress.—*The Declaratory Act (1766):* Parliament reasserts its right to tax colonies.—*The Townshend tax law (1767):* reasons for passage, provisions and new features of policy; nonimportation movement in N.C.; repeal of all taxes (1770), except those on tea; N.C. sets up its first committee of correspondence.—*The Tea Act of 1773:* colonial reaction—tea parties; "Coercive Acts" of 1774; call for a Continental Congress.—*North Carolina's first Provincial Congress; the second Provincial Congress:* the last royal assembly dissolved by Governor Martin.—*The fighting begins in Mass. (April, 1775).—The Mecklenburg patriots act:* the Resolves of May 31, 1775 (controversy about May 20 "Declaration of Independence").—*Provisional government:* Provincial council, congress, and safety committees.—*Revolutionary sentiment and war preparations.—Party divisions:* Whigs, Tories, Moderates.—*Military aid to S.C. and Va.— The War begins in N.C.:* the battle of Moore's Creek Bridge (Feb. 27, 1776).

TEXT—Lefler-Newsome, *North Carolina,* Ch. 12.

BASIC READING—

Lefler, Hugh T. (ed.). *North Carolina History Told by Contemporaries,* 82-98.

Connor, R. D. W. *North Carolina: Rebuilding an Ancient Commonwealth,* I, 289-313.

———. *History of North Carolina,* I, 321-357.

Ashe, S. A. *History of North Carolina,* I, 310-325.

SUGGESTED READING—

Alden, John R. *The South in the Revolution.* (Use index for N.C. references.)

Andrews, Evangeline, and C. M. Andrews (eds.). *The Journal of a Lady of Quality,* 180-215.

Bassett, J. S. "Some New Material Relating to the Mecklenburg Resolves—May 31, 1775," TCHS, *Papers,* V (1905), 65-70.

Boyd, W. K. (ed.). *Some Eighteenth Century Tracts concerning North Carolina,* 101-195.

Cannon, John. "Henry McCulloch and Henry McCulloh," *WMQ,* XV, No. 1 (January, 1955), 71-73.

Carraway, Gertrude. *Historic New Bern,* 1-64.

Clark, Walter. "The Edenton Tea-Party," *Mag. of Hist.,* IX (February, 1909), 86-91.

Connor, R. D. W. *Cornelius Harnett: An Essay in North Carolina History,* 30-119.

———. *Revolutionary Leaders of North Carolina,* 3-125.

Davidson, Philip G. "Sons of Liberty and Stamp Men," *NCHR,* IX, No. 1 (January, 1932), 38-56.

DeMond, R. O. *The Loyalists in North Carolina during the Revolution,* 1-62.

Dillard, Richard. *The Historic Tea-Party of Edenton, October 25th, 1774,* 1-17.

———. "Some North Carolina Memories of the Revolution." *NCB,* VIII (April, 1909), 325-333.

Douglass, Elisha P. *Rebels and Democrats,* 71-100.

Frech, Laura P. "The Wilmington Committee of Public Safety and the Loyalist Rising of February, 1776," *NCHR,* XLI, No. 1 (January, 1964), 21-35.

Harrell, Isaac M. "North Carolina Loyalists," *NCHR,* III, No. 4 (October, 1926), 575-590.

Haywood, C. Robert. "The Mind of the North Carolina Opponents of the Stamp Act," *NCHR,* XXIX, No. 3 (July, 1952), 317-343.

Haywood, M. de L. *Governor William Tryon and His Administration in the Province of North Carolina, 1765-1771,* 9-52.

Henderson, Archibald. *Cradle of Liberty: Historical Essays concerning the Mecklenburg Declaration of Independence. . . ,* 1-56.

———. "The Mecklenburg Declaration of Independence." *Jour. Am. Hist.,* VI, No. 4 (1912), 781-788.

————. *The Revolution in North Carolina in 1775: Transylvania, Craven, Anson, and Mecklenburg,* 1-18.

High, James. "Henry McCulloh: Progenitor of the Stamp Act," *NCHR,* XXIX, No. 1 (January, 1952), 24-38.

Hoyt, W. H. *The Mecklenburg Declaration of Independence,* 1-284.

Lee, E. Laurence, Jr. "Days of Defiance: Resistance to the Stamp Act in the Lower Cape Fear," *NCHR,* XLIII, No. 2 (April, 1966), 186-202.

————. *The Lower Cape Fear in Colonial Days,* 1-334.

McNitt, Virgil V. *Chain of Error and the Mecklenburg Declaration of Independence,* 1-134.

Morgan, Edmund S., and Helen Morgan. *The Stamp Act Crisis,* 38-39, 156, 165-201.

Nevins, Allan. *The American States during and after the Revolution, 1775-1789.* (Use index for N.C. references.)

Olds, Fred A. "The Celebrated Edenton N.C. Tea Party," *D.A.R. Mag.,* LVII (June, 1922), 327-333.

Pittman, Thomas M. "The Revolutionary Congress of North Carolina," *NCB,* II, No. 6 (1902), 3-18.

Quynn, Dorothy M. "Flora Macdonald in History," *NCHR,* XVIII, No. 3 (July, 1941), 236-258.

Rankin, Hugh F. "The Moore's Creek Bridge Campaign, 1776," *NCHR,* XXX, No. 1 (January, 1953), 23-60.

Ritcheson, Charles R. "The Preparation of the Stamp Act," *WMQ,* X, No. 4 (October, 1953), 543-559.

Sellers, Charles G., Jr. "Making a Revolution: The North Carolina Whigs, 1765-1775," J. C. Sitterson (ed.) *Studies in Southern History,* 23-46.

Ubbelohde, Carl W., Jr. "The Vice-Admiralty Court of Royal North Carolina, 1729-1759," *NCHR,* XXXI, No. 4 (October, 1954), 517-528.

Waddell, A. M. *A Colonial Officer and His Times, 1754-1773,* 73-130.

Weir, Robert M. "North Carolina's Reaction to the Currency Act of 1764," *NCHR,* XL, No. 2 (April, 1963), 183-199.

## 14. TRANSITION FROM COLONY TO STATEHOOD

SUMMARY—*The problem of independence:* the compact theory and talk of "reconciliation with England,"—*The Halifax Resolves (April 12, 1776):* first official state action for independence.—*Provisional Government:* Provincial Congress decides not to adopt a state constitution; Council of Safety rules the state; conservative and radical views on government; exponents of different views.—*The State Constitution and Bill of Rights (1776):* sources of ideas; significant provisions of Bill of Rights; the constitution—legislative, executive, and judicial departments; local government; other provisions.—*Emphasis on legislature:* weakness of executive branch; character of the new government.—*Authorship of the constitution.*

TEXT—Lefler-Newsome, *North Carolina,* Ch. 13.

BASIC READING—

Lefler, Hugh T. (ed.). *North Carolina History Told by Contemporaries,* 105-111.

Connor, R. D. W. *North Carolina: Rebuilding an Ancient Commonwealth,* I, 314-346.

———. *History of North Carolina,* I, 389-410.

SUGGESTED READING—

Alden, John R. *The South in the Revolution, 1763-1789.* (Use index for N.C. references.)

Ashe, S. A. *History of North Carolina,* I, 377-416.

Connor, R. D. W. *Cornelius Harnett: An Essay in North Carolina History,* 152-178.

———. "North Carolina's Priority in the Demand for Independence," *Sou. Atl. Quar.,* VIII, No. 3 (July, 1909), 235-254.

———. *Revolutionary Leaders of North Carolina.* (Use index for individuals.)

Douglass, Elisha P. *Rebels and Democrats,* 101-135.

Green, F. M. *Constitutional Development of the South Atlantic States.* (Use index for N.C. references.)

Ketcham, Earle H. "The Sources of the North Carolina Constitution of 1776," *NCHR,* VI, No. 3 (July, 1929), 215-238.

McCurry, Allan J. "Joseph Hewes and Independence: A Suggestion," *NCHR*, XL, No. 4 (October, 1963), 455-464.

McRee, G. J. (ed.). *The Life and Correspondence of James Iredell*, I, 282-339.

Nash, Frank. "The Constitution of 1776 and Its Makers." *JSHP*, XI, No. 2 (1912), 5-23.

Nevins, Allan. *The American States during and after the Revolution, 1775-1789*, 15-170.

Sikes, F. W. *The Transition of North Carolina from Colony to Commonwealth*, 42-84.

Strong, Robert C. "North Carolina's Attitude to the Revolution." *NCB*, VI (April, 1907), 217-226.

Thorpe, F. N. (ed.). *American Charters, Constitutions, and Organic Laws*, V, 2787-2794.

Whitaker, Bessie L. "The Provincial Council and Committees of Safety," *JSHP*, VIII (1908), 1-49.

## 15. *THE NEW STATE AND ITS PROBLEMS*

SUMMARY—*The new state government:* Governor Richard Caswell, Council of State, General Assembly; problems confronting government.—*Defects in constitution become apparent:* weakness of the executive.—*Critical problems:* party division and friction; Tories, their activities, and legislation against them (1777 and 1779); paper money, inflation, and financial chaos; increase in taxes and levying of new taxes, especially on products; the loan system; sale of confiscated Tory property.—*Effects of war on N.C. commerce:* nature of exports and imports.—*The state navy and privateers.*

TEXT—Lefler-Newsome, *North Carolina*, Ch. 14.

BASIC READING—

Lefler, Hugh T. (ed.). *North Carolina History Told by Contemporaries*, 111-115.

Connor, R. D. W. *North Carolina: Rebuilding an Ancient Commonwealth*, 372-437.

Boyd, W. K. *History of North Carolina: The Federal Period,* 1-20.

Ashe, S. A. *History of North Carolina,* I, 497-512.

SUGGESTED READING—

Alden, John R. *The South in the Revolution, 1763-1789.* (Use index for N.C. references.)

Blackwelder, Ruth. "The Attitude of North Carolina Moravians toward the American Revolution," *NCHR,* IX, No. 1 (January, 1932), 1-21.

Bullock, C. J. *Essays in the Monetary History of the United States,* 193-200.

Connor, R. D. W. *Revolutionary Leaders of North Carolina.* (Use index for individuals.)

Coyle, John G. "Cornelius Harnett," *Am. Irish Hist. Soc. Jour.,* XXIX (1931), 148-156.

Crittenden, C. C. *The Commerce of North Carolina, 1763-1789,* 116-170.

Douglass, Elisha P. *Rebels and Democrats.* (Use index for N.C. references.)

Ganyard, Robert L. "Radicals and Conservatives in Revolutionary North Carolina: A Point at Issue, the October Election, 1776," *WMQ,* XXIV, No. 4 (October, 1967), 568-587.

Harrell, Isaac M. "North Carolina Loyalists," *NCHR,* III, No. 4 (October, 1926), 575-590.

Hilldrup, R. L. "The Salt Supply of North Carolina during the American Revolution," *NCHR,* XXII, No. 4 (October, 1945), 393-417.

Hunter, Dard. *Papermaking in Pioneer America.* (Use index for N.C. references.)

McMillan, M. B. *The War Governors in the American Revolution.* (Use index for N.C. references.)

McRee, G. J. (ed.). *The Life and Correspondence of James Iredell,* I, 340-564.

Morris, Francis G., and Phyllis Mary Morris. "Economic Conditions in North Carolina about 1780," *NCHR,* XVI, Nos. 2 and 3 (April and July, 1939), 107-133, 296-327.

Nevins, Allan. *The American States during and after the Revolution, 1775-1789.* (Use index for N.C. references.)

Thorne, Dorothy Gilbert. "North Carolina Friends and the Revolution," *NCHR,* XXXVIII, No. 3 (July, 1961), 323-340.

Wagstaff, H. M. *State Rights and Political Parties in North Carolina, 1776-1861,* 14-31.

Zornow, William F. "North Carolina Tariff Policies, 1775-1789," *NCHR,* XXXII, No. 2 (April, 1955), 151-164.

## 16. THE STATE AT WAR

SUMMARY—*North Carolina troops in the Continental Army:* number of regiments and men, officers, comparison with other states.—*The State Militia:* numbers, how recruited, and activities.—*"Partisans" and their activities.*—*Military activities of N.C. soldiers:* aid to other states, campaign against Indians, second British invasion of South, defeats in Georgia and South Carolina.—*North Carolina prepares for invasion:* "partisan" warfare; Gates takes command of Southern Army; the Board of War; Cornwallis' Plan of Campaign.—*Significant battles and campaigns:* King's Mountain; Greene's historic retreat; Guilford Court House (1781), a strange British victory.—*British surrender at Yorktown, Virginia, October 19, 1781:* war comes to an end.

TEXT—Lefler-Newsome, *North Carolina,* Ch. 15.

BASIC READING—

Lefler, Hugh T. (ed.). *North Carolina History Told by Contemporaries,* 115-119.

Connor, R. D. W. *North Carolina: Rebuilding an Ancient Commonwealth,* I, 347-371.

———. *History of North Carolina,* I, 437-494.

Ashe, S. A. *History of North Carolina,* I, 396-497.

SUGGESTED READING—

Alden, John R. *The South in the Revolution, 1763-1789.* (Use index for N.C. references.)

Allen, Talbot M. "Samuel Johnston in Revolutionary Times," TCHS, *Papers,* V (1905), 39-49.

Allen, W. C. "Whigs and Tories," *NCB,* II, No. 5 (1902), 3-24.

Ashe, S. A. "Some New Light on John Paul Jones," *Sou. Atl. Quar.,* XVII, No. 1 (1918), 44-57.

Bailey, Ralph E. *Guns over the Carolinas: The Story of Nathanael Greene,* 82-150.

Bradbeer, William W. "North Carolina State Currency," *NCB,* XIX (July, 1919), 36-46.

Brown, Alan S. (ed.). "James Simpson's Report on Carolina Loyalists, 1779-1780," *Jour. Sou. Hist.,* XXI (Nov. 1955), 513-519.

"Colonial Coast Forts on the South Atlantic Coast," *Artillery Jour.,* LXX (January, 1929), 41-62.

Connor, R. D. W. *Revolutionary Leaders of North Carolina,* 3-125.

Davidson, Chalmers. *Piedmont Partisan: The Life and Times of Brigadier-General William Lee Davidson,* 91-123.

Davis, Burke. *The Cowpens-Guilford Courthouse Campaign,* 1-208.

———. *The Ragged Ones.* 336 pp. Novel.

Davis, Junius. "Some Facts about John Paul Jones," *Sou. Atl. Quar.,* IV, No. 4 (October, 1905), 378-391; V, No. 1 (January, 1906), 50-64.

Davis, Sallie. "North Carolina's Part in the Revolution," *Sou. Atl. Quar.,* II, No. 4 (October, 1903), 314-324; III, Nos. 1 and 2 (January and July, 1904), 27-38, 154-165.

Delaney, Norman C. "The Outer Banks of North Carolina during the Revolutionary War," *NCHR,* XXXVI, No. 1 (January, 1959), 1-16.

Dickson, William. "A Picture of the Last Days of the Revolutionary War in North Carolina," *NCB,* XXI (1922), 59-67.

Dodd, W. E. "North Carolina in the Revolution," *Sou. Atl. Quar.,* I, No. 1 (January, 1902), 156-161.

———. "The Revolutionary War in North Carolina: Narrative of John Hodges Drake of Nash County," *Publ. Southern History Association,* IV (1900) , 14-21.

Draper, Lyman. *King's Mountain and Its Heroes,* 191-309.

Fox, Luther A. "Patriotism of Germans in the Colonial South," *Luth. Ch. Rev.,* XXXVIII (January-April, 1919), 1-17.

Frech, Laura P. "The Wilmington Committee of Public Safety and the Loyalist Rising of February, 1776," *NCHR,* XLI, No. 1 (January, 1964) , 21-33.

Fries, Adelaide L. "North Carolina Certificates of the Revolutionary War Period," *NCHR,* IX, No. 3 (July, 1932) , 229-241.

Ganyard, Robert L. "Threat from the West: North Carolina and the Cherokee, 1776-1778," *NCHR,* XLV, No. 1 (January, 1968) , 46-66.

Gibson, George H. "Twenty-Seven Tickets," *NCHR,* XXXVII, No. 4 (October, 1960), 477-487.

Gobbel, Luther L. "Militia of North Carolina in Colonial and Revolutionary Times," TCHS, *Papers,* XIII (1919) , 35-61.

Greene, G. W. *The Life of Nathanael Greene, Major General in the Army of the Revolution,* III, 148-218.

Groome, Bailey T. *Mecklenburg in the Revolution, 1740-1783,* 1-114.

Haskins, J. A. "George Washington in Guilford," *NCB,* XIX (January, 1920) , 107-115.

Henderson, Archibald. (ed.). "The Treaty of Long Island of Holston, July, 1777," *NCHR,* VIII, No. 1 (January, 1931), 55-116.

Higginbotham, Don. *Daniel Morgan, Revolutionary Rifleman,* 100-155.

Hinshaw, Ida C. "Cornwallis in North Carolina: Episodes of the Revolutionary Period." *Jour. Am. Hist.,* VI, No. 4 (1912) , 385-389.

Johnston, Hugh B. (ed.). "The Journal of Ebenezer Hazard in North Carolina 1777 and 1778," *NCHR,* XXXVI, No. 3 (July, 1959) , 358-381.

King, Clyde L. "Military Organizations of North Carolina

during and after the Revolution," *NCB,* VIII, No. 1 (July, 1908), 41-55.

Kyte, George W. "Victory in the South: An Appraisal of General Greene's Strategy in the Carolinas," *NCHR,* XXXVII, No. 3 (July, 1960), 321-347.

Lee, Henry. *Memoirs of the War in the Southern Department of the United States,* 194-297.

Lonsdale, R. E. (comp.). *Atlas of North Carolina,* 47-48.

Lutz, Paul V. "A State's Concern for the Soldier's Welfare: How North Carolina Provided for Her Troops during the Revolution," *NCHR,* XLII, No. 3 (July, 1965), 315-318.

Miles, Edwin A. "Benson Lossing and North Carolina's Revolutionary History," *NCHR,* XXXV, No. 1 (January, 1955), 11-19.

Miller, J. C. *Triumph of Freedom, 1775-1783,* 546-553.

Morison, S. E. "The Willie Jones—John Paul Jones Tradition," *WMQ,* XVI, No. 2 (April, 1959), 198-206.

Nash, Frank. "The Continental Line of North Carolina," *NCB,* XVII (January, 1918), 105-134.

Newsome, A. R. (ed.). "A British Orderly Book, 1780-1781," *NCHR,* IX, Nos. 1, 2, 3, 4 (January, April, July, October, 1932), 57-58, 163-186, 273-298, 366-392.

Pugh, Robert C. "The Revolutionary Militia in the Southern Campaigns, 1780-1781," *WMQ,* XIV, No. 2 (April, 1957), 154-175.

Quarles, Benjamin. *The Negro in the American Revolution.* (Use index for N.C. references.)

Rankin, Hugh F. "Cowpens: Prelude to Yorktown," *NCHR,* XXXI, No. 3 (July, 1954), 333-369.

————. *North Carolina in the American Revolution,* 1-75.

Robert Henry's Narrative (1781), TCHS, *Papers,* III (1899), 16-24.

Robinson, B. P. *William R. Davie,* 1-495.

Rodman, Lida T. "Patriotic Women of North Carolina in the Revolution," *D.A.R. Mag.,* XLVI (August, 1914), 145-152.

Ross, Charles (ed.). *Correspondence of Charles, First Marquis Cornwallis,* I, 84-98, 501-510.

Schenck, David. *North Carolina, 1780-1781,* 199-426.

Smith, Helen Burr, and Elizabeth Moore. "John Mare: A Composite Portrait," *NCHR,* XLIV, No. 1 (January, 1967), 18-52.

Treacy, M. F. *Prelude to Yorktown,* 3-202.

Wallace, Willard M. *Appeal to Arms: A Military History of the American Revolution,* 89-91, 228-245.

Ward, Christopher. *The War of the Revolution,* II, 755-802.

Washburn, George C. "Cornwallis in the Carolinas, 1780, from a Contemporary British Account," *Jour. Am. Hist.,* XXIV, No. 2 (April, 1930), 107-113.

————. "Our Victory at King's Mountain, October 7, 1780: Narrated from the British Point of View in 1781." *Jour. Am. Hist.,* XXIV, No. 4 (October, 1930), 216-219.

Wheeler, E. Milton. "Development and Organization of the North Carolina Militia," *NCHR,* XLI, No. 3 (July, 1964), 307-323.

## 17. *AFTERMATH OF THE REVOLUTION*

SUMMARY—*Problems of North Carolina in 1783:* political strife and chaos; Conservatives and Radicals; prisoners of war; veteran's legislation—land grants; Loyalists and their property—case of Bayard vs. Singleton and its significance; location of the state capital at Raleigh—purchase of Joel Lane plantation and laying out of the "new city."—*Cultural recovery:* newspapers, books, and literature; founding of many academies; founding the University of North Carolina (chartered, 1789; opened to students, 1795).—*Religious developments:* Anglican Church disestablished; growth of Baptist, Methodist, Presbyterian, and other sects; general state of organized religion.—*Economic conditions:* loss of trade and bounties as result of Revolution; state debt and public expenditures; taxes; laws designed to improve economic conditions; shipbuilding; foreign and local trade.—*Growth and expansion of population:* population statistics; settlement of mountain region and Tennessee country.

TEXT—Lefler-Newsome, *North Carolina,* Ch. 16.

BASIC READING—

Lefler, Hugh T. (ed.). *North Carolina History Told by Contemporaries,* 125-133, 157-162.

Connor, R. D. W. *North Carolina: Rebuilding an Ancient Commonwealth,* I, 372-400.

Boyd, W. K. *History of North Carolina: The Federal Period,* 1-46, 66-82.

SUGGESTED READING—

Alden, John R. *The South in the Revolution,* 1763-1789. (Use index for N.C. references.)

Amis, Moses. *Historical Raleigh from Its Foundation in 1792,* 11-77.

Bates, Whitney K. "Northern Speculators and Southern State Debts," *WMQ,* IX, No. 1 (January, 1962), 30-48.

Battle, K. P. *History of the Supreme Court of North Carolina,* 5-39.

————. *History of the University of North Carolina,* I, 1-162.

Chamberlain, Hope. *History of Wake County,* 17-115.

Chambers, William N. "As the Twig is Bent: The Family and the North Carolina Years of Thomas Hart Benton," *NCHR,* XXVI, No. 4 (October, 1949), 385-416.

Clark, Walter. "History of the Superior and Supreme Courts of North Carolina," *NCB,* II, No. 2 (October, 1918), 79-104.

Connor, R. D. W. *A Documentary History of the University of North Carolina, 1784-1800,* 2 vols. Edited by L. R. Wilson and Hugh T. Lefler.

————. "The Genesis of Higher Education in North Carolina," *NCHR,* XXVIII, No. 1 (January, 1951), 1-14.

Coon, Charles L. *The Beginnings of Public Education in North Carolina: A Documentary History, 1790-1840.* 2 vols.

———— (ed.). *North Carolina Schools and Academies, 1790-1840: A Documentary History.* 2 vols.

Corbitt, D. L. "Judicial Districts in North Carolina, 1746-1934," *NCHR,* XII, No. 1 (January, 1936), 45-61.

Crittenden, C. C. *The Commerce of North Carolina, 1763-1789*, 155-170.

DeMond, R. O. *The Loyalists in North Carolina during the Revolution*, 170-201.

Fries, Adelaide L. (ed.). "Report of the Brethren Abraham Steiner and Friederich Christian von Schweinitz of their Journey to the Cherokee Nation and in the Cumberland Settlements in the State of Tennessee, from 28th October to 28th December, 1799," *NCHR*, XXI, No. 4 (October, 1944), 330-375.

Green, F. M. "Listen to the Eagle Scream: One Hundred Years of the Fourth of July in North Carolina (1766-1876)," XXXI, Nos. 3 and 4 (July and October, 1954), 295-320, 529-549.

Hecht, Arthur. "Postal History of North Carolina, 1789-1795," *NCHR*, XXXV, No. 2 (April, 1958), 125-152.

Henderson, Archibald. *The Campus of the First State University*, 5-33.

Keith, Alice B. (ed.). *The John Gray Blount Papers*, I, 13-563.

———. "John Gray and Thomas Blount, Merchants, 1783-1800," *NCHR*, XXV, No. 2 (April, 1948), 194-205.

Nash, Frank. "Governor Abner Nash," *NCB*, XXII (1923), 3-11.

Nevins, Allen. *The American States during and after the Revolution*, 606-678.

Ratchford, Bill. "An International Debt Settlement: The North Carolina Debt to France," *AHR*, XII (1934), 163-169.

Rippy, J. Fred. "A View of the Carolinas in 1783," *NCHR*, VI, No. 4 (October, 1929), 362-370.

Sondley, Foster A. *Samuel Davidson* [1736?-1784], 1-22.

## 18. NORTH CAROLINA AND THE FEDERAL UNION

SUMMARY—*North Carolina and the Confederation:* ratification of Articles of Confederation (1778); attitude toward Confederation government: state rights views of North Carolina delegates in Continental Congress—illustrations.—*Western lands and the "Lost State of Franklin":* state makes "conditional cession" of western lands to U.S. and then revokes Cession Act (1784); organization of State of Franklin under leadership of John Sevier; collapse of State of Franklin—due to opposition of N.C., Virginia, and Continental Congress.— *The movement for a "More Perfect Federal Union":* opposition to the Articles of Confederation; the Annapolis Trade Convention (1786) ; increasing demands for a stronger central government—economic and social groups advocating such.— *North Carolina delegation at Federal Convention (1787):* sketch of five N.C. delegates and their activities and contributions.—*North Carolina refuses to ratify Constitution:* Hillsborough Convention (1788) ; leading Federalists (for ratification) ; Willie Jones and other Anti-Federalists; why N.C. refused to ratify.—*Ratification at Fayetteville Convention (1789):* the "campaign of education"; why N.C. ratified.

TEXT—Lefler-Newsome, *North Carolina,* Ch. 17.

BASIC READING—

Lefler, Hugh T. (ed.). *North Carolina History Told by Contemporaries,* 120-125, 133-139.

Connor, R. D. W. *North Carolina: Rebuilding an Ancient Commonwealth,* I, 378-408.

Boyd, W. K. *History of North Carolina: The Federal Period,* 66-82.

SUGGESTED READING—

Alden, John R. *The South in the Revolution, 1763-1789.* (Use index for N.C. references.)

Best, James A. "The Adoption of the Federal Constitution by North Carolina," TCHS, *Papers,* V (1905), 12-30.

Blanchard, J. C. "North Carolina in the First National Congress," *Trinity Archive,* XV (1902), 389-410.

Boyd, Julian P. "A North Carolina Citizen on the Federal Constitution, 1788," *NCHR,* XVI, No. 1 (January, 1939), 36-53.

Boyd, W. K. (ed.). "Letters of Sylvius [Hugh Williamson],"
TCHS, *Papers,* XI (1915), 5-46.

———— (ed.). "News, Letters and Documents concerning
North Carolina and the Federal Constitution," TCHS,
*Papers,* XIV (1922), 75-95.

Burnett, E. C. *The Continental Congress,* 669-721.

———— (ed.). *Letters of Members of the Continental Congress.*
(II-VII for North Carolina references.)

————. "Southern Statesmen and the Confederation," *NCHR,*
XIV, No. 4 (October, 1937), 343-360.

Douglass, Elisha P. "Thomas Burke, Disillusioned Democrat,"
*NCHR,* XXVI, No. 2 (April, 1949), 150-186.

Driver, Carl. *John Sevier, Pioneer of the Old Southwest,* 16-
116.

Elliot, Jonathan (ed.). *The Debates in the Several State Conventions on the Adoption of the Federal Constitution,* IV,
1-251.

Gilpatrick, D. H. "Contemporary Opinion of Hugh Williamson," *NCHR,* XVII, No. 1 (January, 1940), 26-36.

Jensen, Merrill. *The Articles of Confederation: An Interpretation of the Social-Constitutional History of the American
Revolution, 1774-1781,* 25-28, 84-85, 102, 147-149, 172, 185-
186, 195, 216-217.

————. *The New Nation: A History of the United States
during the Confederation, 1781-1789,* 132, 263, 286, 299-
305, 319-324.

Keith, Alice B. "William Blount in North Carolina Politics,
1781-1789," J. C. Sitterson (ed.). *Studies in Southern
History,* pp. 47-61.

Lefler, Hugh T. (ed.). *A Plea for Federal Union, 1788,* 7-73.

Lester, W. S. *The Transylvania Colony,* 1-83, 255-275.

McRee, G. J. (ed.). *The Life and Correspondence of James
Iredell,* I, 340-564.

Masterson, W. H. *William Blount,* 110-179.

Neal, John W. "Life and Public Services of Hugh Williamson," TCHS, *Papers,* XIII (1919), 62-111.

———— (ed.). "Unpublished Letters of Hugh Williamson,"
TCHS, *Papers,* XIII (1919), 112-115.

Nevins, Allan. *The American States during and after the Revolution,* 544-565.

Newsome, A. R. "North Carolina's Ratification of the Federal Constitution," *NCHR,* XVII, No. 4 (October, 1940), 287-301.

Pierson, W. W., Jr. "The Sovereign State of North Carolina, 1787-1789," *N.C. Lit. and Hist. Assoc. Proc.,* XVII (1917), 58-69.

Pool, William C. "An Economic Interpretation of the Ratification of the Federal Constitution in North Carolina. Part I: The Hillsboro Convention; Part II: The Fayetteville Convention," *NCHR,* XXVII, Nos. 2, 3 and 4 (April, July, October, 1950), 119-141, 289-313, 437-461.

Raper, Charles L. "Why North Carolina at First Refused to Ratify the Federal Constitution," *AHA Annual Report,* I (1895), 99-108.

Robinson, B. P. "Willie Jones of Halifax," *NCHR,* Nos. 1 and 2 (January and April, 1941), 1-26, 133-170.

Sanders, Jennings B. "Thomas Burke and the Continental Congress," *NCHR,* IX, No. 1 (January, 1932), 22-37.

Trenholme, Louis Irby. *North Carolina and the Ratification of the Federal Constitution,* 1-282.

Wagstaff, H. M. *State Rights and Political Parties in North Carolina, 1776-1861,* 14-31.

Williams, S. C. *History of the Lost State of Franklin,* 1-378.

## 19.  POLITICS AND PERSONALITIES, 1789-1800

summary—*Origin of political parties:* "party divisions" in colonial era, during Revolution, and in the struggle over the U.S. Constitution.—*The Federalist Party:* Alexander Hamilton's political philosophy; national and state leaders; sources of support.—*The Anti-Federalist (Republican) Party:* Thomas Jefferson's political philosophy; national and state leaders; sources of support.—*N.C. votes Federalist and then reacts against Federalism:* opposition to Judiciary Act of 1789; Judge Iredell's dissent in Chisholm versus Georgia (1794) ; how N.C.

delegation in Congress reacted to Hamilton's fiscal policies—funding national debt, assumption of state debts, national bank, high tariff, and excise taxes; opposition to Federalist foreign policy—Washington's Proclamation of Neutrality (1793), Neutrality Law (1794), and Jay's Treaty (1795).—*North Carolina state politics:* leaders, issues, and election trends.—*Temporary revival of Federalism, 1798-1800:* reaction against federal Alien and Sedition Acts; attitude toward Virginia and Kentucky Resolutions (1798); Davie's mission to France (1800).—*Decline of Federalism in state and nation:* the *Raleigh Register,* strong Republican journal; the "political revolution" of 1800 and the election of Thomas Jefferson to the presidency.

TEXT—Lefler-Newsome, *North Carolina,* Ch. 18.

BASIC READING—

Lefler, Hugh T. (ed.). *North Carolina History Told by Contemporaries,* 139-142.

Connor, R. D. W. *North Carolina: Rebuilding an Ancient Commonwealth,* I, 426-434.

Boyd, W. K. *History of North Carolina: The Federal Period,* 47-65.

Ashe, S. A. *History of North Carolina,* II, Chs. 8-12.

SUGGESTED READING—

Armytage, W. H. G. "The Editorial Experience of Joseph Gales, 1786-1794," *NCHR,* XXVIII, No. 3 (July, 1951), 332-361.

Dodd, W. E. *The Life of Nathaniel Macon,* 1-100.

Elliott, Robert N., Jr. *The Raleigh Register, 1799-1863,* 1-133.

Fordham, Jeff B. "Iredell's Dissent in Chisholm v. Georgia: Its Political Significance," *NCHR,* VIII, No. 2 (April, 1931), 155-167.

Gilpatrick, D. H. *Jeffersonian Democracy in North Carolina, 1789-1816,* 11-127.

Hamilton, J. G. de R. (ed.). "Letters of John Rust Eaton [1794-1815]," *JSHP,* IX (1910), 25-59.

Harmon, George D. "Benjamin Hawkins and the Federal Factory System," *NCHR,* IX, No. 2 (April, 1932), 138-152.

Henderson, Archibald. "John Steele," *NCB,* XVIII (January-April, 1919), 123-133, 159-177.

————. *Washington's Southern Tour, 1791,* 70-125, 277-327.

Hines, E. A. "Hugh Williamson, M.D., LL.D., North Carolina Physician, Statesman, and Historian," *Am. Med. Hist.,* VII (1935), 323-326.

Hoyt, William Dana, Jr. (ed.). "Letters from Willie Jones to His Son at the University of North Carolina, 1796-1801," *NCHR,* XIX, No. 4 (October, 1942), 375-379.

Lycan, Gilbert L. "Alexander Hamilton and the North Carolina Federalists," *NCHR,* XXV, No. 4 (October, 1948), 442-465.

McPherson, Elizabeth G. (ed.). "Unpublished Letters from North Carolinians to Washington," *NCHR,* XII, No. 2 (April, 1935), 149-172.

McRee, G. J. (ed.). *The Life and Correspondence of James Iredell,* II, 1-277.

Newsome, A. R. (ed.). "John Brown's Journal of Travel in Western North Carolina in 1795," *NCHR,* XI, No. 4 (October, 1934), 284-313.

Pound, Merritt B. "Colonel Benjamin Hawkins—North Carolinian—Benefactor of the Southern Indians," *NCHR,* XIX, Nos. 1 and 2 (January and April, 1942), 1-21, 168-186.

Powell, William S. (ed.). "The Diary of Joseph Gales, 1794-1795," *NCHR,* XXVI, No. 3 (July, 1949), 335-347.

Richards, Leonard L. "John Adams and the Moderate Federalists: The Cape Fear Valley As a Test Case," *NCHR,* XLIII, No. 1 (January, 1966), 14-30.

Stewart Joseph (ed.). "Extract from a Letter by Pastor Storch in North Carolina, dated Salisbury, January 20-February 25, 1796," *NCHR,* XX, No. 4 (October, 1943), 336-340.

Stokes, Durward. "North Carolina and the Great Revival of 1800," *NCHR,* XLIII, No. 4 (October, 1966), 401-412.

Wagstaff, H. M. "Federalism in North Carolina," *JSHP,* IX, No. 2 (1910), 3-44.

———— (ed.). *The Papers of John Steele,* 2 vols.

———. *State Rights and Political Parties in North Carolina, 1776-1861*, 1-155.

———. "William Richardson Davie and Federalism," *N.C. Lit. and Hist. Assoc. Proc.,* XX-XXI (1922), 46-71.

## 20. TRIUMPHANT JEFFERSONIAN DEMOCRACY, 1801-1815

SUMMARY—*North Carolina becomes strong Republican state:* reasons for decline of Federalism—loss of leaders, lack of patronage, unpopularity of policies, lack of popular appeal; increasing Republican strength—young aggressive leaders, control of patronage, able political journalism, influence of Nathaniel Macon.—*A one-party system:* Republican governors, legislatures, and Congressional delegation; emphasis on personalities rather than issues; economy in government and failure to support progressive measures.—*N.C. opposition to national Republican policies:* attitude on Yazoo lands, Embargo and Non-Intercourse Acts, and other measures.—*State politics:* politicalizing the University—case of University versus Foy (North Carolina's "Dartmouth College Case") ; the establishment of banks of Cape Fear and New Bern (1804) and Bank of North Carolina (1810) ; manipulation of the electoral system—"general ticket" versus "district ticket" systems; Indian removal by treaties and western land policy.—*Reorganization of the judiciary:* weaknesses of court system; the Court of Conference; the evolution of the State Supreme Court—Act of 1818.—*North Carolina and the War of 1812-1815:* opposition to national foreign policy; "War Hawks" in Congress and "agrarian imperialism"; the state's contributions of men and money for the war; defenseless condition of coast—British fleet lands (1813); the state's heroes of the war—Benjamin Forsythe, Johnston Blakeley, Otway Burns.—*Criticism of war and Treaty of Peace:* views of William Gaston and other North Carolina leaders.

BASIC READING—

Lefler, Hugh T. (ed.). *North Carolina History Told by Contemporaries,* 140-146.

Connor, R. D. W. *North Carolina: Rebuilding an Ancient Commonwealth,* I, 382-394, 428-459.

Boyd, W. K. *History of North Carolina: The Federal Period,* 83-104.

Ashe, S. A. *History of North Carolina,* II, Ch. 3 and 216-238.

SUGGESTED READING—

Battle, K. P. (ed.). "Letters of Nathaniel Macon, John Steele, and William Barry Grove," *JSHP,* No. 3 (1902), 1-22.

———. "The Trial of James Glasgow and the Supreme Court of North Carolina," *NCB,* III (May, 1903), 1-11.

Boyd, W. K. "Currency and Banking in North Carolina," *TCHS, Papers,* X (1914), 52-86.

Burwell, Mrs. A. M. "Shipwreck Off Hatteras, 1812," *NCB,* XXI (1922), 90-100.

Connor, R. D. W. (ed.). *Documentary History of the University of North Carolina.* 2 vols.

Corbitt, D. L. "Congressional Districts of North Carolina, 1789-1934," *NCHR,* XII, No. 2 (April, 1935), 173-188.

——— (ed.). "The Robert J. Miller Papers, 1813-1831," *NCHR,* XXV, No. 4 (October, 1938), 485-521.

Dodd, W. E. *The Life of Nathaniel Macon,* 100-250.

Franklin, Earl R. "The Instruction of United States Senators by North Carolina," *TCHS, Papers,* VII (1907), 5-15.

Gilpatrick, D. H. *Jeffersonian Democracy in North Carolina,* 127-239.

———. "North Carolina Congressional Elections, 1803-1810," *NCHR,* X, No. 3 (July, 1933), 168-185.

Green, F. M. "Electioneering 1802 Style," *NCHR,* XX, No. 3 (July, 1943), 238-246.

Henderson, Archibald. *The Campus of the First State University,* 37-82.

Keith, Alice B. (ed.). "William Maclean's Travel Journal from Lincolnton, North Carolina, to Nashville, Tennessee,

May-June, 1811," *NCHR,* XV, No. 4 (October, 1938), 378-388.

Knight, E. W. (ed.). *A Documentary History of Education in the South before 1860:* Part III. *The Rise of the State University,* 1-5, 9-30, 43, 51, 273-304.

————. *Public School Education in North Carolina,* 1-101.

Link, Eugene P. "The Democratic Societies in the Carolinas," *NCHR,* XVIII, No. 3 (July, 1941), 259-277.

McPherson, Elizabeth G. (ed.). "Unpublished Letters from North Carolinians to Jefferson," *NCHR,* XII, Nos. 3 and 4 (July and October, 1935), 352-383, 354-380.

———— (ed.). "Unpublished Letters from North Carolinians to James Madison and James Monroe," *NCHR,* XIV, No. 2 (April, 1937), 156-187.

Malone, Henry T. "Cherokee-White Relations on the Southern Frontier in the Early Nineteenth Century," *NCHR,* XXXIV, No. 1 (January, 1957), 1-14.

Mitchell, H. H. "A Forgotten Institution—Private Banks in North Carolina," *NCHR,* XXV, No. 1 (January, 1958), 34-49.

Morgan, J. A. "State Aid to Transportation in North Carolina—The Pre-Railroad Era," *NCB,* X, No. 3 (January, 1911), 122-154.

Newsome, A. R. (ed.). "A Miscellany from the Thomas Henderson Letter Book, 1810-1811," *NCHR,* VI, No. 4 (October, 1929), 398-410.

———— (ed.). "Twelve North Carolina Counties, 1810-1811," *NCHR,* V, Nos. 1, 2, 4 (January, April, October, 1929), 67-99, 171-189, 413-446; VI, No. 3 (July, 1929), 281-309.

————. "Udna Maria Blakeley," *NCHR,* IV, No. 2 (April, 1927), 158-171.

Pratt, Fletcher. "Johnston Blakeley, the Carolina Sea Raider," *U.S. Naval Inst. Proc.,* LXXVI (September, 1950), 996-1007.

Pratt, J. W. *Expansionists of 1812.* (Use index for N.C. references.)

Purcell, James S. "A Book Pedlar's [Mason Weems] Progress

in North Carolina," *NCHR,* XXIX, No. 1 (January, 1952), 8-23.

Schauinger, Joseph H. "William Gaston and the Supreme Court of North Carolina," *NCHR,* XXI, No. 2 (April, 1944), 97-117.

Wagstaff, H. M. (ed.). "Letters of William Barry Groves [to James Hogg]," *JSHP,* IX (1910), 45-88.

————. *State Rights and Political Parties in North Carolina 1776-1861,* 1-155.

Weaver, C. C. *History of Internal Improvements in North Carolina Previous to 1860,* 1-94.

Wilson, E. M. "The Congressional Career of Nathaniel Macon," *JSHP,* No. 2 (1900), 1-115.

## 21. THE "RIP VAN WINKLE STATE"

SUMMARY—*Problems of North Carolina after 1815:* geographic handicaps, backwardness of agriculture and industry, inadequate transportation facilities, small trade, low per capita income, backwardness in education, and political apathy.— *Agriculture:* tobacco, corn, cotton, and other crops; areas of production; methods; value of farm lands.—*Commerce:* reasons for state's small trade; leading markets; efforts to improve trade.—*Roads:* lack of good roads, high freight costs.—*Manufacturing:* household industry; beginnings of cotton textile manufactures.—*Finance:* small number of banks, state revenues and expenditures; opposition to taxes.—*Intellectual conditions:* no public schools; academies did not reach masses; high illiteracy rate and educational apathy; University trained only small number of students.—*Emigration:* reasons why thousands left N.C., where they went, *émigrés* who become famous.—*Major causes of the state's backwardness:* natural handicaps and unprogressive government; effects of physical features—coast, sounds, rivers, etc. on the state.—*Undemocratic local government:* appointive county court, dominated by landed aristocracy, in control in most counties; illustrations of "family" control.—*Undemocratic state government:* property qualifications for voting and officeholding; dominance of East in legislature and governorship; evils of the one-party system.—*Nathaniel Macon, champion of the status quo, the dominant figure in North Carolina politics.*

TEXT—Lefler-Newsome, *North Carolina,* Ch. 20.

BASIC READING—

Lefler, Hugh T. (ed.). *North Carolina History Told by Contemporaries,* 140-146.

Connor, R. D. W. *North Carolina: Rebuilding an Ancient Commonwealth,* I, 438-446, 455-474, 498-506.

Boyd, W. K. *History of North Carolina: The Federal Period,* 105-138.

SUGGESTED READING—

Bassett, J. S. (ed.). "General Slade's Journal of a Trip to Tennessee (1819)," TCHS, *Papers,* VI (1906), 37-56.

———— (ed.). "Some Unpublished Letters of Nathaniel Macon," TCHS, *Papers,* VI (1906), 57-65.

Boyd, W. K. (ed.). "Letters of Nathaniel Macon to Judge Charles Tait," TCHS, *Papers,* VIII (1908-1909), 3-5.

————. "Nathaniel Macon in National Legislation," TCHS, *Papers,* IV (1900), 72-88.

Brown, C. K. *A State Movement in Railroad Development,* 1-14.

Cathey, C. O. *Agricultural Developments in North Carolina, 1783-1860,* 30-47.

Connor, R. D. W. *Ante-Bellum Builders of North Carolina,* 3-31.

Dodd, W. E. *The Life of Nathaniel Macon,* 291-369.

Freund, Suzanne H., and Alice B. Keith (trans. and eds.). "Prince Bernhard's Travels in the Carolinas, December, 1825," *NCHR,* XXVI, No. 4 (October, 1949), 446-459.

Hamilton, J. G. de R. "Party Politics in North Carolina, 1815-1860," *JSHP,* XV, Nos. 1 and 2 (1916), 17-29.

Haywood, M. de L. "An Early Peace Society in North Carolina, 1819-1822," *NCB,* VII (April, 1908), 290-300.

Hobbs, S. H., Jr. *North Carolina: Economic and Social,* 67-87.

Johnson, Guion G. *Ante-Bellum North Carolina,* 3-51.

Johnson, William P. "Migration to and from North Carolina, 1650-1950," *North Carolinian,* I (June, 1955), 35-42.

Monaghan, Jay. "North Carolinians in Illinois History," *NCHR,* XXII, No. 4 (October, 1945), 418-459.

Parker, Robert J. (ed.). "A Yankee in North Carolina: Observations of Thomas Oliver Larkin, 1821-1826," *NCHR,* XIV, No. 4 (October, 1937), 325-342.

Parramore, Thomas C. "The North Carolina Background of Richard Jordan Gatling," *NCHR,* XLI, No. 1 (January, 1964), 54-61.

Poe, Clarence. "Nathaniel Macon, The Cincinnatus of America," *Sou. Atl. Quar.,* XXXVII, No. 1 (January, 1938), 12-21.

Silver, James W. "North Carolinians in Mississippi History," *NCHR,* XXII, No. 1 (January, 1945), 43-57.

Stokes, Durward T. "Nathaniel Rochester in North Carolina," *NCHR,* XXXVIII, No. 4 (October, 1961), 467-481.

Wager, Paul W. *County Government and Administration in North Carolina,* 1-18.

Wallis, P. J. "A Further Note on Joseph Gales of Newark, Sheffield, and Raleigh," *NCHR,* XXX, No. 4 (October, 1953), 561-563.

## 22. *THE MURPHEY PROGRAM FOR STATE DEVELOPMENT*

SUMMARY—*Archibald DeBow Murphey and his program:* Murphey's career; his supporters; his prescription for a sick state in reports to the legislature.—*State program of internal improvements:* improvement of inlets, building of canals, improvement of navigability of rivers, system of improved roads. —*State system of public education:* state fund for schools and state board to manage fund; primary schools in each county, ten regional academies, and the state university; appraisal of the Murphey plan.—*Constitutional reform:* necessary before other reforms could be achieved.—*Drainage of swamp lands.— Writing of a state history.—State response to Murphey's plans:* partial adoption of internal improvements plan—some legislative aid for roads and navigation companies, but no unified program; Literary Board and Literary Fund established, but public schools not established for some decades; agitation for education by Joseph Caldwell; temporary failure of the movement for constitutional reform—people had little voice in government; caucus system; general ticket system; sectionalism on state issues.—*Sectional division of opinion in N.C. on three national issues:* internal improvements, protective tariff, slavery extension.

TEXT—Lefler-Newsome, *North Carolina,* Ch. 21.

BASIC READING—

Lefler, Hugh T. (ed.). *North Carolina History Told by Contemporaries,* 146-148, 150-152, 164-177, 198-212.

Connor, R. D. W. *North Carolina: Rebuilding an Ancient Commonwealth,* I, 474-497.

Boyd, W. K. *History of North Carolina: The Federal Period,* 91-104.

SUGGESTED READING—

Barnhart, John D. "Southern Contributions to the Social Order of the Old Northwest," *NCHR,* XVII, No. 3 (July, 1940), 237-248.

Boyd, W. K. "The Finances of the North Carolina Literary Fund," *Sou. Atl. Quar.,* XIII, No. 4 (October, 1914), 361-370.

———. "The North Carolina Fund for Internal Improvements," *Sou. Atl. Quar.,* XV, No. 1 (January, 1916), 52-67.

Caldwell, Joseph. *Letters on Popular Education, Addressed to the People of North Carolina,* 1-102.

Connor, R. D. W. *Ante-Bellum Builders of North Carolina,* 32-60.

Coon, Charles L. (ed.). *The Beginnings of Public Education in North Carolina,* I, ix-xxxvii, 99-282.

Cunningham, Noble E., Jr. "Nathaniel Macon and the Southern Protest against National Consolidation," *NCHR,* XXXII, No. 3 (July, 1953), 376-384.

Haywood, M. De L. "Canova's Statue of Washington," *Sou. Atl. Quar.,* I, No. 3 (1902), 278-287.

Hoyt, W. H. (ed.). *The Papers of Archibald D. Murphey*, I, xix-xxiv, II, 18-195.

Knight, E. W. *Public School Education in North Carolina,* 13-111.

Konkle, B. A. *John Motley Morehead and the Development of North Carolina, 1796-1866,* 63-101.

McFarland, Daniel M. "North Carolina Newspapers, Editors, and Journalistic Politics, 1815-1835," *NCHR,* XXX, No. 3 (July, 1953), 376-414.

Miller, Zane L. "Senator Nathaniel Macon and the Public Domain, 1815-1828," *NCHR,* XXXVIII, No. 4 (October, 1961), 482-499.

Moore, John H. "Jared Sparks in North Carolina," *NCHR,* XL, No. 3 (July, 1963), 285-294.

Morgan, J. A. "State Aid to Transportation in North Carolina: The Pre-Railroad Era," *NCB,* X, No. 3 (January, 1911), 122-154.

Newsome, A. R. *The Presidential Election of 1824 in North Carolina, JSHP,* XXIII, No. 1 (1939), 1-44.

Noble, M. C. S. *A History of Public Schools in North Carolina,* 25-55.

Vinson, John C. "Electioneering in North Carolina, 1800-1835," *NCHR,* XXIX, No. 2 (April, 1952), 171-188.

Weaver, C. C. *History of Internal Improvements in North Carolina Previous to 1860,* 9-75.

Wooten, Hugh H. "A Fourth Creek Farm from 1800 to 1830," *NCHR,* XXX, No. 2 (April, 1953), 167-175.

———. "The Land Valuations of Iredell County in 1800," *NCHR,* XXIX, No. 4 (October, 1952), 523-539.

———. "Westward Migration from Iredell County, 1800-1850," *NCHR,* XXX, No. 1 (January, 1953), 61-71.


## 23. THE STATE'S CHANGING ROLE IN NATIONAL POLITICS, 1824-1835

SUMMARY—*The presidential campaign of 1824:* why considered a turning point in N.C. politics; revolt against caucus domination and subservience to Virginia.—*The 1824 candidates for the presidency:* William H. Crawford (choice of Congressional caucus and the "Virginia" candidate), John Quincy Adams, John C. Calhoun, Henry Clay, and Andrew Jackson; the Calhoun movement in N.C., the Jackson movement and the "People's Ticket" victorious in state; Adams chosen president; Jackson elected in 1828.—*The East becomes Jackson stronghold, due partially to his opposition to internal improvements—Formation of the Whig party in state (1835):* state and national leaders; Whig advocacy of internal improvements, national bank, protective tariff, and other policies; Democrats in state and nation, champions of strict construction of Constitution, state rights, and economy.—*Party machinery and political methods:* leading Whig and Democratic newspapers.

TEXT—Lefler-Newsome, *North Carolina,* Ch. 22.

BASIC READING—

Lefler, Hugh T. (ed.). *North Carolina History Told by Contemporaries,* 148-150.

Connor, R. D. W. *North Carolina: Rebuilding an Ancient Commonwealth,* I, 506-517.

Boyd, W. K. *History of North Carolina: The Federal Period,* 166-184.

SUGGESTED READING—

Cole, A. C. *The Whig Party in the South.* (Use index for N.C. references.)

Foster, William O. "The Career of Montfort Stokes in North Carolina," *NCHR,* XVI, No. 3 (July, 1939), 237-272.

Hamilton, J. G. de R. (ed.). *The Papers of William A. Graham,* I, 144-246.

Hay, Thomas R. "John C. Calhoun and the Presidential Campaign of 1824," *NCHR,* XII, No. 1 (January, 1935), 20-44.

Jones, H. G. "Bedford Brown: State Rights Unionist," *NCHR,* XXXII, Nos. 3 and 4 (July and October, 1955), 321-345, 483-511.

Konkle, B. A. *John Motley Morehead and the Development of North Carolina,* 170-198.

Newsome, A. R. (ed.). "Correspondence of John C. Calhoun, George McDuffie, and Charles Fisher, relative to the presidential Campaign of 1824," *NCHR,* IV, No. 4 (October, 1927), 428-470; VII, No. 4 (October, 1930), 477-504.

———. "Debate on the Fisher Resolutions," *NCHR,* V, Nos. 1, 2, 3 (January, April, July, 1928), 65-96, 204-223, 310-318.

——— (ed.). "Letters of Romulus M. Saunders to Bartlett Yancey, 1821-1828," *NCHR,* VIII, No. 4 (October, 1931), 427-462.

———. *The Presidential Election of 1824 in North Carolina,* 45-173.

Rice, Philip M. "The Early Development of the Roanoke Waterway—A Study in Interstate Relations," *NCHR,* XXXI, No. 1 (January, 1954), 50-74.

Shanks, Henry T. (ed.). *The Papers of Willie P. Mangum.* Vols. I and II.

## 24. THE CONVENTION OF 1835 AND THE TWO-PARTY SYSTEM

SUMMARY—*Increasing criticism of state Constitution:* undemocratic requirements for suffrage and officeholding; borough representation; illiberal religious provisions; free Negro suffrage; inequitable representation in the General Assembly; wasteful and inefficient government.—*Fifty-year campaign for a constitutional convention:* convention necessary because Constitution contained no provision for amendment; convention could be called only by legislature, but this body, fearing change in government and loss of power, refused to call a convention.—*Why convention was finally called in 1835:* question of state capital and building of a new capitol (old one burned in 1831); some eastern opposition to Negro suffrage; decreasing differences between East and West; realization of some eastern leaders of dire need of reform in order to improve economic conditions of state; leadership of David

L. Swain, William Gaston, and others.—*The convention bill and referendum of 1834:* sectional alignment in legislature and in popular vote (West for, East against) .—*Amendments to Constitution, 1835:* equal county representation abolished (especially in Senate); borough representation abolished; governor to be elected by popular vote and for two-year term; word Protestant was changed to "Christian" in suffrage section; other changes. Changes adopted by popular referendum.—*Significance of 1835 changes:* victory for democracy; rise of two-party system, more popular interest in government. —*Whig-Democratic rivalry:* leaders, issues, methods.

TEXT—Lefler-Newsome, *North Carolina,* Ch. 23.

BASIC READING—

Lefler, Hugh T. (ed.). *North Carolina History Told by Contemporaries,* 152-154.

Connor, R. D. W. *North Carolina: Rebuilding an Ancient Commonwealth,* I, 518-540.

Boyd, W. K. *History of North Carolina: The Federal Period,* 139-165.

SUGGESTED READING—

Boyd, W. K. "Federal Politics in North Carolina, 1824-1836," *Sou. Atl. Quar.,* XVIII (January-April, 1948), 41-51, 167-174.

Connor, H. G. "The Convention of 1835," *NCB,* VIII, No. 2 (October, 1908), 89-110.

Connor, R. D. W. *Ante-Bellum Builders of North Carolina,* 60-92.

Dodd, W. E. *The Life of Nathaniel Macon,* 370-401.

Green, F. M. *Constitutional Development of the South Atlantic States,* 176-179, 183-187, 200-208, 265-272.

Hamilton, J. G. de R. *Party Policies in North Carolina, 1835-1860,* 1-16.

Hoffman, William S. *Andrew Jackson and North Carolina Politics.* 1-134.

Hurley, James M. "The Political Status of Roman Catholics in North Carolina," *Am. Cath. Hist. Soc. Rec.,* XXXVIII (September, 1927), 237-296.

Konkle, B. A. *John Motley Morehead and the Development of North Carolina,* 144-169.

McSweeney, Edward F. "Judge William Gaston of North Carolina," *U.S. Catholic Hist. Soc. Rec.,* XVII (1926), 172-188.

Nash, Francis. "The Borough Towns of North Carolina, *NCB,* VI (October, 1906), 83-102.

Schauinger, Joseph H. *William Gaston, Carolinian,* 1-242.

————. "William Gaston: Southern Statesman," *NCHR,* XVIII, No. 2 (April, 1941), 99-132.

————. "William Gaston and the Supreme Court of North Carolina," *NCHR,* XXI, No. 2 (April, 1944), 97-117.

Smith, Mary P. "Borough Representation in North Carolina," *NCHR,* VII, No. 2 (April, 1930), 177-191.

Wagstaff, H. M. *State Rights and Political Parties in North Carolina, 1776-1861,* 60-69.

————. "State Rights in North Carolina through Half a Century," *NCB,* IX (October, 1909), 79-97.

## 25. THE WHIGS INAUGURATE AN AGE OF PROGRESS

SUMMARY—*Whig control of state government, 1835-1850:* Whig governors—Edward B. Dudley, John M. Morehead, William A. Graham, and Charles Manly; closeness of elections for governor, legislature, and Congress; significance of 1840 election—first state party conventions and platforms; first canvass and joint debates by gubernatorial candidates.—*State aid to railroads:* agitation for railroads by Joseph Caldwell and others; the Wilmington and Weldon Railroad and the Raleigh and Gaston, both completed in 1840; extent of state aid.—*The North Carolina Railroad:* demands for more railroads after 1840; proposals for a state-owned railroad; routes suggested; North Carolina Railroad Co. chartered by legislature, 1849; route from Raleigh to Charlotte; effects of its construction.—*The Public School System begun:* Joseph Caldwell's "Letters on Public Education" (1832) ; state receives almost $1,500,000 as its share of federal surplus (1837) ; the public school law of 1839; weaknesses of the public school system.—*Humanitarian reforms:* state hospital for the insane (1849); poor relief—county poor houses; criminal law liberalized—number of capital offenses reduced.—*Rights of free Negroes restricted:* laws become more severe, though some liberality was in evidence in decisions of Judge Gaston.— *Fiscal reform:* increase in taxes and state revenues.

TEXT—Lefler-Newsome, *North Carolina,* Ch. 24.

BASIC READING—

Lefler, Hugh T. (ed.) *North Carolina History Told by Contemporaries,* 185-189, 212-216, 236-243, 264-277.

Connor, R. D. W. *North Carolina: Rebuilding an Ancient Commonwealth,* I, 541-555, 581-590; II, 7-48.

Boyd, W. K. *History of North Carolina: The Federal Period,* 225-262.

SUGGESTED READING—

Ashe, S. A. "A Turning Point in the Life of the People of the State: The Legislation of 1848," *NCB,* XXII (1923), 12-31.

Betz, Eva (Kelly). *William Gaston, Fighter for Social Justice,* 1-190.

Brown, C. K. *A State Movement in Railroad Development,* 15-94.

Caldwell, Joseph. *The Numbers of Carlton,* 3-232.

Connor, R. D. W. *Ante-Bellum Builders of North Carolina,* 93-149.

Coon, Charles L. (ed.). *Beginnings of Public Education in North Carolina,* II, 545-613.

Hamilton, J. G. de R. (ed.). *The Papers of William A. Graham.* Vols. II and III.

———. *Party Politics in North Carolina, 1835-1860,* 30-135.

Hinshaw, C. R., Jr. "North Carolina Canals before 1860," *NCHR,* XXV, No. 1 (January, 1948), 1-57.

Hoffman, William S. "The Downfall of the Democrats: The Reaction of North Carolinians to Jacksonian Land Policy," *NCHR,* XXXIII, No. 2 (April, 1956), 166-180.

————. "The Election of 1836 in North Carolina," *NCHR*, XXXII, No. 1 (January, 1955), 31-51.

————. "John Branch and the Origins of the Whig Party in North Carolina," *NCHR*, XXXV, No. 3 (July, 1958), 299-315.

Horn, James J. "Trends in Historical Interpretation: James K. Polk," *NCHR*, XLII, No. 4 (October, 1965), 454-464.

Hoyt, Elizabeth S. "Reactions in North Carolina to Jackson's Banking Policy, 1829-1832," *NCHR*, XXV, No. 2 (April, 1948), 167-178.

Johnson, Guion G. *Ante-Bellum North Carolina*, 259-282, 493-521, 560-581, 613-673.

Klebner, Benjamin J. "Some Aspects of North Carolina Public Poor Relief, 1700-1860," *NCHR*, XXXI, No. 4 (October, 1954), 479-492.

Knight, E. W. *Public School Education in North Carolina*, 113-156.

Konkle, B. A. *John Motley Morehead and the Development of North Carolina, 1796-1866*, 199-344.

London, Laurence F. "George Edmund Badger in the United States Senate, 1846-1849," *NCHR*, XV, No. 1 (January, 1938), 1-22.

————. "George Edmund Badger, Member of the Harrison-Tyler Cabinet, 1841," *Jour. Sou. Hist.*, IV (1938), 307-327.

McCulloch, Margaret C. "Founding the North Carolina Asylum for the Insane," *NCHR*, XIII, No. 3 (July, 1936), 185-201.

McDuffie, Penelope. "Some Chapters in the Life of Willie Person Mangum," TCHS, *Papers*, XV (1925), 5-54.

McPherson, Elizabeth G. (ed.). "Unpublished Letters from North Carolinians to Polk," *NCHR*, XVI, Nos. 1, 2, 3, 4 (January, April, July, October, 1939), 54-79, 174-200, 328-357, 428-457; XVII, Nos. 1, 2, 3 (January, April, July, 1940), 37-66, 139-166, 249-266.

———— (ed.). "Unpublished Letters from North Carolinians to Van Buren," *NCHR*, XV, Nos. 1 and 2 (January and April, 1938), 53-81, 131-155.

Marshall, Helen. *Dorothea Dix, Forgotten Samaritan*, 1-298.

Newsome, A. R. (ed.). "Simeon Colton's Railroad Report, 1840," *NCHR,* XI, No. 3 (July, 1934), 205-238.

Noble, M. C. S. *A History of the Public Schools of North Carolina,* 56-129.

Norton, C. C. *The Democratic Party in Ante-Bellum North Carolina, 1835-1861,* 3-106.

Paulson, John D. "A Jewel of the Greek Revival Style [N.C. Capitol]," *Art. and Archeol.,* XXXV (1934), 69-71.

Shanks, Henry T. (ed.). *The Papers of Willie P. Mangum.* Vol. III.

Smith, C. Alphonso. "John Motley Morehead," *Sou. Atl. Quar.,* V, No. 1 (January, 1906), 35-43.

Sellers, Charles G. *James K. Polk, Jacksonian, 1795-1843,* 1-526.

Tucker, Glenn. "For Want of a Scribe," *NCHR,* XLIII, No. 2 (April, 1966), 174-185.

Wagstaff, H. M. *State Rights and Political Parties in North Carolina, 1776-1861,* 69-80.

Waugh, Elizabeth. *North Carolina's Capital: Raleigh.* xi, 1-216.

Williams, Max R. "William A. Graham and the Election of 1844: A Study in North Carolina Politics," *NCHR,* XLV, No. 1 (January, 1968), 23-46.

## 26. CONTINUED PROGRESS UNDER THE DEMOCRATS, 1850-1860

SUMMARY—*Democratic ascendancy in state and nation:* reasons for decline of Whig party—relaxation of zeal for constructive policies such as railroads and schools; failure to appeal to common people; unpopularity of Whigs in nation because of opposition to Mexican War and Manifest Destiny. —*Growing strength of Democratic party:* the more dependable friend of slavery and "Southern interests"; new leadership; W. W. Holden and the *North Carolina Standard.*—*The free suffrage issue:* David S. Reid leads Democrats to victory; narrow Democratic defeat in 1848; Democrats gain control of state government in 1850; free suffrage amendment (abolition of 50 acre qualification to vote for state senators) adopted, 1857.—*State aid to internal improvements:* railroads; plank roads or the "farmer's railroads"; effects on transportation and trade.—*Advances in public education:* Calvin H. Wiley's capable administration of public school system.—*Humanitarian institutions:* increased support.—*Tax reform:* taxes increased with public approval.—*Democratic unity and dominance threatened:* Eastern "slavocracy" takes charge; the Ellis-Holden contest for Democratic choice for governorship (1858); the Whig advocacy of *ad valorem* taxation in the "pots and pans campaign" of 1860 threatens Democratic supremacy; Democrats win perhaps due to slavery and other national questions, rather than because of opposition to "democratic reforms."

TEXT—Lefler-Newsome, *North Carolina,* Ch. 25.

BASIC READING—

Lefler, Hugh T. (ed.). *North Carolina History Told by Contemporaries,* 228-236.

Connor, R. D. W. *North Carolina: Rebuilding an Ancient Commonwealth,* II, 49-90.

Boyd, W. K. *History of North Carolina: The Federal Period,* 288-297, 308-322, 344-353.

SUGGESTED READING—

Battle, George Gordon. "The State of North Carolina v. Negro Will, a Slave of James S. Battle: a Cause Célébre of Ante-Bellum Times," *Va. Law Rev.,* VI, No. 7 (April, 1920), 515-530.

Boyd, W. K. "Ad Valorem Slave Taxation," TCHS, *Papers,* V (1905), 31-38.

———. "William W. Holden," TCHS, *Papers,* Series III (1899), 39-78, 90-130.

Brown, C. K. *A State Movement in Railroad Development,* 95-147.

Carr, J. W. "The Manhood Suffrage Movement in North Carolina, 1835-1860," TCHS, *Papers,* XI, 47-78.

Folk, Edgar E. "W. W. Holden and the Election of 1858," *NCHR*, XXI, No. 4 (October, 1944), 294-318.

Hamilton, J. G. de R. *Party Politics in North Carolina, 1835-1860,* 136-210.

Knight, E. W. *Public School Education in North Carolina,* 158-216.

Morrill, James R. "The Presidential Election of 1852: Death Knell of the Whig Party in North Carolina," *NCHR*, XLIV, No. 4 (October, 1967), 342-359.

Newsome, A. R. (ed.). "The A. S. Merrimon Journal, 1853-1854," *NCHR*, VIII, No. 3 (July, 1931), 300-330.

Norton, C. C. "Democratic Newspapers and Campaign Literature in North Carolina, 1835-1861," *NCHR*, VI, No. 4 (October, 1929), 345-361.

Wagstaff, H. M. *State Rights and Political Parties in North Carolina, 1776-1861,* 81-119.

Weeks, S. B. *The Beginnings of the Common School System in North Carolina, or Calvin Henderson Wiley and the Organization of the Common Schools of North Carolina. Report of the Commissioner of Education for 1896/97.* 1379-1414.

## 27. *ECONOMIC DEVELOPMENT, 1835-1860*

SUMMARY—*Economic prosperity of the 1850's:* reasons for this in state and nation.—*Improvements in agriculture:* bright-leaf tobacco developed first in North Carolina; corn, cotton, wheat, rice, and other crops; agricultural journals and societies; first State Fair, 1853.—*The "Golden State":* North Carolina takes the lead in gold mining; areas of production; amounts coined and made into jewelry; private mint of the Bechtlers; branch United States Mint at Charlotte.—*Iron and Coal:* areas of production, amount produced.—*Commercial fisheries:* location and value.—*Manufactures:* decline of household manufactures and decreasing self-sufficiency after 1815; leading commercial industries, location, and products; turpentine, flour and meal, tobacco, cotton textiles; pioneers in textile and tobacco industries; iron manufactures.—*Growth of towns:* largest towns in 1860—Wilmington, New Bern, Fayetteville, Raleigh, Salisbury, and Charlotte.—*How North Carolina ranked; various economic aspects in 1860.*

TEXT—Lefler-Newsome, *North Carolina,* Ch. 26.

BASIC READING—

Lefler, Hugh T. (ed.). *North Carolina History Told by Contemporaries,* 226-228.

Boyd, W. K. *History of North Carolina: The Federal Period,* 331-353.

SUGGESTED READING—

Bardolph, Richard. "A North Carolina Farm Journal of the Middle Fifties," *NCHR,* XXV, No. 1 (January, 1948), 58-90.

Brown, C. K. *A State Movement in Railroad Development,* 1-148.

Cappon, Lester. "Iron-Making—A Forgotten Industry of North Carolina," *NCHR,* IX, No. 4 (October, 1932), 331-348.

Cathey, C. O. *Agricultural Developments in North Carolina, 1783-1860,* 30-205.

————. "Sidney Weller, Ante-Bellum Promoter of Agricultural Reform," *NCHR,* XXXI, No. 1 (January, 1954), 1-17.

Corbitt, D. L. (ed.). "Letters from Hugh Lackey, Raleigh Hatter, 1843," *NCHR,* XXV, No. 2 (April, 1948), 179-192.

Davidson, Philip G. "Industrialism in the Ante-Bellum South," *Sou. Atl. Quar.,* XXVII, No. 1 (January, 1928), 405-425.

Gray, L. C. *History of Agriculture in the Southern United States to 1860.* (Use index for N.C. references.)

Green, F. M. "Gold Mining: A Forgotten Industry of Ante-Bellum North Carolina," *NCHR,* XI, Nos. 1 and 2 (January and April, 1937), 1-19, 135-155.

Olmsted, F. L. *A Journey in the Seaboard Slave States in the Years 1853-1854,* 305-376.

Phifer, Edward W. "Champagne and Brindletown: The Story

of the Burke County Gold Rush, 1829-1833," *NCHR*, XL, No. 4 (October, 1963), 489-500.

———. "Money, Banking, and Burke County in the Ante-Bellum Era," *NCHR*, XXXVII, No. 1 (January, 1960), 22-37.

Phillips, U. B. *American Negro Slavery*. (Use index for N.C. references.)

———. *Life and Labor in the Old South*. 12, 252-254.

Robert, Joseph C. "The Tobacco Industry in Ante-Bellum North Carolina," *NCHR*, XV, No. 2 (April, 1938), 119-130.

———. *The Tobacco Kingdom, Plantation, Market, and Factory in Virginia and North Carolina, 1800-1860*, 3-52.

Stampp, Kenneth M. *The Peculiar Institution: Slavery in the Ante-Bellum South*. (Use index for N.C. references.)

Stanard, Diffie W., and Richard W. Griffin. "The Cotton Textile Industry in Ante-Bellum North Carolina," *NCHR*, XXXIV, Nos. 1 and 2 (January and April, 1957), 15-35, 131-164.

Starling, Robert B. "The Plank Road Movement in North Carolina," *NCHR*, XVI, Nos. 1 and 2 (January and April, 1939), 1-22, 147-173.

Taylor, Rosser H. *Slaveholding in North Carolina: An Economic View*, 8-98.

Tilley, Nannie May. *The Bright-Tobacco Industry*, 3-36.

——— (ed.). "Journal of the Surry County [N.C.] Agricultural Society," *NCHR*, XXIV, No. 4 (October, 1947), 495-531.

Wallace, Wesley H. "North Carolina's Agricultural Journals, 1835-1861, A Crusading Press," *NCHR*, XXXVI, No. 3 (July, 1959), 275-306.


## 28. AN INTELLECTUAL AWAKENING, 1835-1860

SUMMARY—*Educational advance:* improvements in public schools; increase in number of schools, buildings, teachers, appropriations, and educational standards; academies and other private schools; special schools—law, medicine, military, and manual labor schools.—*The University of North Carolina:* leadership of President David L. Swain; broadening of curricula; increase in enrollment; importance of alumni.— *Church colleges:* Wake Forest founded by Baptists, Trinity College (now Duke) by Methodists, Davidson College by Presbyterians, and New Garden Boarding School (now Guilford) by Quakers; other denominational colleges.—*The education of women:* Salem, Greensboro, Davenport, and other colleges.—*Newspapers:* appearance of first dailies; leading papers, circulation, and significance; importance of "political journalism."—*Magazines and other periodicals:* literary and professional publications.—*History and biography:* leading writers and subjects.—*Humor and fiction:* leading writers and themes of writing.—*General educational and cultural conditions in 1860.*

TEXT—Lefler-Newsome, *North Carolina,* Ch. 27.

BASIC READING—

Lefler, Hugh T. (ed.). *North Carolina History Told by Contemporaries,* 179-185, 189-194.

Connor, R. D. W. *North Carolina: Rebuilding an Ancient Commonwealth,* I, 509-613.

Boyd, W. K. *History of North Carolina: The Federal Period,* 354-392.

SUGGESTED READING—

Barbee, David R. "Hinton Rowan Helper," *Tyler's Quar. Lit. and Gen. Mag.,* XV (1934), 145-172, 228-231.

Battle, K. P. *History of the University of North Carolina,* I, 423-723.

Bergeron, Paul H. (ed.). "My Brother's Keeper: William H. Polk Goes to School," *NCHR,* XLIV, No. 2 (April, 1967), 188-204.

Blair, Marian H. "Contemporary Evidence—Salem Boarding School, 1834-1844," *NCHR,* XXVII, No. 2 (April, 1950), 142-161.

Blauch, L. E. "An Early Normal College in the South," *Peabody Jour. Ed.,* VIII (1931), 297-304.

Boyd, W. K. "Dennis Heartt," TCHS, *Papers*, II (1898), 34-43.

———— (ed.). "Rev. Brantley York on Early Days in Randolph County and Union Institute," TCHS, *Papers*, VIII (1908), 15-34.

Braverman, Howard. "Calvin H. Wiley's North Carolina Reader," *NCHR*, XXIX, No. 4 (October, 1952), 500-522.

Chaffin, Nora. *Trinity College, 1839-1892: The Beginnings of Duke University*, 22-117.

Coon, Charles L. (ed.). *The Beginnings of Public Education in North Carolina: A Documentary History*, II, 548-1048.

———— (ed.). *North Carolina Schools and Academies, 1790-1840: A Documentary History*, 1-846.

Creecy, R. B. "What I Know about 'Shocco Jones,'" TCHS, *Papers*, II (1898), 29-33.

Dent, Sanders. "Francis Lister Hawks," TCHS, *Papers*, I (1897), 56-65.

Dormon, James H., Jr. *Theater in the Ante-Bellum South, 1815-1861*. (Use index for New Bern, Raleigh, Fayetteville, Wilmington, and Salisbury.)

Eaton, Clement. *Freedom of Thought in the Old South*, 200-205, 217.

————. *The Mind of the Old South*, 119-136.

Ellen, John C. "Newspaper Finance in North Carolina's Piedmont and Mountain Region during the 1850's," *NCHR*, XXXVII, No. 4 (October, 1960), 488-505.

Farmer, Fannie M. "The Bar Examination and Beginning Years of Legal Practice in North Carolina, 1820-1860," *NCHR*, XXIX, No. 2 (April, 1952), 159-170.

————. "Legal Education in North Carolina, 1820-1860," *NCHR*, XXVIII, No. 3 (July, 1951), 271-297.

————. "Legal Practice and Ethics in North Carolina, 1820-1860," *NCHR*, XXX, No. 3 (July, 1953), 329-353.

Flowers, R. L. "John Joseph Brown [editor *Carolina Watchman*]," TCHS, *Papers*, III (1899), 1-7.

Folk, Edgar E. "W. W. Holden and the North Carolina Standard, 1843-1848," *NCHR*, XIX, No. 1 (January, 1942), 22-47.

Gilbert, Dorothy. *Guilford, A Quaker College,* 11-79.

Henderson, Archibald. *The Campus of the First State University,* 83-178.

——. "Early Drama and Professional Entertainment in North Carolina," *Reviewer,* V (July-October, 1925), 27-57, 68-77.

Hixson, Iva May. "Academic Requirements of Salem College, 1854-1909," *NCHR,* XXVII, No. 4 (October, 1950), 419-429.

Johnson, Guion G. *Ante-Bellum North Carolina,* 283-330.

King, Emma. "Some Aspects of the Work of the Society of Friends for Negro Education in North Carolina," *NCHR,* I, No. 4 (October, 1924), 403-411.

Knight, E. W. "Braxton Craven: Pioneer in Teacher Education," *School and Society,* LXXVI (July, 1952), 33-37.

——. "Interest in the South in Lancasterian Methods," *NCHR,* XXV, No. 3 (July, 1948), 377-402.

——. "Notes on John Chavis," *NCHR,* VII, No. 3 (July, 1930), 326-345.

——. *Public School Education in North Carolina,* 158-191.

Lefler, Hugh T. *Hinton Rowan Helper: Advocate of a "White America,"* 1-45.

McIver, George W. "North Carolinians at West Point before the Civil War," *NCHR,* VII, No. 1 (January, 1930), 15-45.

Marshall, Roger P. "A Mythical Mayflower Competition: North Carolina Literature in the Half-Century Following the Revolution," *NCHR,* XXVII, No. 2 (April, 1950), 178-192.

Menhold, Lucy L. "The Salem Boarding School between 1802 and 1822," *NCHR,* XXVII, No. 1 (January, 1950), 32-45.

Miles, Edwin A. "Joseph Seawell Jones of Shocco—Historian and Humbug," *NCHR,* XXXIV, No. 4 (October, 1957), 483-506.

*North Carolina Authors: A Selective Handbook.* 1-135. (Use index for individual authors.)

Paschal, George W. "Baptist Academies in North Carolina," *NCHR,* XXVIII, No. 1 (January, 1951), 47-62.

————. *History of Wake Forest College,* I, 1-653.

Patton, James W. (ed.) . "New England Tutors in Granville County, North Carolina, 1845-1850," *NCHR,* XXXVII, No. 4 (October, 1960), 544-567.

Phifer, Edward W. "Certain Aspects of Medical Practice in Ante-Bellum Burke County," *NCHR,* XXXVI, No. 1 (January, 1959) , 28-46.

Polk, W. T. "The Hated Helper," *Sou. Atl. Quar.,* XXX, No. 2 (April, 1931) , 177-190.

Raper, Charles L. *The Church and Private Schools of North Carolina,* 9-247.

Rulfs, Donald J. "The Ante-Bellum Professional Theater in Fayetteville," *NCHR,* XXXI, No. 2 (April, 1954) , 125-133.

————. "The Ante-Bellum Professional Theater in Raleigh," *NCHR,* XXIX, No. 3 (July, 1952), 344-358.

————. "The Era of the Opera House in Piedmont North Carolina," *NCHR,* No. 3 (July, 1958) , 328-346.

————. "The Professional Theater in Wilmington, 1858-1870," *NCHR,* No. 2 (April, 1951) , 119-136.

Sanders, John L. (ed.) . "The Journal of Ruffin Wirt Tomlinson, The University of North Carolina, 1841-1842," *NCHR,* XXX, Nos. 1 and 2 (January and April, 1953), 86-114, 233-260.

Sellers, Charles G., Jr. "Jim Polk Goes to Chapel Hill," *NCHR,* XXIX, No. 2 (April, 1952) , 189-203.

Shaw, Cornelia. *Davidson College,* 1-98.

Smiley, David L. "Educational Attitude of North Carolina Baptists," *NCHR,* XXXV, No. 3 (July, 1958) , 316 327.

Walser, Richard. "Letters of a Young Novelist: Calvin Henderson Wiley," *NCHR,* XXXI, No. 3 (July, 1954) , 180-201.

————. "The Mysterious Case of George Higby Throop (1818-1896) ; or, The Search for the Author of the Novels *Nag's Head, Bertie,* and *Lynde Weiss,*" *NCHR,* XXXIII, No. 1 (January, 1956), 12-44.

————. "The North Carolina Sojourn of the First American Novelist," *NCHR,* XXVIII, No. 2 (April, 1951) , 138-155.

————. "Senator Strange's Indian Novel," *NCHR,* XXVI, No. 1 (January, 1949) , 1-27.

Wiley, Mary C. "Childhood Recollections of My Father," *NCHR*, XXXIV, No. 4 (October, 1957), 517-529.

———— (ed.). "Unpublished Letters of Calvin Henderson Wiley," *NCHR*, XXIX, No. 1 (January, 1952), 91-103.

———— (ed.). "With Calvin H. Wiley in Tennessee through Unpublished Letters," *NCHR*, XXXVI, No. 1 (January, 1959), 72-95.

Williams, Max R. "The Education of William A. Graham," *NCHR*, XL, No. 1 (January, 1963), 1-14.

Yearns, Wilfred B. "François X. Martin and His *History of North Carolina*," *NCHR*, XXXVI, No. 1 (January, 1959), 17-27.


## 29. *RELIGION AND SOCIETY IN ANTE-BELLUM NORTH CAROLINA*

SUMMARY—*Growth of church membership:* Causes and effects.—*The Protestant Episcopal Church:* slow growth following Revolution; Diocese of North Carolina organized (1817); first bishop, Ravenscroft (1823); second bishop, Ives, becomes Roman Catholic (1853), and is succeeded by Atkinson; statistics on churches, membership, and value of church property.—*Baptists:* rapid growth; various divisions; organization of State Convention (1830); founding of Wake Forest College.—*Methodists:* slow growth at first; rapid growth later; various divisions; chief rival of Baptists for numbers and in appeal to common people.—*Presbyterians:* third largest sect.—*Other religious groups:* Lutherans, Moravians, Reformed, Quakers, Catholics, Jews.—*The "Great Revival" and camp meetings:* causes and effects.—*Church work and influence:* attitude toward slavery and various social problems.—*Dominant social characteristics of North Carolina:* provincialism, conservatism, sectionalism, individualism, and social stratification.—*Social classes:* gentry or planter aristocracy, small farmers, yeomen and mechanics, "poor whites," free Negroes, and slaves.—*The social life of each class:* houses; furniture and furnishings; food and drink; clothing; pleasures and amusements.—*Free Negroes:* origin, numbers, location, laws relating to them.—*Negro slavery:* numbers, percentage of population, counties with heaviest density, prices; treatment of slaves; plantation rules; laws relating to slaves; court decisions concerning slaves.—*Town life:* outstanding characteristics; influence of towns in state.—*Family life:* attitude toward women, who had few legal rights.—*Most prevalent crimes and punishments.*

TEXT—Lefler-Newsome, *North Carolina,* Ch. 28.

BASIC READING

Lefler, Hugh T. (ed.). *North Carolina History Told by Contemporaries,* 195-198, 216-225.

Connor, R. D. W. *North Carolina: Rebuilding an Ancient Commonwealth,* II, 152-173.

Boyd, W. K. *History of North Carolina: The Federal Period,* 185-224.

SUGGESTED READING—

Allcott, John V. "Architectural Developments at 'Montrose' in the 1850's," *NCHR,* XLII, No. 1 (January, 1965), 85-95.

Bassett, J. S. *Anti-Slavery Leaders of North Carolina,* 7-74.

———. "The Case of State v. Will," *TCHS, Papers,* II (1898), 12-20.

———. *History of Slavery in the State of North Carolina,* 7-109.

———. "Methodism and Slavery," *TCHS, Papers,* IV (1900), 1-11.

Bonner, James C. (ed.). "Plantation Experiences of a New York Woman," *NCHR,* XXXIII, Nos. 3 and 4 (July and October, 1956), 384-412, 529-546.

Boyd, W. K. (ed.). "The Autobiography of Brantley York," *The John Lawson Monographs,* I (1910), 1-139.

———. "Methodist Expansion in North Carolina after the Revolution," *TCHS, Papers,* XII (1916), 37-55.

Brewer, James H. "Legislation Designed to Control Slavery in Wilmington and Fayetteville," *NCHR,* XXX, No. 2 (April, 1953), 155-166.

Browning, James B. "The Free Negro in Ante-Bellum North Carolina," *NCHR,* XV, No. 1 (January, 1938), 23-33.

Carroll, Kenneth L. "The Nicholites of North Carolina," *NCHR,* XXXI, No. 4 (October, 1954), 453-462.

Chavis, John. "The Influence of John Chavis and Lunsford Lane on the History of North Carolina," *Jour. Negro Hist.,* XXV (1940), 14-24.

Clowes, Chorley E. "John Stark Ravenscroft, first Bishop of North Carolina," *Am. Church Mo.,* XXIII (March, 1928), 37-47.

Davidson, Chalmers. "Catawba Springs—Carolina's Spa," *NCHR,* XXVIII, No. 4 (October, 1951), 414-425.

Des Champs, Margaret B. "John Chavis As a Preacher to Whites," *NCHR,* XXXII, No. 2 (April, 1955), 165-172.

Falk, Stanley L. "The Warrenton Female Academy of Joseph Mordecai, 1809-1818," *NCHR,* XXXV, No. 3 (July, 1958), 281-298.

Farrison, William E. "The Negro Population of Guilford County, North Carolina, before the Civil War," *NCHR,* XXI, No. 4 (October, 1944), 319-329.

Ford, Paul M. "Calvin H. Wiley's View of the Negro," *NCHR,* XLI, No. 1 (January, 1964), 1-20.

Fox, L. A. "Decline and Revival of the Lutheran Consciousness in the Carolinas," *Luth. Ch. Rev.,* XXXI (October, 1912), 658-677.

Franklin, John Hope. "The Free Negro in the Economic Life of Ante-Bellum North Carolina," *NCHR,* XIX, Nos. 3 and 4 (July and October, 1942), 239-259, 358-374.

————. *The Free Negro in North Carolina,* 14-271.

Hamilton, John B. (ed.). "Diary of Thomas Miles Garrett at the University of North Carolina, 1849," *NCHR,* XXXVIII, Nos. 1, 2, 3, 4 (January, April, July, October, 1961), 64-93, 241-262, 380-410, 534-563.

Hamlin, Griffith A. "Educational Activities of the Disciples of Christ in North Carolina, 1852-1902," *NCHR,* XXXIII, No. 3 (July, 1956), 310-331.

Howerton, R. T., Jr. "The Rose of Sharon Baptist Church," TCHS, *Papers,* VII (1907), 39-47.

Jameson, J. F. (ed.). "Autobiography of Omar ibn Said, Slave in North Carolina, 1831," *AHR*, XXXI (July, 1925), 787-795.

Johnson, Guion G. *Ante-Bellum North Carolina*, 331-467, 522-559, 582-612.

———. "The Ante-Bellum Town in North Carolina," *NCHR*, V, No. 4 (October, 1928), 372-389.

———. "The Camp Meeting in Ante-Bellum North Carolina," *NCHR*, X, No. 2 (April, 1933), 95-110.

———. "Courtship and Marriage Customs in Ante-Bellum North Carolina," *NCHR*, VIII, No. 4 (October, 1931), 384-402.

———. "Recreational and Cultural Activities in the Ante-Bellum Town of North Carolina," *NCHR*, VI, No. 1 (January, 1929), 17-37.

———. "Revival Movements in Ante-Bellum North Carolina," *NCHR*, X, No. 1 (January, 1933), 21-43.

———. "Social Characteristics of Ante-Bellum North Carolina," *NCHR*, VI, No. 2 (April, 1929), 140-157.

Lemmon, Sarah M. "The Genesis of the Protestant Episcopal Diocese of North Carolina, 1701-1823," *NCHR*, XXVIII, No. 4 (October, 1951), 426-462.

Owsley, Frank. *Plain Folk of the Old South*, 45-51, 58-61.

Padgett, James A. "From Slavery to Prominence in North Carolina," *Jour. Negro Hist.*, XXII (1937), 433-487.

Paschal, George W. "Morgan Edwards' Materials toward a History of the Baptists in the Province of North Carolina," *NCHR*, VII, No. 3 (July, 1930), 365-399.

Ravenscroft, John Stark. "Manuscript Journal of John Stark Ravenscroft, First Bishop of North Carolina," *P.E. Church Hist. Mag.*, V (1936), 42-46.

Rives, Ralph H. "Panacea Springs: Fashionable Spa," *NCHR*, XLII, No. 4 (October, 1965), 430-439.

Roberts, W. C. "Cockfighting: An Early Entertainment in North Carolina," *NCHR*, XLII, No. 3 (July, 1965), 306-314.

Shryock, Richard H. "Medical Practice in the Old South," *Sou. Atl. Quar.*, XXIX (1930), 160-178.

Sowle, Patrick. "The North Carolina Manumission Society, 1816-1834," *NCHR*, XLII, No. 1 (January, 1965), 47-69.

Stroupe, Henry S. "The Beginnings of Religious Journalism in North Carolina, 1823-1865," *NCHR*, XXX, No. 1 (January, 1953), 1-22.

————. "North Carolina Baptist Convention History," *Quar. Rev.* (Bapt.), XVI (January-March, 1907), 60-76.

———— (comp.). "The Religious Press in the South Atlantic States, 1802-1865. An Annotated Bibliography," TCHS, *Papers*, XXXII (1956), 1-172.

Taylor, Rosser H. *The Free Negro in North Carolina*, 5-26.

————. "Humanizing the Slave Code of North Carolina," *NCHR*, II, No. 3 (July, 1925), 323-331.

————. "Slave Conspiracies in North Carolina," *NCHR*, V, No. 1 (January, 1928), 20-34.

Todd, Willie G. "North Carolina Baptists and Slavery," *NCHR*, XXIV, No. 2 (April, 1947), 135-159.

Turner, Charles W. (ed.). "Reuben Knox Letters, 1848-1851," *NCHR*, XXXVII, Nos. 1, 2, 3 (January, April, July, 1960), 66-93, 245-270, 397-418.

Turner, Joseph K. "Slavery in Edgecombe County," TCHS, *Papers*, XII (1916), 5-36.

Wall, Bennett H. "Charles Pettigrew, First Bishop-Elect of the North Carolina Episcopal Church," *NCHR*, XXVIII, No. 1 (January, 1951), 15-46.

Ware, Charles C. *North Carolina Disciples of Christ*, 1-377.

Yamuck, Julius. "Thomas Ruffin and North Carolina Slave Law," *Jour. Sou. Hist.*, XXI (November, 1955), 447-475.


## 30. SECTIONAL DIFFERENCES AND CONFLICTS IN THE UNION

SUMMARY—*Geographical basis of sectionalism.*—*Northern economic development:* free labor, diversified agriculture, development of manufactures and trade; growth of cities; *Southern economic development*: emphasis on cotton, tobacco, and other staple crops; slave labor—but not all; little development of manufactures and commerce; the South as a "conscious minority" after 1820.—*Federal economic legislation unfavorable to South:* tariff, banking, and other legislation.— *The sectional controversy over slavery extension:* the principle of compromise (Missouri Compromise of 1820 and "Great Compromise" of 1850).—*Change in Southern attitude toward slavery after 1830:* shift from apologetic to defensive attitude —due to rise of abolition movement, slave uprisings, and opening of rich cotton lands in Lower South; Southern leaders defend slavery as a "positive good"; stricter laws concerning free Negroes.—*The slavery issue in national politics:* the Texas-Oregon questions (1844-1846) and the Wilmot Proviso (1846); the Compromise of 1850; Personal Liberty laws of Northern states; the Kansas-Nebraska Act (1854); the presidential election of 1856; the Dred Scott decision (1857); the Lincoln-Douglas debates (1858); John Brown's raid at Harper's Ferry (1859); the presidential election of 1860.— *Secession of Lower South (1860-1861):* causes and reaction.

TEXT—Lefler-Newsome, *North Carolina,* Ch. 29.

SUGGESTED READING—

Bassett, J. S. "The Congressional Career of Thomas L. Clingman," TCHS, *Papers,* IV (1900), 48-63.

Craven, Avery O. *The Coming of the Civil War,* 21-25, 58, 96, 153-154, 213, 262-270, 352, 414.

Crenshaw, Ollinger. "The Psychological Background of the Election of 1860 in the South," *NCHR,* XIX, No. 3 (July, 1942) 260-279.

Elliott, Robert N., Jr. "The Nat Turner Insurrection As Reported in the Northern Press," *NCHR,* XXXVIII, No. 1 (January, 1961), 1-18.

Franklin, Earl R. "Henry Clay's Visit to Raleigh [1844]," TCHS, *Papers,* VII (1907), 55-63.

Johnston, Clifton H. "Abolitionist Missionary Activities in North Carolina," *NCHR,* XL, No. 3 (July, 1963), 295-320.

London, Lawrence F. "George Edmund Badger and the Compromise of 1850," *NCHR,* XV, No. 2 (April, 1938), 99-118.

———. "George Edmund Badger, His Last Years in the

United States Senate, 1851-1855," *NCHR*, XV, No. 3 (July, 1938), 231-250.

Milton, George Fort. *Douglas and the Needless War,* 1-608.

Newsome, A. R. (ed.). "Letters of Lawrence O'Bryan Branch, 1856-1861," *NCHR*, X, No. 1 (January, 1933), 44-79.

Parker, Robert J., and David L. Corbitt (eds.). "California's Larkin Settles Old Debts: A View of North Carolina," *NCHR*, XVII, No. 4 (October, 1940), 332-346.

Peterson, Owen M. "W. W. Avery in the Democratic National Convention of 1860," *NCHR*, XXXI, No. 4 (October, 1954), 463-478.

Randall, J. G. *The Civil War and Reconstruction,* 3-258.

Sitterson, J. C. "Economic Sectionalism in Ante-Bellum North Carolina," *NCHR*, XVI, No. 2 (April, 1939), 134-146.

Stampp, Kenneth M. "The Southern Refutation of the Pro-slavery Argument," *NCHR*, XXI, No. 1 (January, 1944), 35-45.

Wallace, Lee A. "Raising a Volunteer Regiment for Mexico, 1846-1847," *NCHR*, XXXV, No. 1 (January, 1958), 20-33.

Weaver, C. C. "The North Carolina Manumission Society," TCHS, *Papers,* I (1897), 71-76.

## 31. A STATE IN THE CONFEDERACY, 1861-1865

SUMMARY—*North Carolina less Southern than states of Lower South:* its role in formation of the Union and its relation to that Union.—*The two-party system—Whigs and Democrats:* leaders and issues; party alignments on protective tariff, internal improvements, national bank, and other national issues; Democratic party considered most dependable defender of slavery and other "Southern interests," "Unionist Whigs"— Badger, Graham, Morehead, and others; "State Rights" Whigs-Mangum, Clingman, and others.—*Party views on major national issues:* the Mexican War (1846-1848), the Wilmot Proviso (1846), the Compromise of 1850, the Kansas-Nebraska Act (1854); the presidential election of 1856 and talk of secession in North Carolina in case of Republican victory.—*North*

*Carolina's anti-slavery leaders:* Helper, Hedrick, Goodloe, and others.—*The presidential election of 1860:* state goes for Breckinridge and "Southern Democrats," but Unionist vote very large.—*North Carolina opposes secession (1860):* votes against convention to consider secession; failure of peace movement.—*North Carolina secedes, May 20, 1861:* causes and events which led to secession; nature of secession ordinance; state's reaction to secession.

TEXT—Lefler-Newsome, *North Carolina,* Ch. 30.

BASIC READING—

Lefler, Hugh T. (ed.). *North Carolina History Told by Contemporaries,* 262-289.

Connor, R. D. W. *North Carolina: Rebuilding an Ancient Commonwealth,* II, 91-151.

Boyd, W. K. *History of North Carolina: The Federal Period,* 263-287, 297-330.

SUGGESTED READING—

Bassett, J. S. *Anti-Slavery Leaders of North Carolina,* 7-74.

Boyd, W. K. "North Carolina on the Eve of Secession," *AHA Ann. Rept.* (1910), 165-177.

Gibbons, J. P. "Bart F. Moore on Secession and Reconstruction," TCHS, *Papers,* II (1898), 75-82.

Hamilton, J. G. de R. "Benjamin Sherwood Hedrick," *JSHP,* X, No. 1 (1910), 1-42.

———. *Reconstruction in North Carolina,* 1-36.

Hill, D. H. *North Carolina in the War Between the States: Bethel to Sharpsburg,* I, 1-45.

Hoffman, William S. *North Carolina in the Mexican War, 1846-1848,* 1-48.

Holt, Bryce R. "The Supreme Court of North Carolina and Slavery," TCHS, *Papers,* XVII (1927), 7-77.

Johnston, Frontis (ed.). *The Papers of Zebulon Baird Vance, 1843-1862,* I, xvii-lxxiv, 1-100.

Lefler, Hugh T. *Hinton Rowan Helper: Advocate of a "White America,"* 5-42.

Parramore, Thomas C. "The Ironic Fate of the 'Southern Star,'" *NCHR,* XLII, No. 3 (July, 1965), 335-344.

Sherrill, Paul M. "The Quakers and the North Carolina Manumission Society," TCHS, *Papers,* X (1914), 32-51.

Sitterson, J. C. *The Secession Movement in North Carolina,* 24-249.

## 32. THE WAR FOR SOUTHERN INDEPENDENCE, 1861-1865

SUMMARY—*Comparative strength of the contestants:* population, wealth, industry, trade, railroads, and other aspects of economic life.—*Military strategy of North:* (1) blockade Southern ports; (2) cut Confederacy in two by gaining control of Mississippi Valley; (3) conquest of individual Southern states.—*Major campaigns and "decisive battles":* in East, in West; significance of the Confederate loss of Vicksburg and Gettysburg, in summer of 1863; war of attrition.—*England and the Confederacy:* landed aristocracy friendly to South; industrial labor favored North; policy of Queen Victoria and government to stay out of war; ships built for Confederacy in British shipyards.—*Lincoln's Emancipation Proclamation (1862-1863):* effects on Negroes, on North and South, on England.—*The war ends, 1865:* general situation in North and South.—*North Carolina contributions to the Confederacy:* men, money, and supplies; N.C. officers in army and navy; civil officials in State and Confederate governments; heavy casualties—40,275 deaths of approximately 125,000 men in service.—*Important military operations in North Carolina:* (1) Federal conquest of Sound region; (2) capture of Fort Fisher and Wilmington; (3) Sherman's invasion; (4) Stoneman's raid.—*Problems of the home front:* agriculture, industry, trade, and transportation; inflation; increase in taxes; relief work.—*Contributions of women to the war effort:* nature and extent of this work.—*Blockade-running:* how these operations were conducted; value of goods brought in; the "life line of the Confederacy."

BASIC READING—

Lefler, Hugh T. (ed.). *North Carolina History Told by Contemporaries,* 296-304, 308-314.

Connor, R. D. W. *North Carolina: Rebuilding an Ancient Commonwealth,* II, 232-260.

Hamilton, J. G. de R. *North Carolina Since 1860,* 7-38.

Ashe, S. A. History of North Carolina, II 620-1012.

SUGGESTED READING—

Alexander, Violet G. "The Confederate States Navy Yard at Charlotte, North Carolina, 1862-1865," *NCB,* XXIII (1926), 128-137.

Anderson, Mrs. John H. "The Confederate Arsenal at Fayetteville, North Carolina," *Confed. Vet.,* XXXVI (June, 1928), 222-228.

———. "What Sherman Did to Fayetteville," *Confed. Vet.,* XXXII (April, 1924), 138-140.

Barrett, John G. *The Civil War in North Carolina,* 3-392.

———. *General Sherman's March through the Carolinas,* 1-325.

———. "General Sherman's March through North Carolina," *NCHR,* XLII, No. 2 (April, 1965), 192-207.

———. *North Carolina as a Civil War Battleground, 1861-1865,* 1-99.

———. "Sherman and Total War in the Carolinas," *NCHR,* XXXVII, No. 3 (July, 1960), 367-381.

Barry, Richard S. "Fort Macon: Its History," *NCHR,* XXVII, No. 2 (April, 1950), 163-177.

Black, Wilfred W. (ed.). "Civil War Letters of E. N. Boots from New Bern and Plymouth," *NCHR,* XXXVI, No. 2 (April, 1959), 205-223.

Blair, Marian H. (ed.). "Civil War Letters of Henry W. Barrow Written to John W. Fries, Salem," *NCHR,* XXXIV, No. 1 (January, 1957), 68-85.

Bradlee, F. B. C. "Blockade Running during the Civil War," *Essex Inst. Hist. Soc. Coll.,* LXII (January-October, 1926), 33-64, 129-160, 321-352.

Brooks, A. L., and Hugh T. Lefler. (eds.). *The Papers of Walter Clark,* I, 49-146.

Brown, Louis A. (ed.). "The Correspondence of David Olando McRaven and Amanda Nantz McRaven, 1864-1865," *NCHR,* XXVI, No. 1 (January, 1949), 41-98.

Clark, Walter. (ed.). *Civil War Regiments.* 5 vols.

————. *North Carolina at Gettysburg, and Pickett's Charge a Misnomer,* 1-31.

————. "North Carolina Troops at Gettysburg," *NCB,* XXII (1923), 91-108.

————. "The Raising, Organization, and Equipment of North Carolina Troops during the Civil War," *N.C. Lit. and Hist. Assoc. Proc.,* XVII (1919), 104-11.

Corbitt, D. L., and Elizabeth Wilborn (eds.). *Civil War Pictures,* 1-90.

Coulter, E. M. *The Confederate States of America, 1861-1865.* (Use index for N.C. references.)

Cunningham, H. H. *Doctors in Gray.* (Use index for N.C. references.)

————. "Edmund Burke Haywood and Raleigh's Confederate Hospitals," *NCHR,* XXXV, No. 2 (April, 1958), 153-166.

————. "Organization and Administration of the Confederate Medical Department," *NCHR,* XXXI, No. 3 (July, 1954), 385-409.

Earnhart, Hugh G. (ed.). "Aboard a Blockade Runner: Some Civil War Experiences of Jerome Du Shane," *NCHR,* XLIV, No. 4 (October, 1967), 392-399.

Flowers, R. L. "Fort Hamby on the Yadkin," TCHS, *Papers,* I (1897), 1-9.

Graham, W. A. "The North Carolina Businessmen of Eighteen Hundred and Sixty-One," *NCB,* XI (July, 1911), 3-16.

Harmon, George D. (ed.). "Letters of Luther Rice Mills—A Confederate Soldier," *NCHR,* IV, No. 3 (July, 1927), 285-310.

————. "The Military Experiences of James A. Peifer, 1861-1865," *NCHR,* XXXII, Nos. 2 and 3 (July and October, 1955), 385-409, 544-572.

Hesseltine, W. B. *Civil War Prisons: A Study in War Psychology.* (Use index for Salisbury prison.)

Hill, D. H. *North Carolina in the War Between the States: Bethel to Sharpsburg,* I, 46-397; II, 1-418.

Hoffman, Ural. "Major W. A. Graham," TCHS, *Papers,* VI (1906), 22-26.

Iobst, Richard, and Louis H. Manarin. *The Bloody Sixth: The Sixth North Carolina Regiment, Confederate States of America,* 3-450.

Johnston, Frontis. "The Courtship of Zeb Vance," *NCHR,* XXXI, No. 2 (April, 1954), 222-239

———— (ed.). *The Papers of Zebulon Baird Vance, Volume One, 1843-1862,* xvii-lxxiv, 1-459.

————. "Zeb Vance: A Personality Sketch," *NCHR,* XXX, No. 2 (April, 1953), 178-190.

Lonsdale, R. E. (comp.). *Atlas of North Carolina,* 49-51.

Luvaas, Jay. "Johnston's Last Stand—Bentonville," *NCHR,* XXXIII, No. 3 (July, 1956), 332-358.

Merrill, James M. (ed.). "The Fort Fisher and Wilmington Campaign: Letters from Rear Admiral David D. Porter," *NCHR,* XXXV, No. 4 (October, 1958), 461-475.

————. "The Hatteras Expedition, August, 1861," *NCHR,* XXIX, No. 2 (April, 1952), 204-219.

Murray, Paul, and Stephen R. Bartlett (eds.). "The Letters of Stephen Chaulker Bartlett Aboard U.S.S. 'Lenapee,' January to August, 1865," *NCHR,* XXXIII, No. 1 (January, 1965), 66-92.

Nichols, Roy F. (ed.). "Fighting in North Carolina Waters," *NCHR,* XL, No. 1 (January, 1963), 75-84.

Padgett, James A. (ed.). "With Sherman through Georgia and the Carolinas: Letters of a Federal Soldier," *Ga. Hist. Quar.,* XXXIII (March, 1949), 49-81.

Rights, Douglas L. "Salem in the War between the States," *NCHR,* XXVII, No. 3 (July, 1950), 277-288.

Robinson, William M., Jr. "Admiralty in 1861: The Confederate States District Court for the Division of the Pamlico of the District of North Carolina," *NCHR,* XVII, No. 2 (April, 1940), 132-138.

Silver, James W. "The Confederate Preacher Goes to War," *NCHR*, XXXIII, No. 4 (October, 1956), 499-509.

Spencer, Cornelia P. *The Last Ninety Days of the War in North Carolina*, 1-287.

Spraggins, Tinsley L. "Mobilization of Negro Labor for the Department of Virginia and North Carolina," *NCHR*, XXIV, No. 2 (April, 1947), 160-197.

Still, William H. "The Career of the Confederate Ironclad 'Neuse,'" *NCHR*, XLIII, No. 1 (January, 1966), 1-13.

Tolbert, Noble J. (ed.). *The Papers of John W. Ellis*. 2 vols.

Tucker, Glenn. "Some Aspects of North Carolina's Participation in the Gettysburg Campaign," *NCHR*, XXXV, No. 2 (April, 1958), 191-212.

Vandiveer, Frank E. (ed.). "The Capture of a Confederate Blockade Runner: Extracts from the Journal of a Confederate Naval Officer," *NCHR*, XXI, No. 2 (April, 1944), 136-138.

Van Noppen, Ina W. "The Significance of Stoneman's Last Raid," *NCHR*, Nos. 1, 2, 3, 4 (January, April, July, October, 1961), 19-44, 149-172, 341-361, 500-526.

Wiley, Bell I. "Camp Newspapers of the Confederacy," *NCHR*, XX, No. 4 (October, 1948), 327-335.

## 33. *INTERNAL DIVISION AND WRECKAGE, 1861-1865*

SUMMARY—*Political divisions in state, 1861-1865:* Confederates and Conservatives; leaders and views of each group; Zebulon B. Vance (Conservative) elected governor in 1862; popularity of the "War Governor."—*Vance's controversy with Confederate President Jefferson Davis:* accusations against Confederacy: discrimination against state in civil and military appointments; neglect of local defense; conscription laws and policies; impressment of property by Confederate agents; Confederate taxes, especially those "in kind"; the controversy over supplying North Carolina troops; disputes over blockade-running; suppression of free speech and suspension of the writ of habeas corpus.—*The problem of desertion:* increasing "disaffection";

causes of desertion, methods used, results; Governor Vance's efforts to solve the problem.—*Holden and the "peace movement"*: Vance defeats Holden for governorship in 1864; Vance's policy to "fight the Yankees and fuss with the Confederacy." —*The devastating effects of the war*: losses of men, money, and property.—*The social revolution resulting from the war*: the problem of the "freedmen"; the Freedmen's Bureau and its work.—*Future relations with the United States.*

TEXT—Lefler-Newsome, *North Carolina*, Ch. 32.

BASIC READING—

Lefler, Hugh T. (ed.). *North Carolina History Told by Contemporaries*, 289-296, 306-331.

Connor, R. D. W. *North Carolina: Rebuilding an Ancient Commonwealth*, II, 183-192, 204-231.

Hamilton, J. G. de R. *North Carolina Since 1860*, 39-55.

SUGGESTED READING—

Anderson, Mrs. John H. *North Carolina Women of the Confederacy.* 1-141.

Bardolph, Richard. "Inconstant Rebels: Desertion of North Carolina Troops in the Civil War," *NCHR*, XLI, No. 2 (April, 1964), 163-189.

Black, Robert D. *The Railroads of the Confederacy*, 3-10, 148-154.

Boyd, W. K. "Fiscal and Economic Conditions in North Carolina during the Civil War," *NCB*, XIV (April, 1915), 195-219.

———. "Running the Blockade from Confederate Ports," TCHS, *Papers*, II (1898), 62-67.

Brown, Norman D. "A Union Election in Civil War North Carolina," *NCHR*, XLIII, No. 4 (October, 1966), 381-400.

Burkhead, L. S. "History of the Difficulties of the Pastorate of the Front Street Methodist Church, Wilmington, N.C. for the Year 1865," TCHS, *Papers*, VIII (1908-1909), 35-118.

Cathey, C. O. "The Impact of the Civil War on Agriculture in North Carolina," J. C. Sitterson (ed.). *Studies in Southern History*, 97-110.

Cunningham, H. H. "Edmund Burke Haywood and Raleigh's Confederate Hospitals," *NCHR*, XXXV, No. 2 (April, 1958), 153-166.

Daniel, W. Harrison. "Southern Presbyterians in the Confederacy," *NCHR*, XLIV, No. 3 (July, 1967), 231-255.

Delaney, Norman C. "Charles Henry Foster and the Unionists of Eastern North Carolina," *NCHR*, XXXVII, No. 3 (July, 1960), 348-366.

Douglas, Clarence D. "Conscription and the Writ of Habeas Corpus in North Carolina during the Civil War," TCHS, *Papers*, XIV (1922), 5-39.

Dowd, Clement. *Life of Zebulon B. Vance*, 62-101.

Fisher, Clyde O. "The Relief of Soldiers' Families in North Carolina during the Civil War," *Sou. Atl. Quar.*, XVI (January, 1917), 60-72.

Hamilton, J. G. de R. "The Freedmen's Bureau in North Carolina," *Sou. Atl. Quar.*, VIII, Nos. 1 and 2 (January and April, 1909), 53-67, 154-163.

————. "The North Carolina Courts and Confederacy," *NCHR*, IV, No. 4 (October, 1927), 366-403.

————. *Reconstruction in North Carolina*, 36-80.

Johnston, Frontis W. (ed.). *The Papers of Zebulon B. Vance, 1843-1862*, I, 100-459.

Klingberg, Frank W. "Operation Demonstration: A Report on Southern Unionist Planters," *NCHR*, XXV, No. 4 (October, 1948), 466-484.

————. *The Southern Claims Commission*, 157-169.

Knight, E. W. "The Influence of the Civil War on Education in North Carolina," *N.C. Lit. and Hist. Assoc. Proc.*, XVIII (1919), 52-60.

Lonn, Ella. *Desertion in the American Civil War*. (Use index for N.C. references.)

Marcum, A. W. "History of the Salisbury, N.C. Confederate Prison," *Publ. Sou. Hist. Assoc.*, III, No. 1 (January, 1899), 307-336.

Massey, Mary E. "Confederate Refugees in North Carolina," *NCHR*, XL, No. 2 (April, 1963), 158-182.

————. *Ersatz in the Confederacy.* (Use index for N.C. references.)

————. "The Food and Drink Shortage on the Confederate Homefront," *NCHR,* XXVI, No. 3 (July, 1949), 306-334.

————. "Southern Refugee Life during the Civil War," *NCHR,* Nos. 1 and 2 (January and April, 1943), 1-21, 132-156.

Mitchell, Memory F. *Legal Aspects of Conscription and Exemption in North Carolina, 1861-1865,* 1-91.

Moore, A. B. *Conscription and Conflict in the Confederacy,* 47, 79, 95-107, 202-203, 279-296, 317-320.

Moser, Harold D. "Reaction in North Carolina to the Emancipation Proclamation," *NCHR,* XLIV, No. 1 (January, 1967), 53-71.

Nelson, B. H. "Some Aspects of Negro Life in North Carolina during the Civil War," *NCHR,* XXV, No. 2 (April, 1948), 143-166.

Owsley, F. L. *State Rights in the Confederacy.* (Use index for N.C. references.)

Patton, James W. "Serious Reading in Halifax County, 1861-1865," *NCHR,* XLII, No. 2 (April, 1965), 169-179.

Quarles, Benjamin. *The Negro in the Civil War.* (Use index for N.C. references.)

Raper, Horace W. "William W. Holden and the Peace Movement in North Carolina," *NCHR,* XXXI, No. 4 (October, 1954), 493-516.

St. Clair, Kenneth E. "Judicial Machinery in North Carolina in 1865," *NCHR,* XXX, No. 3 (July, 1953), 415-539.

Sellew, Robert A. "The Peace Movement in North Carolina," *MVHR,* XI (September, 1924), 190-199.

Sharpe, John H. (ed.). "Diary of a Confederate Refugee," TCHS, *Papers,* III (1899), 8-15.

Sikes, E. W. "Social and Economic Legislation in North Carolina during the Civil War," *N.C. Lit. and Hist. Assoc. Proc.,* XVI (1916), 42-49.

Smith, Mary B. *Union Sentiment in North Carolina during the Civil War,* 1-21.

Spencer, Cornelia P. *The Last Ninety Days of the War in North Carolina*, 1-287.

Stover, John F. *The Railroads of the South, 1865-1900*. (Use index for N.C. references.)

Todd, Richard C. "The Produce Loans: A Means of Financing the Confederacy," *NCHR*, XXVII, No. 1 (January, 1950), 46-74.

Webb, Elizabeth Yates. "Cotton Manufacturing and State Regulation in North Carolina, 1861-1865," *NCHR*, IX, No. 2 (April, 1932), 117-137.

Wilson, L. R. (ed.). *Selected Papers of Cornelia Phillips Spencer*, 107-154.

Yates, Richard E. *The Confederacy and Zeb Vance*, 1-132.

————. "Governor Vance and the End of the War in North Carolina," *NCHR*, XVIII, No. 4 (October, 1941), 315-338.

————. "Governor Vance and the Peace Movement," *NCHR*, XVII, Nos. 1 and 2 (January and April, 1940), 1-25, 89-113.

————. *Zebulon B. Vance as War Governor of N.C., 1862-1865*, 1-33.

Yearns, Wilfred B. "North Carolina in the Confederate Congress," *NCHR*, XXIX, No. 3 (July, 1952), 359-378.

## 34. *RETURN TO THE UNION*

SUMMARY—*The presidential plan of reconstruction:* Lincoln's theory of "forfeited rights"; his 10 per cent plan; classes which were not to be pardoned immediately.—*President Johnson puts the 10 per cent plan into effect:* appointment of Holden as "provisional governor," 1865; the Convention of 1865 and its work; Jonathan Worth defeats Holden for governorship; Congress refuses to seat Southerners.—*The Black Code:* authorship, provisions, Northern reaction.—*The Fourteenth Amendment (1868):* provisions, state reaction.—*The Congressional plan of reconstruction (1867-1877):* South divided into five military districts; military rule; role of carpetbaggers and scalawags.—*Organization of the Republican party in North*

*Carolina:* Holden and other leaders; membership.—*The 1868 Convention and the new State Constitution:* personnel of convention, provisions of Constitution; appraisal; state reaction; the 1868 election.

TEXT—Lefler-Newsome, *North Carolina,* Ch. 33.

BASIC READING

Lefler, Hugh T. (ed.). *North Carolina History Told by Contemporaries,* 306-324, 331-340.

Connor, R. D. W. *North Carolina: Rebuilding an Ancient Commonwealth,* II, 261-274, 280-305.

Hamilton, J. G. de R. *North Carolina Since 1860,* 56-113.

SUGGESTED READING—

Bell, John L., Jr. "Baptists and the Negro in North Carolina during Reconstruction," *NCHR,* XLII, No. 4 (October, 1965), 391-401.

———. "The Presbyterian Church and the Negro in North Carolina during Reconstruction," *NCHR,* XL, No. 1 (January, 1963), 15-36.

Brooks, A. L., and Hugh T. Lefler (eds.). *The Papers of Walter Clark,* I, 145-193.

Chaffin, Nora C. "A Southern Advocate of Methodist Unification in 1865," *NCHR,* XVIII, No. 1 (January, 1941), 38-47.

Coulter, E. M. *The South during Reconstruction, 1865-1877.* (Use index for N.C. references.)

Evans, William McKee. *Ballots and Fence Rails: Reconstruction on the Lower Cape Fear,* 4-102.

Ewing, Cortez A. M. "Two Reconstruction Impeachments," *NCHR,* XV, No. 3 (July, 1938), 204-230.

Hamilton, J. G. de R. "The Elections of 1872 in North Carolina," *Sou. Atl. Quar.,* XI, No. 2 (April, 1912), 143-152.

———. "The North Carolina Convention of 1865-1866," *N.C. Lit. and Hist. Assoc. Proc.,* XIV (1914), 56-68.

——— (ed.). *The Papers of Randolph Shotwell,* 3 vols.

———. "The Prison Experiences of Randolph Shotwell," *NCHR,* II, Nos. 2, 3, 4 (April, July, October, 1925), 147-161, 332-350, 459-474.

Heckman, O. S. "The Presbyterian Church in the United States of America in Southern Reconstruction, 1860-1880," *NCHR*, XX, No. 3 (July, 1943), 219-237.

Heyman, Max L. " 'The Great Reconstructor'; General E. R. S. Canby and the Second Military District," *NCHR*, XXXI, No. 1 (January, 1955), 52-80.

McPherson, Elizabeth G. (ed.). "Letters from North Carolina to Andrew Johnson," *NCHR*, XXVII, Nos. 3 and 4 (July, and October, 1950), 336-363, 462-490; XXVIII, Nos. 1, 2, 3, 4 (January, April, July, October, 1951), 63-87, 219-237, 362-375, 486-516; XXIX, Nos. 1, 2, 3, 4 (January, April, July, October, 1952), 104-119, 259-268, 400-431, 569-578.

Morrill, John R., Jr. "North Carolina and the Administration of Brevet Major General Sickles," *NCHR*, XLII, No. 3 (July, 1965), 291-305.

Padgett, James A. (ed.). "Reconstruction Letters from North Carolina: Letters to Benjamin Franklin Butler," *NCHR*, XIX, No. 4 (October, 1942), 380-403; XX, Nos. 1, 2, 3, 4 (January, April, July, October, 1943), 54-82, 157-180, 259-282, 341-370; XXI, No. 1 (January, 1944), 46-71.

——— (ed.). "Reconstruction Letters from North Carolina: Letters to Carl Schurz," *NCHR*, XIX, No. 3 (July, 1942), 280-302.

——— (ed.). "Reconstruction Letters from North Carolina: Letters to Edward McPherson," *NCHR*, XIX, No. 2 (April, 1942), 187-208.

——— (ed.). "Reconstruction Letters from North Carolina: Letters to Elihu Benjamin Washburne," *NCHR*, XVIII, No. 4 (October, 1941), 373-397.

——— (ed.). "Reconstruction Letters from North Carolina: Letters of James Abram Garfield," *NCHR*, XXI, No. 2 (April, 1941), 139-157.

——— (ed.). "Reconstruction Letters from North Carolina: Letters to John Sherman," *NCHR*, XVIII, Nos. 3 and 4 (July and October, 1941), 278-300, 373-397.

——— (ed.). "Reconstruction Letters from North Carolina: Letters to Salmon Portland Chase," *NCHR*, XXI, No. 3 (July, 1944), 232-247.

——— (ed.). "Reconstruction Letters from North Carolina: Letters to Thaddeus Stephens," *NCHR*, XVIII, No. 3 (April, 1941), 171-195.

——— (ed.). "Reconstruction Letters from North Carolina: Letters to William E. Chandler," *NCHR*, XIX, No. 1 (January, 1942), 59-94.

——— (ed.). "Reconstruction Letters from North Carolina: Letters to William Tecumsch Sherman," *NCHR*, XVIII, No. 4 (October, 1941), 373-397.

Ruark, Bryant W. "Some Phases of Reconstruction in Wilmington and New Hanover County," TCHS, *Papers*, XI (1915), 79-112.

Russ, William A., Jr. "Radical Disfranchisement in North Carolina, 1867-1868," *NCHR*, XI, No. 4 (October, 1934), 271-283.

St. Clair, Kenneth E. "Debtor Relief in North Carolina during Reconstruction," *NCHR*, XVIII, No. 3 (July, 1941), 215-235.

## 35. RECONSTRUCTION POLITICS, 1868-1877

SUMMARY—*Conditions in North Carolina, 1868:* problems confronting Governor Holden and the legislature; steps taken for readmission to the Union.—*The presidential campaign of 1868:* Republican Grant carries state.—*Republican extravagance and corruption:* railroad bond scandals; activities of Littlefield and Swepson; other instances of waste and corruption.—*The problem of preserving law and order:* the Ku Klux Klan and its activities; other secret societies; the Union League (Northern) and its work; the Shoffner Act (1868).—*The Kirk-Holden War:* causes, leaders, results.—*The impeachment and conviction of Governor Holden:* impeachment charges, the trial; results and aftermath.—*More federal interference:* the "Force Acts" of Congress; state reaction.—*Changes in State Constitution:* by legislation (1873) and by amendment (1875); restoration of "white supremacy" and "home rule."—*The gubernatorial election of 1876:* Zebulon B. Vance defeats Republican Thomas Settle.—*The end of political reconstruction (1877):* President Hayes withdraws Federal troops from South; state government in complete control of Democrats.—*Effects of Reconstruction on state and its people:* appraisal of the period.

TEXT—Lefler-Newsome, *North Carolina,* Ch. 34.

BASIC READING—

Lefler, Hugh T. (ed.). *North Carolina History Told by Contemporaries,* 341-345, 350-355.

Connor, R. D. W. *North Carolina: Rebuilding an Ancient Commonwealth,* II, 305-352.

Hamilton, J. G. de R. *North Carolina Since 1860,* 114-160, 170-191.

SUGGESTED READING—

Atchison, R. M. *"The Land We Love:* A Southern Post-Bellum Magazine of Agriculture, Literature, and Military History," *NCHR,* XXXVII, No. 4 (October, 1960), 506-515.

Bernstein, Leonard. "The Participation of Negro Delegates in the Constitutional Convention of 1868," *Jour. Negro Hist.,* XXXIV, No. 4 (October, 1949), 391-409.

Boyd, W. K. (ed.). *Memoirs of W. W. Holden,* 31-130.

———. "William W. Holden," TCHS, *Papers,* III (1899), 39-78, 90-130.

Carlton, Luther M. "The Assassination of John Walter Stephens," TCHS, *Papers,* II (1898), 1-11.

Dailey, Douglass C. "The Elections of 1872 in North Carolina," *NCHR,* XL, No. 3 (July, 1963), 338-360.

Daniels, Jonathan. *Prince of Carpetbaggers,* [Milton Littlefield], 1-319.

Davis, Jedith Ross. "Reconstruction in Cleveland County," TCHS, *Papers,* X (1914), 5-36.

Dent, Sanders. "The Origin and Development of the Ku Klux Klan," TCHS, *Papers,* I (1897), 10-27.

Evans, William McKee. *Ballots and Fence Rails: Reconstruction on the Lower Cape Fear,* 103-175.

Ewing, Cortez A. M. "Two Reconstruction Impeachments," *NCHR*, XV, No. 3 (July, 1938), 204-230.

Farris, James Joseph. "The Lowrie Gang—An Episode in the History of Robeson County," TCHS, *Papers*, XV (1925), 55-93.

Hamilton, J. G. de R. *Reconstruction in North Carolina*, 343-667.

Olsen, Otto H. "Albion W. Tourgée: Carpetbagger," *NCHR*, XL, No. 4 (October, 1963), 434-454.

————. *Carpetbagger's Crusade: The Life of Albion Winegar Tourgée*, 1-395.

————. "The Ku Klux Klan: A Study in Reconstruction Politics and Propaganda," *NCHR*, XXXIX, No. 3 (July, 1962), 340-362.

Randolph, Bessie C. "Foreign Bondholders and the Repudiated Debts of the Southern States," *Am. Jour. Int. Law*, XXV (1931), 63-82.

Ruark, Bryant W. "Some Phases of Reconstruction in Wilmington and the County of New Hanover," TCHS, *Papers*, XI (1915), 79-112.

Smith, Samuel D. *The Negro in Congress*, 1870-1901. (Use index for N.C. references.)

Tourgée, A. W. *A Fool's Errand*, 1-521. Reconstruction novel.

Whitener, D. J. "Public Education in North Carolina during Reconstruction, 1865-1876," in *Essays in Southern History Presented to J. G. de R. Hamilton*, 67-91.

## 36. THE INDUSTRIAL REVOLUTION IN NORTH CAROLINA, 1870-1900

SUMMARY—*Development of factory industry in state:* factors which favored its development; retarding forces and factors. —*Postwar economic optimism:* arguments for a diversified economy.—*The beginnings of industrial recovery:* tobacco, textiles, and other industries; individuals and localities which took the lead.—*Rapid industrialization after 1800:* the gospel of the "New South"; the "industrial balance sheet"—capital, value of products, numbers of workers, wages.—Cotton textiles: significant developments, leaders, and problems.—*Phenomenal development of the tobacco industry:* the Dukes, Reynolds, and other leaders; "Buck" Duke and the "Tobacco Trust" (despite Sherman Anti-Trust Act of 1890).—*The furniture industry:* leaders, localities, types of furniture made.—*The growth of towns:* largest cities, rural and urban population ratios; state still largely rural.—*The social and cultural lag:* backwardness in education and general cultural progress; reasons for this situation.—*Capital and labor:* beginnings of labor organizations in state—Knights of Labor in the 1880's and American Federation of Labor in late nineties; little labor legislation; State Bureau of Labor Statistics (1887) and its ineffectiveness.—*Railroad transportation:* abandonment of policy of state aid to railroads; North Carolina Railroad and others leased to private companies; railroad consolidation and emergence of three major systems—Southern, Atlantic Coast Line, and Seaboard.—*Slow development of highways:* the "labor tax" system and its inadequacy.—*Improvements in communication:* telephones; rural free delivery mail service; increased circulation of newspapers and magazines.

TEXT—Lefler-Newsome, *North Carolina,* Ch. 35.

BASIC READING—

Lefler, Hugh T. (ed.). *North Carolina History Told by Contemporaries,* 357-366, 391-393.

Connor, R. D. W. *North Carolina: Rebuilding an Ancient Commonwealth,* II, 353-375, 420-453.

Hamilton, J. G. de R. *North Carolina Since 1860,* 384-403.

SUGGESTED READING—

Bassett, J. S. "Old Durham Traditions," TCHS, *Papers,* VI (1906), 27-36.

Boyd, W. K. *The Story of Durham, City of the New South,* 1-96.

Bradsher, A. B. "The Manufacture of Tobacco in North Carolina," TCHS, *Papers,* VI (1906), 12-31.

Brown, C. K. "A History of the Piedmont Railroad Company," NCHR, III, No. 2 (April, 1926), 198-222.

Collins, Herbert. "The Idea of a Cotton Textile Industry in the South, 1870-1900," *NCHR*, XXXIV, No. 3 (July, 1957), 358-392.

Davidson, Elizabeth H. "The Child-Labor Problem in North Carolina, 1883-1903," *NCHR*, XIII, No. 3 ( April, 1936), 105-121.

————. "Early Development of Public Opinion Against Southern Child Labor," *NCHR*, XIV, No. 3 (July, 1937), 230-250.

Douty, H. M. "Early Labor Organizations in North Carolina, 1880-1900," *Sou. Atl. Quar.*, XXXIV, No. 3 (July, 1935), 260-268.

Evans, William McKee, *Ballots and Fence Rails: Reconstruction on the Lower Cape Fear*, 176-210.

Few, William P. "Washington Duke," *Sou. Atl. Quar.*, IV, No. 3 (July, 1905), 203-208.

Fries, Adelaide L. "One Hundred Years of Textiles in Salem," *NCHR*, XXVII, No. 1 (January, 1950), 1-19.

————. *The Townbuilders*, 1-19.

Griffin, Richard W. "Reconstruction of the North Carolina Textile Industry, 1865-1885," *NCHR*, XLI, No. 1 (January, 1964), 34-53.

Jenkins, J. W. *James B. Duke, Master Builder*, 1-98.

Jolley, Harley E. "The Labor Movement in North Carolina, 1880-1922," *NCHR*, XXX, No. 3 (July, 1953), 354-375.

Kilgo, John C. "William H. Branson," TCHS, *Papers*, IV (1900), 21-30.

Lemmon, Sarah M. "Entertainment in Raleigh in 1890," *NCHR*, XL, No. 3 (July, 1963), 321-337.

————. "Raleigh—An Example of the 'New South,' " *NCHR*, XLIII, No. 3 (July, 1966), 261-285.

Logan, Frenise A. "The Colored Industrial Association of North Carolina and Its Fair of 1886," *NCHR*, XXXIV, No. 1 (January, 1957), 58-67.

————. "The Economic Status of the Town Negro in Post-Reconstruction North Carolina," *NCHR*, XXXV, No. 4 (October, 1958), 448-460.

————. *The Negro in North Carolina, 1876-1894*, 3-219.

McGuire, P. S. "The Seaboard Air Line," *NCHR*, XI, No. 2 (April, 1934), 94-115.

Mitchell, Broadus. *The Rise of Cotton Mills in the South.* (Use index for N.C. references.)

Sitterson, J. C. "Business Leaders in Post-Civil War North Carolina, 1865-1900," J. C. Sitterson (ed.). *Studies in Southern History*, 111-121.

Thomas, David N. "Getting Started at High Point," *Forest History*, II (July, 1967), 23-32.

Thompson, Holland. *From the Cotton Field to the Cotton Mill: A Study of the Industrial Transition in North Carolina*, 1-250.

———. "Some Effects of Industrialization in an Agricultural State," *Sou. Atl. Quar.*, IV, No. 1 (January, 1905), 71-77.

Winston, George T. *Builder of the New South, Being the Story of the Life and Work of Daniel Augustus Tompkins*, 3-403.

## 37. AGRICULTURAL PROBLEMS AND DEPRESSION, 1865–1900

SUMMARY—*The rapid postwar recovery of agriculture:* crop statistics.—*The rise and spread of farm tenancy:* reasons for evolution of the sharecropper system; tenancy not a racial matter; sharecroppers and cash tenants; areas and counties with largest percentage of tenants; advantages and disadvantages of tenancy.—*Problems of farmers in state and nation:* fall in price of farm crops; high cost of fertilizers, farm equipment, and other manufactured goods; declining farm income; high taxes; exorbitant credit costs—interest rates and "time prices," and a national monetary and currency situation unfavorable to the farmer.—*Criticism of the "Money Power":* protective tariffs, corporations and monopolistic trusts, merchants, and middlemen, railroads, banks.—*Demands for railroad regulation:* complaints against high and discriminatory rates, poor service, rebates, pools, and other unfair practices.— *The farmers begin to organize:* The State Grange incorporated, 1875; local granges and total membership; the Farmers Alliance in the state after 1887; demands of the "embattled farmers"; achievements.

TEXT—Lefler-Newsome, *North Carolina,* Ch. 36.

BASIC READING—

Lefler, Hugh T. (ed.). *North Carolina History Told by Contemporaries,* 356-357, 372-379.

Connor, R. D. W. *North Carolina: Rebuilding an Ancient Commonwealth,* II, 356-358, 420-428.

Hamilton, J. C. de R. *North Carolina Since 1860,* 376-384.

SUGGESTED READING—

Applewhite, Majorie M. "Sharecropper and Tenant in the Courts of North Carolina," *NCHR,* XXXI, No. 2 (April, 1954), 134-149.

Buck, S. J. *The Agrarian Crusade.* (Use index for N.C. references.)

———. *The Granger Movement.* (Use index for N.C. references.)

Carson, W. W. "Agricultural Reconstruction in North Carolina after the Civil War," *AHA Annual Rept.* (1921), 217-225.

Hicks, John D. "The Farmers' Alliance in North Carolina," *NCHR,* II, No. 2 (April, 1925), 162-187.

———. *The Populist Revolt,* 36-95.

Lockmiller, David A. "The Establishment of the North Carolina College of Agriculture and Mechanic Arts," *NCHR,* XVI, No. 3 (July, 1939), 273-295.

———. *History of the State College of Agriculture and Engineering of the University of North Carolina,* 1-310.

Noblin, Stuart. *Leonidas Lafayette Polk, Agrarian Crusader,* 73-108.

———. "Leonidas Lafayette Polk and the North Carolina Department of Agriculture," *NCHR,* XX, Nos. 2 and 3 (April and July, 1943), 103-121, 197-218.

Poe, Clarence. "L. L. Polk: A Great Agrarian Leader in a Fifty-Year Perspective," *Sou. Atl. Quar.,* XLI, No. 4 (October, 1942), 405-415.

Taylor, Joseph H. "The Great Migration from North Carolina in 1879," *NCHR*, XXXI, No. 1 (January, 1954), 18-33.

Taylor, Rosser H. "Fertilizers and Farming in the Southeast, 1840-1950," *NCHR*, Nos. 3 and 4 (July and October, 1953), 305-328, 483-523.

## 38.  SLOW RECOVERY OF EDUCATION AFTER THE CIVIL WAR

SUMMARY—*Effects of the war on education:* public schools, academies, higher education.—*Education during Reconstruction:* Trinity, Wake Forest, and Davidson reopened soon after war; University closed, 1870-1875; collapse of state system of common schools, 1865-1868; the Republican party and education; educational provisions of the 1868 Constitution; the progressive school law of 1869 and reasons for its nonenforcement; the problems of higher education—small student bodies, inadequate funds, and other difficulties.—*The movement for a College of Agriculture and Mechanic Arts:* the Land Grant College (Morrill) Act of 1862; the University's attitude toward agricultural and technical education; the movement for a separate agricultural and mechanical college; the A. & M. College chartered, 1887, and opened to students two years later.—*Other colleges established:* Fayetteville Colored Normal (1877), the State Normal and Industrial School at Greensboro (1891), the North Carolina Agricultural and Mechanical College for the Colored Race at Greensboro (1891), and the Elizabeth City Colored Normal (1891-1892).—*Trinity College moved to Durham* (1892): reasons for transfer; role of Carr, Duke, and others—*The plight of the public schools:* inadequate funds, scarcity of teachers, and other problems; beginning of a teacher-training program; school statistics reveal backwardness of state.—*Reasons for state's low rank in education:* general apathy and indifference; aversion to taxation; unprogressive political leadership; legislative indifference; state supreme court decisions adverse to public schools.—*Freedmen's Bureau schools:* operated for a few years only.—

*The Peabody Fund assists schools of a few towns:* nature, extent, and effects of this aid.—*Increasing sentiment for public schools:* progress of other states; influence of farm organizations and leaders; activities of Walter Hines Page, Charles D. McIver, Edwin A. Alderman, and other champions of schools.

TEXT—Lefler-Newsome, *North Carolina,* Ch. 37.

BASIC READING—

Lefler, Hugh T. (ed.). *North Carolina History Told by Contemporaries,* 304-306, 345-391.

Connor, R. D. W. *North Carolina: Rebuilding an Ancient Commonwealth,* II, 376-398, 414-420.

Hamilton, J. G. de R. *North Carolina Since 1860,* 347-375.

SUGGESTED READING—

Atchison, Ray M. *"Our Living and Our Dead:* A Post-Bellum North Carolina Magazine of Literature and History," *NCHR,* XL, No. 4 (October, 1963) , 423-433.

Battle, K. P. *History of the University of North Carolina,* II, 1-589.

Bowles, Elisabeth Ann. *A Good Beginning: The First Four Decades of the University of North Carolina at Greensboro,* 3-28.

Chaffin, Nora C. *Trinity College, 1839-1892: The Beginnings of Duke University,* 217-542.

Connor, R. D. W. "The Peabody Educational Fund," *Sou. Atl. Quar.,* IV, No. 2 (April, 1905), 169-181.

Coon, Charles L. "The Beginnings of the North Carolina City Schools, 1867-1881," *Sou. Atl. Quar.,* XII, No. 3 (July, 1913) , 235-247.

Ferguson, Robert L. "Colonel William J. Hicks," TCHS, *Papers,* VII (1907), 48-54. (Hicks built the State Penitentiary.)

Garber, Paul N. *John Carlisle Kilgo, President of Trinity College,* 1-412.

Gatewood, Willard B., Jr. "North Carolina and Federal Aid to Education: Public Reaction to the Blair Bill, 1881-1890," *NCHR,* XL, No. 4 (October, 1963) , 465-488.

Gilbert, Dorothy. *Guilford, A Quaker College,* 84-287.

Henderson, Archibald. *The Campus of the First State University,* 181-215.

Holder, Rose Howell. *McIver of North Carolina,* 1-283.

Huggins, M. A. *A History of North Carolina Baptists, 1727-1932,* 191-298.

Knight, E. W. "The Peabody Fund and Its Early Operation in North Carolina," *Sou. Atl. Quar.,* XIV, No. 2 (April, 1915), 168-180.

————. *Public School Education in North Carolina,* 238-327.

Lockmiller, David A. *History of the North Carolina State College of Agriculture and Engineering, 1889-1939,* 19-68.

Logan, Frenise A. "The Movement in North Carolina to Establish a State-Supported College for Negroes," *NCHR,* XXXV, No. 2 (April, 1958), 167-180.

Mayo, A. D. "The Final Establishment of the American Common School System in North Carolina, South Carolina, and Georgia, 1863-1900," *U.S. Bur. Educ. Rept.* (1904), 909-1090.

Morton, Richard L. (ed.). "A 'Yankee Teacher' in North Carolina, by Margaret Newbold Thorpe," *NCHR,* XXX, No. 4 (October, 1953), 564-582.

Noble, M. C. S. *A History of the Public Schools of North Carolina,* 233-439.

Paschal, George W. "The Educational Convention of February, 1873, and the Common Schools," *NCHR,* XXVI, No. 2 (April, 1949), 208-215.

————. *A History of Wake Forest College,* Vol. II (1865-1905), 3-308.

Rondthaler, Howard E. "New Plans against an Old Background, Salem College, 1866-1884," *NCHR,* XXVII, No. 4 (October, 1950), 430-436.

Sellers, Charles G., Jr. "Walter Hines Page and the Spirit of the New South," *NCHR,* XXIX, No. 4 (October, 1952), 481-499.

Whitener, Daniel J. "The Republican Party and Public Education in North Carolina, 1867-1900," *NCHR,* XXXVIII, No. 3 (July, 1960), 382-396.

Wilson, L. R. (ed.). *Selected Papers of Cornelia Phillips Spencer*, 612-728.

## 39. CONSERVATIVE DEMOCRACY AND POLITICAL REVOLUTION, 1872–1894

SUMMARY—*Emergence of "Solid South" and "Bourbon Democracy":* explanation of these terms; impairment of local self-government; local government under control of Democratic legislatures; most of state debt repudiated; conflicting opinions about this and other policies of state government.— *Conservatives control Democratic party:* alliance between business and politics; champion of *laissez faire;* opposition to social legislation and expansion of system of public education.— *Unwholesome political practices:* partisan legislation; manipulation of elections; emphasis on "white supremacy"; gerrymandering of state senatorial and national congressional districts.—*Republican opposition:* composition of party; lack of aggressive leaders and party newspapers; failure to champion constructive program for the state; many of leaders apparently chiefly interested in federal jobs.—*"Liberal Democrats":* the Anti-Prohibition party (1882); statewide prohibition defeated by overwhelming vote.—*Intra-party divisions:* "Liberals" and "Conservatives"—leaders and issues.—*The Agrarian Revolt:* the Grangers—their demands and achievements, the Farmers' Alliance—leaders, demands, accomplishments; the "farmers' legislature" of 1891 and its constructive work.—*Formation of the Populist or People's Party:* Colonel L. L. Polk, Marion Butler, and other leaders; Populist platform of 1892 and defeat; Democratic denunciation of Populists.—*Fusion of Republicans and Populists defeats Democrats:* legislative victory of 1894.

TEXT—Lefler-Newsome, *North Carolina*, Ch. 38.

BASIC READING—

Lefler, Hugh T. (ed.). *North Carolina History Told by Contemporaries*, 372-382.

Connor, R. D. W. *North Carolina: Rebuilding an Ancient Commonwealth,* II, 399-414.

Hamilton, J. G. de R. *North Carolina Since 1860,* 192-246.

SUGGESTED READING—

Connor, H. G. "Thomas Jordan Jarvis and the Rebuilding of North Carolina," *NCB,* XV (April, 1916), 81-97.

Dailey, Douglas C. "The Election of 1872 in North Carolina," *NCHR,* XL, No. 2 (1963), 338-360.

Daniels, Josephus. *Tar Heel Editor,* 247-510.

De Santis, Vincent P. "President Garfield and the Solid South," *NCHR,* XXXVI, No. 4 (October, 1959), 442-465.

Flowers, R. L. "Matthew Whitaker Ransom: A Senator of the Old Regime," *Sou Atl. Quar.,* IV, No. 2 (April, 1905), 159-168.

Hendrick, B. J. (ed.). *The Earlier Life and Letters of Walter Hines Page,* I, 1-444.

Hicks, John D. "The Farmers' Alliance in North Carolina," *NCHR,* II, No. 2 (April, 1925), 162-187.

————, and John D. Barnhart. "The Farmers' Alliance," *NCHR,* VI, No. 3 (July, 1929), 254-280.

————. *The Populist Revolt.* (Use index for N.C. references.)

Logan, Frenise A. "The Movement of Negroes from North Carolina, 1876-1894," *NCHR,* XXXIII, No. 1 (January, 1956), 45-65.

Noblin, Stuart. *Leonidas Lafayette Polk, Agrarian Crusader,* 73-298.

Ratchford, B. U. "The Adjustment of the North Carolina Public Debt, 1879-1883," *NCHR,* X, No. 3 (July, 1933), 157-167.

————. "The Conversion of the North Carolina Public Debt after 1879," *NCHR,* X, No. 4 (October, 1933), 251-272.

————. "The North Carolina Public Debt, 1870-1878," *NCHR,* X, No. 1 (January, 1933), 1-20.

Steelman, Joseph F. "Vicissitudes of Republican Party Politics: The Campaign of 1892 in North Carolina," *NCHR,* XLIII, No. 4 (October, 1966), 430-442.

Whitener, D. J. "North Carolina Prohibition Election of 1881 and Its Aftermath," *NCHR,* XI, No. 1 (January, 1934), 71-93.

————. *Prohibition in North Carolina, 1715-1945,* 34-132.

Woodward, C. Vann. *Origins of the New South, 1877-1913.* (Use index for N.C. references.)

Zimmerman, Jane. "The Formative Years of the North Carolina State Board of Health, 1877-1893," *NCHR,* XXI, No. 1 (January, 1944), 1-34.

## 40. FUSION RULE AND THE RETURN OF A CHASTENED DEMOCRACY TO POWER

SUMMARY—*Record of the Fusion legislature of 1895:* local self-government largely restored to counties; new election law; greater appropriations for education; other reforms.—*Increased Negro political activity:* some Negro officeholders—local, state, and federal.—*The election of 1896:* state elects Republican Daniel Russell governor, but votes for Democrat W. J. Bryan for president.—*Governor Russell's administration, 1897-1901:* progressive program of public education; powers of railroad commission increased; lack of harmony among Fusionists.—*The Spanish American War, 1898:* North Carolina's contribution.—*Party conventions and platforms, 1898:* promises made by Democrats, Populists, and Republicans.—*The White Supremacy Campaign of 1898:* Democratic leadership of F. M. Simmons and others; nature of the campaign; editorial in Negro paper and white reaction; activities of the Red Shirts; Governor Russell's appeal for law and order; Simmons' final appeal to the voters; "White Supremacy" as a factor in the election; the role of business interests in the campaign; aftermath of the election—the Wilmington "race riot."—*The Democratic legislature of 1899:* laws enacted and suffrage amendment passed.—*The suffrage amendment and the "grandfather clause":* provisions and possible effects. —*The 1900 election:* candidates and platforms; Red Shirt activity again; Democrats win a decisive victory; Charles B.

Aycock elected governor; suffrage amendment adopted; the political revolution of 1900.

TEXT—Lefler-Newsome, *North Carolina,* Ch. 39.

BASIC READING—

Lefler, Hugh T. (ed.). *North Carolina History Told by Contemporaries,* 396-402.

Connor, R. D. W. *North Carolina: Rebuilding an Ancient Commonwealth,* II, 445-498.

Hamilton, J. G. de R. *North Carolina Since 1860,* 244-315.

SUGGESTED READING—

Connor, R. D. W., and Clarence Poe (eds.). *The Life and Speeches of Charles Brantley Aycock,* 1-89.

Daniels, Josephus. *Editor in Politics,* 85-157, 202-264, 381-439.

Delap, Simeon A. "The Populist Party in North Carolina," TCHS, *Papers,* XIV (1922) , 40-74.

Durden, Robert F. "The Battle of the Standards in 1896 and North Carolina's Place in the Mainstream," *Sou. Atl. Quar.,* LXIII, No. 3 (July, 1964) , 336-350.

———. "Governor Daniel L. Russell Explains His 'South Dakota Bond' Scheme," *NCHR,* XXXVIII, No. 4 (October, 1961) , 527-533.

———. *Reconstruction Bonds & Twentieth Century Politics: South Dakota v. North Carolina,* 3-62.

Edmonds, Helen G. *The Negro and Fusion Politics in North Carolina, 1895-1901,* 8-214.

Gibson, George H. "Attitudes of North Carolina Regarding the Independence of Cuba," *NCHR,* XLIII, No. 1 (January, 1966), 43-65.

Harlan, Louis. *Separate But Unequal.* (Use index for N.C. references.)

Hayden, Harry. *The Story of the Wilmington Rebellion,* 1-32.

Johnson, Guion G. "The Ideology of White Supremacy, 1876-1910," *Essays in Southern History Presented to J. G. de R. Hamilton,* 124-156.

Mabry, William A. "The Negro in North Carolina Politics

Since Reconstruction," TCHS, *Papers*, XXIII (1940), 3-87.

———. "Negro Suffrage and Fusion Rule in North Carolina," *NCHR*, XII, No. 2 (April, 1935), 79-102.

———. " 'White Supremacy' and the North Carolina Suffrage Amendment," *NCHR*, XIII, No. 1 (January, 1936), 1-24.

Tompkins, D. A. "The Real Grievances against the Railroads," *Sou. Atl. Quar.*, VI, No. 4 (October, 1907), 317-322.

Woodward, C. Vann. *Origins of the New South, 1877-1913*, 260-261, 276-284, 331-355, 380-382.

———. *The Strange Career of Jim Crow.* (Use index for N.C. references.)

## 41. *A NEW ERA IN NORTH CAROLINA POLITICS, 1901–1920*

SUMMARY—*Democratic monopoly of public offices after 1900:* governors, legislators, delegations in Congress; size of Democratic majorities.—*Republicans in control of national government, 1901-1913:* problems of patronage in North Carolina; friction between state and federal governments.—*Divisions within the Democratic party:* "Conservatives" and "Liberals"; policies of the two factions; leaders of the two wings of the party; significant struggles for control.—*Divisions within the Republican party:* "Lily White" Republicans; party control by federal officeholders; failure to become a strong opposition party—*Democratic partisanship:* impeachment of two Republican judges.—*The off-year election of 1902:* Democrats make a clean sweep; the contest for Chief Justiceship of Supreme Court; Walter Clark wins after a bitter fight.—*The South Dakota Bond Case (1904):* facts in case; decision of United States Supreme Court and reaction of Governor Aycock and the state.—*The "attempted larceny" of the Atlantic and North Carolina Railroad:* facts in case; reaction of Governor Aycock and Josephus Daniels to federal court's action; final lease of the railroad.—*The 1904 election:* election of Robert B. Glenn as governor.—*The "Progressively Conservative" Administration of Glenn (1901-1905):* significant legislation; the passenger rate controversy: President Theodore Roosevelt helps arrange a compromise; state-wide prohibition adopted, 1908; other legislation relating to sale of liquor.— *The 1908 election:* divisions within Democratic party; W. W. Kitchin elected governor.—*The 1912 election:* gubernatorial and senatorial contests; Woodrow Wilson elected President.— *North Carolinians in the Wilson Administration (1913-1921):* Josephus Daniels, Secretary of the Navy; role of North Carolinians in Congress.—*The Quiet Election of 1916:* Thomas W. Bickett elected governor.—*North Carolina's role in World War I, 1917-1918:* military contributions, civilian contributions; political leaders in state and national governments; effects of the war on North Carolina.—*Changes in the state's tax structure:* the "Bickett Revaluation" of 1920; adoption of income taxes; state ceases to levy general property tax.— *Woman Suffrage:* North Carolina opposition; adoption of Nineteenth Amendment (1920) makes woman suffrage effective.

TEXT—Lefler-Newsome, *North Carolina,* Ch. 40.

BASIC READING—

Lefler, Hugh T. (ed.). *North Carolina History Told by Contemporaries,* 407-414.

Connor, R. D. W. *North Carolina: Rebuilding an Ancient Commonwealth,* II, 490-541.

SUGGESTED READING—

Alderman, Edwin A. "Charles Brantley Aycock—An Appreciation," *NCHR,* I, No. 3 (July, 1924), 243-250.

Arnett, A. M. *Claude Kitchin and the Wilson War Policies,* 47-300.

———. Claude Kitchin versus the Patrioteers," *NCHR,* XIV, No. 1 (January, 1937), 20-30.

Brooks, A. L. *Walter Clark: Fighting Judge,* 129-192.

———, and Hugh T. Lefler (eds.). *The Papers of Walter Clark.* 2 vols.

Clark, Walter, "North Carolina in the World War," *Proc. of N.C. Bar Assoc.* (1923), 57-72.

Daniels, Josephus. "Charles Brantley Aycock—Historical Address," *NCHR,* I, No. 3 (July, 1924), 251-276.

————. *Editor in Politics,* 313-626.

————. *Tar Heel Editor,* 1-544.

————. *The Wilson Era.* 2 vols.

Durden, Robert F. *Reconstruction Bonds & Twentieth Century Politics,* 63-260.

Grantham, Dewey W., Jr. "The Southern Senators and the League of Nations, 1918-1920," *NCHR,* XXVI, No. 2 (April, 1949), 187-205.

Heard, Alexander. *A Two Party South?* (Use index for N.C. references.)

Herring, Harriet L. "Cycles of Cotton Mill Criticism," *Sou. Atl. Quar.,* XXVII, No. 2 (April, 1930), 113-125.

House, Robert B. "Preserving North Carolina's World War Records As a State Enterprise," *Sou. Atl. Quar.,* XIX, No. 2 (April, 1920), 109-117.

Lefler, Hugh T. (ed.). "Selected William E. Dodd—Walter Clark Letters," *NCHR,* XXV, No. 1 (January, 1948), 91-100.

Lonsdale, Richard E. (comp.). *Atlas of North Carolina,* 52-53.

McCain, William D. "The Papers of the Food Administration for North Carolina, 1917-1919, in the National Archives," *NCHR,* XV, No. 1 (January, 1938), 34-40.

Nash, Francis. "Revaluation and Taxation in North Carolina," *Sou. Atl. Quar.,* XIX, No. 4 (October, 1920), 289-301.

Newton, I. G. "Expansion of Negro Suffrage in North Carolina [1900-1927]," *Jour. Negro Hist.,* XXVI (Spring, 1957), 351-358.

Orr, Oliver H., Jr. *Charles Brantley Aycock,* 3-363.

Raper, Charles L. "North Carolina's Taxation Problem and Its Solution," *Sou. Atl. Quar.,* XIV, No. 1 (January, 1915), 1-14.

Roller, David C. "Republican Factionalism, 1904-1906," *NCHR,* XLI, No. 1 (January, 1964), 62-73.

Steelman, Joseph F. "Republicanism in North Carolina: John Motley Morehead's Campaign to Revive a Moribund Party, 1908-1910," *NCHR,* XLII, No. 2 (April, 1965), 113-168.

————. "Richmond Pearson, Roosevelt Republicans, and the Campaign of 1912 in North Carolina," *NCHR,* XLIII, No. 2 (April, 1966), 122-139.

————. "The Trials of a Republican State Chairman: John Motley Morehead and North Carolina Politics, 1910-1912," *NCHR,* XLIII, No. 1 (January, 1966), 31-42.

Stephenson, Gilbert T. "The War Savings Campaign of 1918," *NCHR,* I, No. 1 (January, 1924), 26-34.

Taylor, A. Elizabeth. "The Woman Suffrage Movement in North Carolina," *NCHR,* XXXVIII, Nos. 1 and 2 (January and April, 1961), 46-62, 173-189.

Thompson, Holland. "The Southern Textile Situation," *Sou. Atl. Quar.,* XXIX, No. 2 (April, 1930), 113-125.

Tindall, George B. *The Emergence of the New South, 1913-1945.* (Use index for N.C. references.)

Vance, Rupert. "Aycock of North Carolina," *Southern Rev.,* XVIII (1913), 288-306.

War Camp Community Service in North Carolina, *NCHR,* I, No. 4 (October, 1924), 412-448.

Watson, Richard L., Jr. "Furnifold M. Simmons: Jehovah of the Tar Heels," *NCHR,* XLIV, No. 2 (April, 1967), 166-187.

Whitener, D. J. "The Dispensary Movement in North Carolina," *Sou. Atl. Quar.,* XXXVI, No. 1 (January, 1937), 33-48.

————. *The Prohibition Movement in North Carolina, 1715-1945,* 50-183.

————. "The Temperance Movement in North Carolina," *Sou. Atl. Quar.,* XXXIV, No. 3 (July, 1935), 305-313.

Wilson, W. S. "Suffrage in North Carolina," *N.C. Lit. and Hist. Assoc. Proc.,* XVII (1917), 70-77.

Winston, Robert W. "The Passenger Rate War in North Carolina," *Sou. Atl. Quar.*, VI, No. 4 (October, 1947), 342-347.

## 42. *A QUARTER CENTURY OF ECONOMIC GROWTH*

SUMMARY—*Population trends after 1900:* population, rural and urban; growing urbanization and industrialization.—*A state of small farms:* decrease in size of farms; value of farm land; percentage of white and Negro farmers; tenancy—totals and percentages; white and Negro tenants—totals and percentages.—*North Carolina's cash crops: tobacco, cotton, and corn:* areas of production, value of crops, national rank; other significant crops—hay, wheat, Irish potatoes, sweet potatoes, and others.—*Livestock:* beef cattle and milk cows; low national rank.—*Values of farm property:* low rank in nation.—*The North Carolina Farmers' Union (1908-1920):* objectives and accomplishments.—*Other efforts to solve farm problems:* farm colonies of European immigrants; tobacco experiment station; credit unions; Tobacco Growers Cooperative Marketing Association (1920-1926).—*Federal aid to agriculture:* the A. and M. College, Experiment Station, extension work; vocational education in public schools.—*Remarkable development of manufactures:* value of manufactures exceed that of agriculture; increase in number of workers and in wages.—*The development of electric power:* role of James B. ("Buck") Duke and Duke Power Company; other power companies; effects of increased use of electricity. *The state's leading industries: textiles, tobacco, and furniture:* total value, nature of products, rank of state in the nation; location of factories.—*Other industries:* lumber, flour and meal, cottonseed oil, and others. —*Slow growth of organized labor:* reasons for this; labor unions in state: State Federation of Labor; union activity—strikes and their results.—*Mining:* total value; leading minerals; importance of granite, brick, gravel, and stone products. —*Commercial fisheries:* food fish and nonfood fish.—*Total and per capita wealth:* low rank of state.—*Banking progress:*

banks, building and loan associations, and insurance.—*Railroad construction and consolidation:* the three major railways systems, Southern, Seaboard Air Line, and Atlantic Coast Line; development of fourth system, Norfolk Southern; two new railroads—Winston-Salem Southbound and Carolina, Clinchfield and Ohio; total railway mileage in state.—*The movement for state regulation of railroads:* complaints against railways; the work of the Corporation Commission.—*Highways and motor cars:* beginnings of the "good roads" movement; creation of State Highway Commission.

TEXT—Lefler-Newsome, *North Carolina,* Ch. 41.

BASIC READING—

Lefler, Hugh T. (ed.). *North Carolina History Told by Contemporaries,* 427-437, 445-450.

Connor, R. D. W. *North Carolina: Rebuilding an Ancient Commonwealth,* II, 597-621.

Hamilton, J. G. de R. *North Carolina Since 1860,* 383-393.

SUGGESTED READING—

Blythe, LeGette. *William Henry Belk: Merchant of the South,* 3-78.

Boyd, W. K. *The Story of Durham, City of the New South,* 1-345.

Brown, C. K. "The Southern Railway Security Company, an Early Instance of a Holding Company," *NCHR,* VI, No 2 2 (April, 1929), 158-170.

Ebert, Charles H. V. "Furniture Making in High Point," *NCHR,* XXXVI, No. 3 (July, 1959), 330-339.

Eutsler, Roland B. "The Cape Fear and Yadkin Railroad," *NCHR,* II, No. 4 (October, 1925), 427-441.

Herring, Harriet. *Passing of the Mill Village,* 3-131.

Hobbs, S. H., Jr. *North Carolina: Economic and Social,* 271-344.

Jenkins, J. W. *James B. Duke: Master Builder,* 98-184.

Loomis, Charles P. "Activities of the North Carolina Farmers' Union," *NCHR,* VII, No. 4 (October, 1930), 443-462.

———. "The Rise and Decline of the North Carolina Farmers' Union," *NCHR,* VII, No. 3 (July, 1930), 305-325.

McGuire, Peter S. "The Seaboard Airline," *NCHR*, XI, No. 2 (April, 1934), 94-115.

Mitchell, G. S. *Textile Unionism and the South.* (Use index for N.C. references.)

Pinkett, Harold T. "Gifford Pinchot at Biltmore," *NCHR*, XXXIV, No. 3 ( July, 1957), 346-357.

Poe, Clarence. "Builders of an Agricultural Commonwealth," *Sou. Atl. Quar.*, VIII, No. 1 (January, 1909), 1-11.

Thompson, Holland. *From the Cotton Field to the Cotton Mill*, 1-284.

————. *The New South.* (Use index for N.C. references.)

————. "Some Effects of Industrialism on an Agricultural State," *Sou. Atl. Quar.*, IV, No. 1 (January, 1905), 71-77.

Tilley, Nannie May, "Agitation Against the American Tobacco Company in North Carolina, 1890-1911," *NCHR*, XXIV, No. 3 (April, 1947), 207-223.

## 43. *AN INTELLECTUAL AWAKENING*

SUMMARY—*Progress of public education:* the crusade for public schools; Aycock's program; Supreme Court decision favorable to public schools; achievements of the decade 1901-1910; continued progress of the public schools 1911-1920.—*Negro education:* state support; outside funds.—*Progress of higher education:* the University of North Carolina; the Agricultural and Mechanical College at Raleigh; the State Normal and Industrial Institute (Woman's College) and now U.N.C. at Greensboro; East Carolina, Appalachian, and other state-supported colleges.—*Denominational Colleges:* Wake Forest, Trinity (now Duke), Davidson, others.—*North Carolina's backwardness in library facilities:* public libraries; North Carolina Library Commission and its work.—*Newspapers and magazines:* leading daily papers.—*North Carolina writers:* historical and biographical works; emergence of professional historians; novels, poetry, and drama.

TEXT—Lefler-Newsome, *North Carolina,* Ch. 42.

BASIC READING—

Lefler, Hugh T. (ed.). *North Carolina History Told by Contemporaries,* 407-411, 436-437.

Connor, R. D. W. *North Carolina: Rebuilding an Ancient Commonwealth,* II, 639-695.

Hamilton, J. G. de R. *North Carolina Since 1860,* 347-375.

SUGGESTED READING—

Benjamin, Marcus. "John Henry Boner," *Sou. Atl. Quar.,* III, No. 2 (April, 1904), 166-174.

Blackwelder, Fannie Farmer. "Organization and Early Years of the North Carolina Bar Association," *NCHR,* XXXIV, No. 1 (January, 1957), 36-57.

Bowles, Elisabeth Ann. *A Good Beginning: The First Four Decades of The University of North Carolina at Greensboro,* 29-178.

Branson, Lanier E. *Eugene Cunningham Branson: Humanitarian,* 1-183.

Brooks, E. C. "Charles Brantley Aycock," *Sou. Atl. Quar.,* XI, No. 3 (July, 1912), 279-282.

Brown, William Burlie. "The State Literary and Historical Association, 1900-1950," *NCHR,* XXVIII, No. 2 (April, 1951), 156-197.

Cash, W. J. *The Mind of the South,* 89, 224, 322-326, 341, 354, 372-376.

Connor, R. D. W. "Samuel A'Court Ashe," *NCHR,* III, No. 1 (January, 1926), 132-135.

Coon, Charles L. "School Support and Our North Carolina Schools," *NCHR,* III, No. 3 (July, 1926), 399-438.

Gatewood, Willard B., Jr. *Eugene Clyde Brooks: Educator and Public Servant,* 1-279.

Gibson, John M. "Walter Hines Page Has Been 'Forgiven,'" *Sou. Atl. Quar.,* XXXII (1933), 283-293.

Graham, Edward Kidder. "The Poetry of John Charles McNeill," *Sou Atl. Quar.,* VI. No. 1 (January, 1907), 81-86.

Hammond, Mrs. John D. "The Work of the General Education Board in the South," *Sou. Atl. Quar.*, XIV, No. 4 (October, 1915), 348-357.

Harlan, Louis R. *Separate and Unequal: Public School Campaigns and Racism in the Southern Seaboard States, 1901-1915*, 45-74, 102-134.

Harman, Henry F. "John Charles McNeill and His Work," *Sou. Atl. Quar.*, XVI, No. 4 (October, 1916), 301-308.

Henderson, Archibald. *The Campus of the First State University*, 216-279.

Hobbs, S. H., Jr. *North Carolina: Economic and Social*, 247-279.

House, Robert B. "Aycock and Universal Education," *NCHR*, XXXVII, No. 2 (April, 1960), 211-216.

Johnson, Elmer D. "James Yadkin Joyner, Educational Statesman," *NCHR*, XXXIII, No. 3 (July, 1956), 359-383.

Jones, H. G. *For History's Sake; The Preservation and Publication of North Carolina History, 1663-1903*, 3-287.

————. "Stephen Beauregard Weeks: North Carolina's First 'Professional Historian,'" *NCHR*, XLII, No. 4 (October, 1965), 410-423.

Kennedy, Fronde. "Fighting Adult Illiteracy," *Sou. Atl. Quar.*, XIX, No. 3 (July, 1920), 189-200.

Knight, E. W. *Public School Education in North Carolina*, 329-374.

Leonard, Jacob C. *History of Catawba College*, 1-353.

Linder, S. C. *William Louis Poteat: Prophet of Progress*, 1-224.

*North Carolina Authors: A Selective Handbook.* (Use index for individual authors.)

*North Carolina Fiction, 1734-1957: An Annotated Bibliography.* (Use index for individual authors.)

Orr, Oliver H., Jr. *Charles Brantley Aycock*, 183-334.

Oxendine, Clifton. "Pembroke State Colleges for Indians: Historical Sketch," *NCHR*, XXII, No. 1 (January, 1945), 22-33.

Polk, William T. *Southern Accent: From Uncle Remus to Oak Ridge.* (Use index for N.C. references.)

Rulfs, Donald J. "The Era of the Opera House in Piedmont

North Carolina," *NCHR,* XXXV, No. 3 (July, 1958) , 328-346.

———. "The Theater in Asheville, 1879 to 1931," *NCHR,* XXXVI, No. 4 (October, 1959) , 429-441.

Shaw, Albert. "Walter Hines Page—Memorial Address," *NCHR,* I, No. 1 (January, 1924) , 3-25.

Smith, Willis. "James Robert Bent Hathaway—A Gleaner in North Carolina History," TCHS, *Papers,* VII (1907), 32-38.

Stephenson, Wendell H. "The Negro in the Thinking and Writing of John Spencer Bassett," *NCHR,* XXV, No. 4 (October, 1948) , 427-441.

Wagstaff, H. M. *Impression of Men and Movements at the University of North Carolina,* 1-110.

Walser, Richard. "North Carolina Short Stories," *NCHR,* XXV, No. 2 (April, 1948) , 206-211.

Whitener, D. J. "Education for the People," *NCHR,* XXXVI, No. 2 (April, 1959) , 187-196.

Wilson, Louis Round. "The Acquisition of the Stephen B. Weeks Collection of Caroliniana," *NCHR,* XLII, No. 4 (October, 1965), 424-429.

Winston, Robert W. "North Carolina: A Militant Mediocracy," *Nation,* CXVI (February 21, 1923) , 209-212.

## 44. *POLITICS, 1920-1932: THE ADMINISTRATIONS OF MORRISON, McLEAN, AND GARDNER*

SUMMARY—*Disillusionment and reaction following World War I:* revival of "nativism"—the Ku Klux Klan; the fundamentalist movement and the controversy over evolution; the "noble experiment" of prohibition and repeal of the Eighteenth Amendment (1933) .—*The election of 1920:* Cameron Morrison elected governor.—*Morrison, "Good Roads Governor," 1921-1925:* Highway Act of 1921; bond issues; work of Frank Page and others.—*Remarkable improvements in higher education:* great growth and expansion of the University of North Carolina; the rise of Duke University.—*Progress of the public schools:* achievements under administration of Superintendents of Public Instruction, E. C. Brooks (1919-1923) and A. T. Allen (after 1923).—*Attempts to develop North Carolina ports:* defeat of bond issue for port development.—*The expanding functions of government:* increase in state services, costs, and taxes.—*The election of 1924:* Angus W. McLean elected governor.—*Achievements of the McLean administration (1925-1929):* creation of the Budget Bureau, Department of Conservation and Development, the Tax Commission, the County Government Advisory Commission, the State Board of Equalization and other boards and agencies. —*Use of equalization fund for public schools:* counties which benefited.—*The election of 1928:* Republican Hoover defeats Democrat Alfred E. Smith for the presidency; O. Max Gardner elected governor by large majority.—*The Gardner administration (1929-1933):* the state's economic and financial situation in 1929; achievements of the 1929 General Assembly: Australian (secret) ballot, Workmen's Compensation Act, and other significant legislation; beginnings of the "Great Depression," and its effects on North Carolina.—*Gardner's program:* reduction in number of state officers, creation of central purchasing agency, consolidation of some counties, and consolidation of the University of North Carolina, State College, and the Woman's College: other proposals.—*The General Assembly of 1931:* bitter fight over luxury tax, and failure to pass either a general sales tax or a luxury tax; Gardner's own explanation of how he had "cleaned house": in road legislation (state took over county roads); in public school legislation; in legislation for control of public debt (Local Government Act), and Consolidation of the University of North Carolina.— *The election of 1932:* bitter Democratic primary; J. C. Blucher Ehringhaus nominated and elected; United States Senator Cameron Morrison defeated by Robert R. ("Our Bob") Reynolds.

TEXT—Lefler-Newsome, *North Carolina,* Ch. 43.

BASIC READING—

Lefler, Hugh T. (ed.). *North Carolina History Told by Contemporaries,* 417-424, 431-436.

Connor, R. D. W. *North Carolina: Rebuilding an Ancient Commonwealth*, II, 490-541, 547-549.

SUGGESTED READING—

Corbitt, D. L. (ed.). *Public Papers and Letters of Cameron Morrison, Governor of North Carolina, 1921-1925*, XLVIII, 339.

———— (ed.). *Public Papers and Letters of Angus Wilton McLean, Governor of North Carolina, 1925-1929*, XVI, 899.

———— (ed.). *Public Papers and Letters of Oliver Max Gardner, Governor of North Carolina, 1929-1933*, LIII, 764.

Cronon, E. David. "Josephus Daniels As a Reluctant Candidate," *NCHR*, XXXIII, No. 4 (October, 1956), 457-482.

Gatewood, Willard B., Jr. "Eugene Clyde Brooks: Educational Journalist in North Carolina, 1906-1923," *NCHR*, XXXVI, No. 3 (July, 1959), 307-329.

————. "Eugene Clyde Brooks and Negro Education in North Carolina, 1919-1923," *NCHR*, XXXVIII, No. 3 (July, 1961), 326-379.

————. "Politics and Piety in North Carolina: The Fundamentalist Crusade at High Tide, 1925-1927," *NCHR*, XLII, No. 3 (July, 1965), 275-290.

————. *Preachers, Pedagogues & Politicians: The Evolution Controversy in North Carolina, 1920-1927*, 1-268.

Johnson, LeRoy. *The Evolution Controversy during the 1920's*. 1-210.

Linder, Suzanne. "William Louis Poteat and the Evolution Controversy," *NCHR*, XL, No. 2 (April, 1963), 135-157.

————. *William Louis Poteat: Prophet of Progress*, 1-224.

Moore, John R. "The Shaping of a Political Leader: Josiah W. Bailey and the Gubernatorial Campaign of 1924," *NCHR*, XLI, No. 2 (April, 1964), 190-213.

Morrison, Joseph L. *Josephus Daniels: The Small-d Democrat*, 1-316.

————. "The 'Tar Heel Editor' in North Carolina's Crisis, 1929-1932," *NCHR*, XLIV, No. 3 (July, 1967), 270-282.

Pearson, C. C. "Race Relations in North Carolina: A Field

Study of Moderate Opinion," *Sou. Atl. Quar.*, XXIII, No. 1 (January, 1924), 1-9.

Puryear, Elmer L. *Democratic Party Dissension in North Carolina, 1928-1936*, 1-155.

Ratchford, B. U. "The Public Finances of North Carolina Since 1920," *Sou. Atl. Quar.*, XXVII, No. 1 (January, 1928), 1-15.

Tindall, George B. "Business Progressivism: Southern Politics in the Twenties," *Sou. Atl. Quar.*, LXII, No. 1 (January, 1963), 92-106.

————. *The Emergence of the New South, 1913-1945.* (Use index for N.C. references.)

Watson, Richard L., Jr. "A Political Leader Bolts—F. M. Simmons in the Presidential Election of 1928," *NCHR*, XXXVII, No. 4 (October, 1960), 516-543.

————. "A Southern Democratic Primary: Simmons vs. Bailey in 1930," *NCHR*, XLII, No. 1 (January, 1965), 21-46.

## 45. THE NEW DEAL ERA TO THE OUTBREAK OF WORLD WAR II, 1933–1941

SUMMARY—*The general situation in the state and nation in 1933:* agriculture, industry, trade, and banking; desperate situation of local governments.—*Efforts of Governor Ehringhaus to cope with the "Great Depression":* more drastic economy; reduced salaries and services; state assumes major support of public schools; more state taxes; general sales tax.—*Legislative fight over the 3 per cent general sales tax:* opposition of industrial leaders, merchants, and others groups; reasons for final adoption.—*The end of state-wide prohibition, 1933:* beginnings of state Alcoholic Beverage Control (ABC) stores.—*The New Deal, 1933-1941:* a program of banking reform, enlarged credit facilities, work for the unemployed, agricultural program, labor policy, social security, electric power program; AAA, NRA, TVA, and other alphabetical agencies.—New Deal benefits to North Carolina farmers and other elements of the population.—Conservative opposition to New Deal reforms.—*North Carolinians in the New Deal Administration:* Josephus Daniels, Robert L. Doughton, Lindsay Warren, R. D. W. Connor, and others.—*The election of 1936:* Clyde R. Hoey defeats Dr. Ralph McDonald in heated primary and is later elected governor.—*The Hoey administration (1937-1941):* new election law; other legislation.—*The election of 1940:* J. Melville Broughton elected governor.

TEXT—Lefler-Newsome, *North Carolina,* Ch. 44.

BASIC READING—

Corbitt, D. L. (ed.). *Addresses, Letters, and Papers of John Christoph Blucher Ehringhaus, Governor of North Carolina, 1933-1937,* 1-475.

Whitener, D. J. *Prohibition in North Carolina, 1715-1945,* 184-228.

SUGGESTED READING—

Green, Fletcher M. "Resurgent Southern Sectionalism, 1933-1955," *NCHR,* XXXIII, No. 2 (April, 1956), 222-240.

Lonsdale, Richard E. (comp.). *Atlas of North Carolina,* 70-75. (Election maps).

Ratchford, B. U. "The Financial Crisis of North Carolina," *Sou. Atl. Quar.,* XXXII, No. 1 (January, 1933), 43-62.

Whitener, D. J. *Prohibition in North Carolina, 1715-1945,* 184-288.


## 46. WORLD WAR II AND AFTER:
## PROGRESS AND PROBLEMS, 1941–1952

SUMMARY—*Auspicious beginnings of Broughton administration:* Significant acts of 1941 General Assembly.—*Preparations for national defense:* important Congressional legislation; national boards and agencies.—*The United States becomes "the arsenal of democracy":* American exchange with Great Britain of fifty destroyers for bases in Newfoundland, Bermuda, and other places; the Lend-Lease law (1941); President Roosevelt declares an "unlimited emergency"; repeal of portions of neutrality laws which forbade arming merchant ships; Japanese attack on Pearl Harbor, December 7, 1941; American declaration of war against "Axis partners," Japan, Germany, and Italy.—*North Carolina's role in World War II:* contributions of men and women, money, supplies; camps located in the state; effects of war on agriculture, industry, labor and other aspects of life.—*The state's industrial contributions to the war:* money spent in state for war supplies; value and importance of war materials produced in North Carolina.— *Politics during the war years:* Significant laws of 1943 General Assembly—great increases in support for education; appropriations for art and music; beginnings of medical care program. —*The 1944 election:* Gregg Cherry wins gubernatorial nomination and election.—*The Cherry administration (1945-1949):* Increased legislative appropriations for education and other state services; Five-year Hospital Plan inaugurated (July 8, 1947).—*The 1948 election:* W. Kerr Scott wins gubernatorial nomination in close contest and elected governor.—*The Scott administration (1949-1953):* the "Go Forward" program, with emphasis on secondary road construction and schools; state votes $200,000,000 bond issue for roads and $25,000,000 for construction of school buildings; record breaking legislative appropriations and $7,500,000 in bonds for improvement of ports; Negros admitted to the University of North Carolina, following federal court decisions outlawing segregation; Frank Graham appointed by Scott to United States Senate, following Senator Broughton's death (1949); Graham defeated by Willis Smith (1950) in bitter race.—*North Carolinians in the Truman administration:* Kenneth Royall, Gordon Gray, O. Max Gardner, Jonathan Daniels, and others.

TEXT—Lefler-Newsome, *North Carolina,* Ch. 45.

BASIC READING—
Lefler, Hugh T. (ed.). *North Carolina History Told by Contemporaries,* 464-469, 476-479.

SUGGESTED READING—
Corbitt, D. L. (ed.). *Addresses, Letters and Papers of Clyde*

*Roark Hoey, Governor of North Carolina, 1937-1941*, 1-869.

———— (ed.). *Public Addresses, Letters and Papers of Joseph Melville Broughton, Governor of North Carolina, 1941-1945*, xi, 679.

———— (ed.). *Public Addresses and Papers of Robert Gregg Cherry, Governor of North Carolina, 1945-1949*, lv, 1009.

———— (ed.). *Public Addresses, Letters, and Papers of William Kerr Scott, Governor of North Carolina, 1949-1953*, xxvi, 591.

King, Spencer B., Jr. *Selective Service in North Carolina in World War II*, 3-360.

Lefler, Hugh T. "Robert Digges Wimberly Connor," in Clifford Lord, *Keepers of the Past*, 109-123.

Lemmon, Sarah M. *North Carolina's Role in the First World War*, 1-91.

————. *North Carolina's Role in World War II*, 1-69.

Lerche, Charles O., Jr. *The Uncertain South: Its Changing Patterns of Politics in Foreign Policy.* (Use index for N.C. references.)

## 47. *THE MODERN INDUSTRIAL REVOLUTION AFTER 1930*

SUMMARY—*Increase in value of North Carolina manufactures:* leading industries; value of product; number of plants, number of workers.—*The textile industry:* total value of products, number of establishments, number of workers; rank of state in nation; types of products; geographic location of plants.— *Consolidation of textile mills:* phenomenal growth of Burlington Mills (now Burlington Industries) ; Cone Mills and others. —*The "passing of the mill village":* number and percentage of mills which have sold "company houses" to employees; rise and growth of "stringtowns."—*Tobacco manufacturing:* phenomenal increase; concentration in Winston-Salem, Durham, Reidsville, and Greensboro; rank of state in nation.—

*Forest products industries:* furniture, paper products, lumber; High Point and other "furniture towns"; great increase in production of pulp-paper products.—*Other industries:* food products, chemicals, electronics, machinery, and others; the construction industry; spectacular growth of tourist or travel-serving industry.—*Minerals, stone and gravel, brick and clay:* how state ranks in mineral production; leading products— mica, feldspar, lithium, graphite, tungsten; kaolin, brick and slate; granite, stone, sand, and gravel.—*Total and per capita wealth of North Carolina:* low rank and reasons for this.— *Population trends:* increase in population, but not as rapid as that of nation; out-of-state migration—causes and effects on state; urbanization; largest cities in 1950 and 1960.—*Increasing importance of North Carolina cities:* centers of manufacturing, trade, banking, and other aspects of life; banks, building and loan associations, insurance companies.—*Growth of the labor movement in North Carolina:* labor-management relations; labor troubles at Gastonia, Marion, and other places, 1929-1932.—*Labor policies of the New Deal and the Fair Deal (Truman):* the Wagner Act.—*The State Department of Labor:* the nature of its activities.—*Growth of organized labor in state after 1937:* activities of the CIO (Committee on Industrial Organization); legislature fails to ratify proposed Child Labor Amendment.—North Carolina's labor force in the decade 1950-1960.—*Labor-management relations in the past decades:* state's outstanding record in number of "man-days idle" as a result of strikes.

TEXT—Lefler-Newsome, *North Carolina,* Ch. 46.

BASIC READING—

Lefler, Hugh T. (ed.). *North Carolina History Told by Contemporaries,* 469-474, 510-518.

Hobbs, S. H., Jr. *North Carolina: An Economic and Social Profile,* 3-9, 75-83, 98-130, 157-177.

SUGGESTED READING—

Herring, Harriet. *The Passing of the Mill Village,* 3-131.

————. *Welfare Work in Mill Villages,* 1-406.

Landon, Charles E. "Recent Developments in the Tobacco Manufacturing Industry," *Sou. Atl. Quar.,* XXXI, No. 1 (January, 1932), 88-97.

Lemert, Ben F. *The Tobacco Manufacturing Industry in North Carolina,* 1-107.

Lonsdale, Richard E. (comp.). *Atlas of North Carolina,* 56-60, 116-139.

Mitchell, G. S. *Textile Unionism and the South.* (Use index for N.C. references.)

Morris, J. A. *Woolen and Worsted Manufacturing in the Southern Piedmont.* (Use index for N.C. references.)

## 48. AGRICULTURE, TRANSPORTATION, TRADE IN RECENT YEARS

SUMMARY—*Profound changes in North Carolina agriculture in the past decade:* rapid decline in number of farms; increase in size of farms; increased mechanization; trend toward large-scale agriculture; decline in farm tenancy; increase in value of farms.—*"King Tobacco":* total production, monetary value, and national rank.—*Cotton and corn:* amounts, value of crops, national rank.—*Other cash crops:* hay, soy beans, Irish and sweet potatoes, vegetables and fruits.—*Recent progress in production of livestock, cattle, poultry, and pigs:* value and significance.—*Rapid decline in farm tenancy:* total and percentage decreases; reasons for decline; tenancy not a racial problem.—*Federal aid to North Carolina farmers:* aid for experiment and extension work; federal benefits to North Carolina farmers; rural electrification and its significance.—*Work of State Department of Agriculture:* illustrations of its varied activities.—*Other causes of improved farming in North Carolina:* heavy use of fertilizer; more farm machinery; new varieties of seed; activities of county agents; 4-H Clubs and other organizations; the *Progressive Farmer.*—*Changes in rural life:* economic, social, and cultural improvements.—*A new era in transportation and communication:* North Carolina a "Good Roads State"—extent of highway system, expenditures for roads, effects of improved roads on life of people.—*Motor bus and freight lines:* wholesale trade of state; significance of trucking industry.—*Death on highways:* traffic accidents and fatalities.— *Recent developments in aviation:* importance of air travel to state.—*Improvements in communication:* telephones, radio, television.—*Wholesale and retail trade of North Carolina:* kinds of business, number of establishments, and total sales.

TEXT—Lefler-Newsome, *North Carolina,* Ch. 47.

BASIC READING

Hobbs, S. H., Jr. *North Carolina: An Economic and Social Profile,* 85-97, 138-142, 146-147.

SUGGESTED READING—

Blythe, W. LeGette. *William Henry Belk: Merchant of the South,* 81-219.

Brown, Aycock. *The Birth of Aviation: Kitty Hawk, North Carolina,* 1-63.

Lively, Robert A. *The South in Action: A Sectional Crusade Against Freight Rate Discrimination.* (Use index for N.C. references.)

Lonsdale, Richard E. (comp.). *Atlas of North Carolina,* 61-69, 100-115, 140-158.

Noblin, Stuart. *The Grange in North Carolina, 1929-1954: A Study of Argicultural Progress,* 1-59.

Poe, Clarence. "Exploding Agricultural Myths: Comparing Farm Prosperity South and West," *Sou. Atl. Quar.,* XXXIII, No. 2 (April, 1934), 113-127.

———. "Rural Land Segregation between the Whites and Negroes: A Reply to Mr. Stephenson," *Sou. Atl. Quar.,* XIII, No. 3 (July, 1919), 207-212.

Raper, Charles L. "The Use of Credit by the North Carolina Farmers," *Sou. Atl. Quar.,* XIII, No. 2 (April, 1914), 118-128.

Stephenson, Gilbert T. "The Segregation of the White and Negro Races in Rural Communities in North Carolina," *Sou. Atl. Quar.,* XIII, No. 2 (April, 1914), 107-117.

Taylor, Rosser H. *A Study of Rural Life at the End of the Horse-and-Buggy Era*, 1-172.

## 49. FOR A FINER NORTH CAROLINA

SUMMARY—*Increasing interest in education:* public schools; institutions of higher learning.—*Progress of the public schools:* increase in number of pupils, expenditures, value of school property, teachers' salaries, libraries; the state's rank in public schools; some innovations in recent years.—*State-supported institutions of higher learning:* The University of North Carolina at Chapel Hill—new schools, divisions, and departments; things which have given the University national distinction; great growth and expansion of State College; steady progress of the Woman's College; East Carolina, Appalachian, and other state-supported colleges.—*Church-related colleges:* their number and importance; the growth and expansion of Duke University; the transfer of Wake Forest to Winston-Salem; Davidson, Meredith, Greensboro, and other colleges.—*Expansion of public library facilities:* work of the Library Commission; county and city libraries; "bookmobiles."—*Newspapers:* number and circulation; leading dailies and nondaily papers; appraisal of state's newspapers.—*Book publishing:* University of North Carolina Press; Duke University Press; commercial publishers.—*North Carolina writers: nonfiction:* leading historians and biographers; county histories; distinguished writers in sociology, literature, science, religion, and other fields.— *North Carolina novelists:* James Boyd, Inglis Fletcher, Thomas Wolfe, and others.—*North Carolina poets:* Randall Jarrell, James Larkin Pearson, Carl Sandburg, and others.—*Short stories, pageants, and folklore.—Increasing interest in art:* the North Carolina Art Society; State Art Museum (opened 1956). —*Music in modern North Carolina:* North Carolina Symphony Orchestra; other symphony orchestras; Transylvania Music Camp; Grass Roots Opera; Lamar Stringfield and other North Carolina composers.—*Church membership:* largest denominations—Baptist, Methodist, Presbyterian, Lutheran,

Episcopal, Congregational Christian, Evangelical and Reformed, Friends, Moravians, and others.

TEXT—Lefler-Newsome, *North Carolina,* Ch. 48.

BASIC READING—

Hobbs, S. H., Jr. *North Carolina: An Economic and Social Profile,* 219-241, 245-247.

SUGGESTED READING—

Aydlett, A. Laurence. "The North Carolina State Board of Public Welfare," *NCHR,* XXIV, No. 1 (January, 1947), 1-34.

*The Frank C. Brown Collection of North Carolina Folklore.* 5 vols.

Cash, W. J. *The Mind of the South.* (Use index for N.C. references.)

Crittenden, C. C. "We've Come a Long Way: History and Historical Activities in North Carolina," *NCHR,* XXXVI, No. 1 (January, 1959), 153-161.

Davis, Lambert. "North Carolina and the University Press," *NCHR,* XLIII, No. 2 (April, 1966), 149-156.

Hamilton, William B. *Fifty Years of the South Atlantic Quarterly,* 1-397.

Holman, C. Hugh. *Thomas Wolfe,* 1-47.

Hoyle, Bernadette. *Tar Heel Writers I Know,* 1-215.

Hunter, Kermit. "The Outdoor Historical Drama," *NCHR,* XXX, No. 2 (April, 1953), 218-222.

———. *Unto These Hills.* 1-100.

Knight, E. W. *Public School Education in North Carolina,* 329-366.

Lefler, Hugh T. "Robert Digges Wimberly Connor," in Lord, Clifford L. (ed.). *Keepers of the Past,* 109-123.

Leonard, Samuel L. "The History of the Eastern North Carolina Industrial School for Boys, at Rocky Mount, North Carolina," *NCHR,* XXII, No. 3 (July, 1945), 276-292.

Lonsdale, Richard E. (comp.). *Atlas of North Carolina,* 76-94.

McCoy, George W. "Asheville and Thomas Wolfe," *NCHR,* XXX, No. 2 (April, 1953), 200-217.

Murray, Paul. "Thirty Years of the New History: A Study of the *North Carolina Historical Review*, 1924-1953," *NCHR*, XXXII, No. 2 (April, 1955), 174-193.

Noble, Alice. *The School of Pharmacy of the University of North Carolina*, 3-222.

*North Carolina Authors: A Selective Handbook*, 1-135.

Polk, William T. *The Fallen Angel and Other Stories*, 1-180.

————. *Southern Accent: From Uncle Remus to Oak Ridge*, 1-264.

Ramsey, Annie S. "Utility Regulation in North Carolina, 1891-1941: Fifty Years of History and Progress," *NCHR*, XXII, No. 2 (April, 1945), 125-151.

Stephens, George M. "The Beginnings of the Historical Drama 'Unto These Hills,'" *NCHR*, XXVIII, No. 2 (April, 1951), 212-218.

Stroupe, Henry S. "The North Carolina Department of Archives and History—the First Half Century," *NCHR*, XXXI, No. 2 (April, 1954), 184-200.

Walser, Richard. (ed.). *North Carolina Poetry*, 1-196.

———— (ed.). *Short Stories from the Old North State*, 1-288.

Wilson, L. R. *The University of North Carolina, 1900-1930: The Making of a Modern University*, 3-604.


## 50. THE NEW COMMONWEALTH— FOR THE PUBLIC WELFARE

SUMMARY—*Triumph of the service concept of government:* a nationwide development; illustrations.—*Organization and functions of local government:* county, municipal (mayor-council, commission, and city manager plans).—*Organization of the state government:* executive, legislative, and judicial branches.—*Services of state government:* protection of life and property; education—public schools and higher education; agriculture—Department of Agriculture, colleges, and experiment stations; banks and banking regulations; labor legislation and agencies associated with it, such as Unemployment Compensation Commission; construction, maintenance, and control of highways; protection for consumers; public welfare program; charitable and correctional institutions.— *The war against disease:* the State Board of Health; local health work; the state's hospital and medical care program; the Blue Cross–Blue Shield Plan in North Carolina.—*Development of the State's resources:* work of Department of Conservation and Development; wild life, forest resources, mineral resources, conservation work, state advertising; federal aid; national forests, Great Smoky Mountains Park and other federal parks.—*State parks and historic sites.*—*National parks, sites, and memorials.*—*The State Department of Archives and History:* collection and preservation of historical records; publications; the highway marker program.—*The increasing cost of government:* vast expansion of services and of governmental employees.—*Sources of state revenues:* income taxes, gasoline taxes, sales taxes, motor vehicles taxes, franchise taxes, beverage taxes, and others.—*Major state expenditures:* education, highway construction and maintenance, health and hospitals, retirement and pensions, public welfare, debt service, general government, and other services.—*Total state and local government debt.*

TEXT—Lefler-Newsome, *North Carolina,* Ch. 49.

SUGGESTED READING—

Brown, Roy M. *Public Poor Relief in North Carolina,* 1-184.

Cheek, Roma. *Sleeping Tar Heels,* 1-95.

Davidson, Elizabeth Huey. "Child-Labor Reforms in North Carolina Since 1903," *NCHR,* XIV, No. 2 (April, 1937), 109-134.

Ferrell, John A. "The North Carolina Campaign Against Hookworm Disease," *Sou Atl. Quar.,* XI, No. 2 (April, 1912), 128-135.

Gatewood, Willard B., Jr. "North Carolina's Role in the Establishment of the Great Smoky Mountains National Park," *NCHR,* XXXVII, No. 2 (April, 1960), 165-184.

Maxwell, Allen J., and William O. Suiter. "The North Carolina Department of Revenue," *NCHR,* XXI, No. 4 (October, 1944), 265-293.

Rankin, Robert S. *The Government and Administration of North Carolina,* 1-429.

Scheer, Julian. "Tweetsie," *NCHR,* XXXVI, No. 1 (January, 1959) , 168-172.

Smith, Charles D. "The Appalachian National Park Movement, 1805-1901," *NCHR,* XXXVII, No. 1 (January, 1960), 38-65.

Wager, Paul W. (ed.) . *County Government Across the Nation,* 408-420.

## 51. IN THE MAINSTREAM:
## A DECADE OF GREAT GROWTH AND CHANGE

SUMMARY—*Profound changes in state, nation, and world after 1950:* North Carolina a rural state moving toward industrialization, but state lost ground relatively in the early 1950's.— *The administration of William B. Umstead, (1953-1954):* 1953 General Assembly continues "Go Forward" program.—*The "Bryant Committee's" Report on Higher Education (1955):* summary of its findings.—*The 1954 off-year election:* candidates and results; Governor Umstead dies and Lieutenant Governor Luther H. Hodges becomes governor (Nov. 9, 1954.)—*The "first administration" of Hodges (1954-1957):* the problem of desegregation in the public schools; General Assembly of 1955 makes major changes in public school laws; activities of National Association for the Advancement of Colored People (NAACP) and of the Patriots of North Carolina.—*The state adopts the "Pearsall Plan":* an effort to solve the desegregation problem.—*The 1956 election:* results of the Democratic primary and of the general election.—*The General Assembly of 1957:* changes in organization of state government; changes in tax laws of multistate corporations— effects.—*The Research Triangle:* what it included and its general objectives; the Research Park and progress.—*The 1958 election.—North Carolina's rapid recovery from the 1957-1958 recession:* great increase in industrial investment; industry becoming more diversified; the state's advertising program.—

*The 1959 General Assembly:* record-breaking appropriations; other significant legislation; voters approve a $34,050,000 bond issue.—*The 1960 election:* Terry Sanford wins in bitter second Democratic primary and elected governor on a "Go Forword" program.—*The 1961 General Assembly:* more far-reaching legislation than that of any other legislature in recent state history; illustrations of this; voters overwhelmingly rejected a multipurpose bond issue of $61,500,000.—*The state's economic situation in 1961:* illustrations.—*North Carolinians in the Kennedy Administration.—Public school desegregation:* slow but peaceful adjustment to "integration."—*Integration at eating places and theaters.*

TEXT—Lefler-Newsome, *North Carolina,* Ch. 50.

BASIC READING—

Lefler, Hugh T. (ed.). *North Carolina History Told by Contemporaries,* 487-510.

SUGGESTED READING—

Burgess, M. Elaine. *Negro Leadership in a Southern City* [Durham], 1-231.

Corbitt, D. L. (ed.). *Public Addresses, Letters, and Papers of William Bradley Umstead, Governor of North Carolina, 1953-1954,* xxiv, 388.

Craven, Charles. "The Robeson County Indian Uprising against the KKK," *Sou. Atl. Quar.,* LVII, No. 4 (October, 1958), 433-442.

Fleer, Jack. *North Carolina Politics,* 1-163.

Hamilton, William B. "The Research Triangle of North Carolina: A Study in Leadership for the Common Weal," *Sou. Atl. Quar.,* LXV, No. 2 (April, 1966), 254-278.

Hodges, Luther H. *Businessman in the Statehouse: Six Years As Governor of North Carolina,* 1-320.

Lonsdale, Richard E. (comp.). *Atlas of North Carolina,* 95-99.

Mitchell, Memory F. (ed.). *Messages, Addresses, and Papers of Terry Sanford, Governor of North Carolina, 1961-1965.* xxxvii, 792.

Patton, James W. (ed.). *Messages, Addresses, Letters, and*

*Papers of Luther Hartwell Hodges, Governor of North Carolina, 1954-1961.* 3 vols.

Ross, Malcolm. "North Carolina, Dixie Dynamo," *National Geographic,* Vol. 121, No. 2 (February, 1962), 141-183.

## VII. / BOOKS AND ARTICLES
## RELATING TO
## NORTH CAROLINA COUNTIES
## AND TOWNS

### A. WORKS COVERING SEVERAL COUNTIES

Arthur, J. P. *Western North Carolina 1790 to 1913.* Raleigh, 1914. 710 pp.

Battle, K. P. "Glimpses of History in the Names of Our Counties," *NCB,* VI, No. 11 (July, 1906), 27-48.

Connor, R. D. W. (ed.). *North Carolina Manual, 1913.* Raleigh, 1913. 1053 pp. Contains historical sketches of the state's 100 counties.

Corbitt, D. L. *The Formation of North Carolina Counties, 1663-1943.* Raleigh, 1950. 323 pp. Invaluable for facts relating to the formation of counties.

*How They Began, The Story of North Carolina County, Town, and Other Place Names.* New York, 1941. 73 pp.

Olds, Fred A. *Story of the Counties of North Carolina, with Other Data.* Oxford, 1921. 64 pp.

Powell, William S. *North Carolina: A Students' Guide to Localized History.* New York, 1965. 35 pp.

———. *North Carolina County Histories.* U.N.C. Library, Chapel Hill, 1958. 27 pp.

———. *The North Carolina Gazetteer.* Chapel Hill, 1968. 580 pp. An invaluable work.

———. *Raleigh—Durham—Chapel Hill: A Students' Guide to Localized History.* New York, 1968. 41 pp.

————, and Eva J. Lawrence. *A Bibliography of North Carolina Counties.* Raleigh, 1952. 13 pp.

Robinson, Blackwell P. (ed.). *The North Carolina Guide.* Chapel Hill, 1955. 649 pp. Especially valuable for historical sketches of towns.

Sharpe, Bill. *A New Geography of North Carolina.* 4 vols. Raleigh, 1954, 1958, 1961, 1965. Contains sketches of all North Carolina counties.

————. *North Carolina, A Description by Counties.* Raleigh, 1948. One volume (unpaged).

Smathers, G. H. *History of Land Titles in Western North Carolina.* Asheville, 1938. 148 pp.

Wheeler, John H. *Historical Sketches of North Carolina from 1584 to 1851.* Two vols. in one. Philadelphia, 1851. 138 pp.; 48 pp.


## B. *STUDIES OF INDIVIDUAL COUNTIES AND TOWNS*

ALAMANCE—

Harden, John W. *Alamance County: Economic and Social.* Chapel Hill, 1928. 95 pp.

Sharpe, Bill. *A New Geography of North Carolina.* Raleigh, 1954. I, 1-22.

*State,* May 16, 1953.

Stockard, Sallie W. *History of Alamance County.* Raleigh, 1960. 166 pp.

Whitaker, Walter. *Centennial History of Alamance County, 1849-1949.* Charlotte, 1949. 270 pp.

ALEXANDER—

Crouse, A. L. *Historical Sketches of Alexander County.* Hickory, 1905. 124 pp.

Pittard, Ben L. *Prologue, A History of Alexander County.* Taylorsville, 1958. 67 pp.

Sharpe, Bill. *A New Geography of North Carolina.* IV, 1681-1696.

ALLEGHANY—

Cox, A. B. *Foot Prints on the Sands of Time.* Sparta, 1900. 76-103.

Sharpe, Bill. *A New Geography of North Carolina,* IV, 1697-1712.

*State,* September 5, 1942.

ANSON—

Boylin, Mrs. J. G. "Anson County," *NCB,* XIII, No. 4 (1914), 214-221.

Sharpe, Bill. *A New Geography of North Carolina,* III, 1115-1136.

*State,* October 17, 1942; July 1, 1944.

ASHE—

Newsome, A. R. (ed.). "Twelve North Carolina Counties in 1810-1811," *NCHR,* V, No. 4 (October, 1928), 419-421.

Sharpe, Bill. *A New Geography of North Carolina,* II, 535-550.

*State,* August 29, 1942; April 9, 1949.

AVERY—

Deyton, J. B. "History of the Toe River Valley to 1865," *NCHR,* XXIV, No. 4 (October, 1947), 423-466.

Sharpe, Bill. *A New Geography of North Carolina,* II, 551-572.

BEAUFORT—

Bonner, Lottie H. *Colonial Bath and Pamlico Section.* Aurora, 1939. 46 pp.

Pascal, Herbert, Jr. *A History of Colonial Bath.* Raleigh, 1955. 69 pp.

Reed, C. Wingate. *Beaufort County: Two Centuries of Its History.* Raleigh, 1962. 244 pp.

Sharpe, Bill. *A New Geography of North Carolina,* II, 573-594.

*State,* March 28, 1942; April 29, 1944; December 18, 1948; September 24, 1955.

BERTIE—

Sharpe, Bill. *A New Geography of North Carolina,* IV, 1713-1736.

*State,* January 10, 1942; March 27, 1943.

BLADEN—

McCullough, Norman. "History of Bladen County," *Tar Heel Banker*, XVI, No. 4 (1937), 1-6.

Sharpe, Bill. *A New Geography of North Carolina*, III, 1137-1160.

*State*, January 10, 1942; November 27, 1943; September 9, 1944.

BRUNSWICK—

Battle, K. P. "Brunswick County" in J. H. Wheeler's *Reminiscences and Memoirs of North Carolina*, 38-55.

Lee, Enoch Laurence. "Old Brunswick, The Story of a Colonial Town," *NCHR*, XXIX, No. 2 (April, 1952), 230-245.

Sharpe, Bill. *A New Geography of North Carolina*, II, 595-622.

*State*, August 23, 1941; September 26, 1944; April 30, 1949; May 19, 1956.

BUNCOMBE—

Digges, C. A., Jr. *Historical Facts concerning Buncombe County Government*. Asheville, 1935. 328 pp.

Mead, Martha W. *Asheville in the Land of the Sky*. Richmond, 1942. 188 pp.

Sharpe, Bill. *A New Geography of North Carolina*, II, 623-648.

Sondley, F. A. *Asheville and Buncombe County*. Asheville, 1922. 200 pp.

———. *History of Buncombe County, North Carolina*. 2 vols., Asheville, 1930.

*State*, June 1, 1957.

BURKE—

Sharpe, Bill. *A New Geography of North Carolina*, II, 649-674.

*State*, December 6, 1941; September 25, 1943; April 23,1955.

CABARRUS—

Hammer, Carl, Jr. *Rhinelanders on the Yadkin*. Salisbury, 1943. 130 pp.

Moore, James L., and Thomas Wingate. *Cabarrus Reborn:*

*A Historical Sketch of the Founding and Development of Cannon Mills and Company and Kannapolis.* Kannapolis, 1940. 102 pp.

Sharpe, Bill. *A New Geography of North Carolina,* I, 23-40. *State,* December 8, 1951.

CALDWELL—

Alexander, Nancy. *Here Will I Dwell: The Story of Caldwell County.* Lenoir, 1956. 230 pp.

Scott, W. M. *Annals of Caldwell County and "Gentleman" John Perkins.* Lenoir, 1930. 162 pp.

Sharpe, Bill. *A New Geography of North Carolina,* II, 675-700.

*State,* September 26, 1936; January 31, 1942; May 20, 1944; September 25, 1954.

CAMDEN—

Pugh, Jesse F. *Three Hundred Years Along the Pasquotank: A Biographical History of Camden County.* Old Trap, 1957. 249 pp.

Sharpe, Bill. *A New Geography of North Carolina,* II, 701-720.

*State,* November 29, 1941.

CARTERET—

Lefferts, A., and others. *Carteret County, Economic and Social.* Chapel Hill, 1926. 100 pp.

Sharpe, Bill. *A New Geography of North Carolina,* I, 41-72. *State,* June 27, 1953.

CASWELL—

Newsome, A. R. (ed.). "Twelve North Carolina Counties in 1810-1811," *NCHR,* V, No. 4 (October, 1928), 421-429.

Sharpe, Bill. *A New Geography of North Carolina,* IV, 1751-1766.

*State,* November 28, 1942.

CATAWBA—

Hahn, G. W. *The Catawba Soldier of the Civil War . . . Together with a Sketch of Catawba County from 1860 to 1911.* Hickory, 1911. 385 pp.

Preslar, C. J. (ed.). *A History of Catawba County.* Salisbury, 1954. 526 pp.

Sharpe, Bill. *A New Geography of North Carolina,* III, 1161-1180.

*State,* January 11, 1941; February 12, 1944.

CHATHAM—

London, Henry A. *An Address on the Revolutionary History of Chatham County.* Stanford, 1894. 27 pp.

Sharpe, Bill. *A New Geography of North Carolina,* II, 701-720.

*State,* April 5, 1941; July 10, 1943; May 4, 1957.

CHEROKEE—

Barclay, E. E. *Ducktown Back in Raht's Time.* Chapel Hill, 1946. 286 pp.

Freel, Margaret W. *Our Heritage: The People of Cherokee County, North Carolina, 1540-1955.* Asheville, 1956. 407 pp.

Sharpe, Bill. *A New Geography of North Carolina,* II, 721-736.

*State,* October 25, 1941; March 15, 1949; November 3, 1956.

CHOWAN—

Boyce, W. S. *Economic and Social History of Chowan County, 1880-1915.* New York, 1917. 293 pp.

Parramore, Thomas C. *Cradle of the Colony: The History of Chowan County and Edenton, North Carolina.* Edenton, 1967. 92 pp.

Sharpe, Bill. *A New Geography of North Carolina,* III, 1181-1202.

*State,* July 25, 1942; September 2, 1944; March 12, 1949.

CLAY—

Sharpe, Bill. *A New Geography of North Carolina,* IV, 1767-1782.

*State,* October 4, 1941.

CLEVELAND—

Davis, J. R. "Reconstruction in Cleveland County," TCHS, *Papers,* X (1914), 5-31.

Sharpe, Bill. *A New Geography of North Carolina,* III, 1203-1224.

*State,* February 2, 1935; March 21, 1942; October 9, 1943.

Weathers, Lee B. *The Living Past of Cleveland County, A History.* Shelby, 1956. 269 pp.

COLUMBUS—

Rogers, James A. *Columbus County, North Carolina.* Whiteville, 1946. 108 pp.

Sharpe, Bill. *A New Geography of North Carolina,* II, 737-760.

*State,* March 14, 1942; February 26, 1944.

CRAVEN—

Brinson, S. M. "Early History of Craven County," *NCB,* X, No. 4 (1911), 176-195.

Carraway, Gertrude. *Historic New Bern.* New Bern, 1934, rev. ed., 23 pp. 1957, 11th ed., 75 pp.

Cooper, Francis H. "Some History of Craven County," *JSHP,* XVII (1920), 27-74.

Dill, Alonzo T. "Eighteenth Century New Bern," *NCHR,* XXII and XXIII (January, 1945-October, 1946).

Garden Club of North Carolina. *New Bern, Cradle of North Carolina.* Raleigh, 1941. 86 pp.

Sharpe, Bill. *A New Geography of North Carolina,* III, 1225-1250.

CUMBERLAND—

Oates, John A. *The Story of Fayetteville and the Upper Cape Fear.* Charlotte, 1950. 868 pp.

Sharpe, Bill. *A New Geography of North Carolina,* III, 1251-1278.

*State,* March 3, 1949.

CURRITUCK—

Albertson, Catherine. *In Ancient Albemarle.* Raleigh, 1914. 134-152.

Sharpe, Bill. *A New Geography of North Carolina,* III, 1279-1302.

*State,* August 8, 1942.

DARE—

Sharpe, Bill. *A New Geography of North Carolina,* I, 73-114.

*State,* July 18, 1953.

Stick, David. *Fabulous Dare: The Story of Dare County, Past and Present.* Kitty Hawk, 1949. 71 pp.

DAVIDSON—

Leonard, J. C. *Centennial History of Davidson County.* Raleigh, 1927. 270 pp.

Matthews, Mary G., and M. J. Sink. *Wheels of Faith and Courage.* High Point, 1952. 217 pp.

Sharpe, Bill. *A New Geography of North Carolina,* IV, 1783-1802.

Sink, M. J. *Davidson County, Economic and Social,* Chapel Hill, 1925. 86 pp.

DAVIE—

Sharpe, Bill. *A New Geography of North Carolina,* IV, 1803-1814.

*State,* April 4, 1942; June 10, 1944.

DUPLIN—

Newsome, A. R. (ed.). "Twelve North Carolina Counties in 1810-1811," *NCHR,* V, No. 4 (October, 1928), 429-446.

Sharpe, Bill. *A New Geography of North Carolina,* IV, 1815-1832.

*State,* December 13, 1941; November 13, 1943.

DURHAM—

Boyd, W. K. *The Story of Durham: City of the New South.* Durham, 1925. 345 pp.

Dula, W. C., and A. C. Simpson. *Durham and Her People.* Durham, 1951. 295 pp.

Sharpe, Bill. *A New Geography of North Carolina,* IV, 1833-1852.

Upchurch, W. M., and M. B. Fowler. *Durham County, Economic and Social.* Chapel Hill, n.d. 93 pp.

EDGECOMBE—

Newsome, A. R. (ed.). "Twelve North Carolina Counties, 1810-1811," *NCHR,* VI, No. 1 (January, 1929), 87-99.

Sharpe, Bill. *A New Geography of North Carolina*, III, 1303-1322.

Turner, J. K., and J. L. Bridgers. *History of Edgecombe County*. Raleigh, 1920. 486 pp.

FORSYTH—

Fries, Adelaide L. *Forsyth County*. Winston, 1898. 132 pp.

———— (ed.). *Forsyth, A County on the March*. Chapel Hill, 1949. 248 pp.

Sharpe, Bill. *A New Geography of North Carolina*. I, 115-147.

Siewers, C. M. *Forsyth County, Economic and Social*. Chapel Hill, 1924. 110 pp.

*State,* January 30, 1954.

FRANKLIN—

Davis, Edward H. *Historical Sketches of Franklin County*. Raleigh, 1948. 298 pp.

Newsome, A. R. (ed.). "Twelve North Carolina Counties in 1810-1811," *NCHR,* VI, No. 2 (April, 1929), 171-177.

Sharpe, Bill. *A New Geography of North Carolina*. IV, 1853-1876.

GASTON—

Cope, Robert F., and Manly W. Wellman. *The County of Gaston: Two Centuries of a North Carolina Region*. Gastonia, 1961. 274 pp.

Puett, Minnie S. *History of Gaston County*. Charlotte, 1939. 218 pp.

Separk, Joseph H. *Gastonia and Gaston County, North Carolina, Past, Present, and Future*. Kingsport, Tenn., 1936. 141 pp.

————. *Gastonia and Gaston County, 1849-1949*. Gastonia, 1949. 237 pp.

Stowe, R. L. *Early History of Belmont and Gaston County, North Carolina,* 1951. 61 pp.

GATES—

Harrell, Isaac S. "Gates County to 1860," TCHS, *Papers,* XII (1916), 56-106.

Sharpe, Bill. *A New Geography of North Carolina*. IV, 1877-1890.

*State,* January 24, 1942.

GRAHAM—
Sharpe, Bill. *A New Geography of North Carolina.* III, 1323-1344.
*State,* July 11, 1942.

GRANVILLE—
Caldwell, J. R., Jr. "A History of Granville County, North Carolina: The Preliminary Phase, 1746-1800" (dissertation, U.N.C. 1950), 268 pp.
Sharpe, Bill. *A New Geography of North Carolina.* II, 787-808.
*State,* February 14, 1942; June 12, 1943; November 30, 1957.
Tilley, Nannie May. "Industries of Colonial Granville County," *NCHR,* XII, No. 4 (October 1936), 273-289.
———. "Political Disturbances in Colonial Granville County," *NCHR,* XVIII, No. 4. (October, 1941), 339-359.
———. "The Settlement of Granville County," *NCHR,* XI, No. 1 (January, 1934), 1-19.

GREENE—
Newsome, A. R. (ed.). "Twelve North Carolina Counties in 1810-1811," *NCHR,* VI, No. 2 (April, 1929), 177-179.
Sharpe, Bill. *A New Geography of North Carolina.* IV, 1891-1904.
*State,* December 5, 1942.

GUILFORD—
Albright, James W. *Greensboro, 1808-1904.* Greensboro, 1904. 134 pp.
Arnett, Ethel S., and W. C. Jackson. *Greensboro: County Seat of Guilford, North Carolina.* Chapel Hill, 1955. 494 pp.
Caldwell, Bettie D. *Founders and Builders of Greensboro, 1808-1908.* Greensboro, 1925. 356 pp.
High Point Chamber of Commerce. *The Building and Builders of a City—High Point, North Carolina.* High Point, 1947. 329 pp.
Sharpe, Bill. *A New Geography of North Carolina.* II, 809-840.
*State,* April 26, 1941; July 17, 1941; May 15, 1943; July 30, 1955.
Stockard, Sallie W. *History of Guilford County.* Knoxville, 1902. 197 pp.

HALIFAX—

Allen, S. B., and R. S. Travis, Jr. *Halifax County, Economic and Social*. Chapel Hill, 1920. 106 pp.

Allen, W. C. *History of Halifax County*. Boston, 1918. 106 pp.

Sharpe, Bill. *A New Geography of North Carolina*, I, 148-174.

*State,* February 23, 1952.

HARNETT—

Fowler, Malcolm. *They Passed This Way: A Personal Narrative of Harnett County History*. Lillington, 1955. 167 pp.

Sharpe, Bill. *A New Geography of North Carolina*, III, 1345-1362.

*State,* January 30, 1937; July 2, 1941; May 15, 1943.

HAYWOOD—

Allen, W. C. *Annals of Haywood County*. Waynesville, 1935. 628 pp.

Sharpe, Bill. *A New Geography of North Carolina*, I, 175-204.

*State,* August 15, 1943.

HENDERSON—

Patton, Sadie S. *The Story of Henderson County*. Asheville, 1947. 290 pp.

Sharpe, Bill. *A New Geography of North Carolina*, II, 841-864.

*State,* April 21, 1956.

HERTFORD—

Parker, Joseph Roy. *The Ahoskie Era of Hertford County*. Ahoskie, 1939. xxxii, 751 pp.

Sharpe, Bill. *A New Geography of North Carolina*, II, 865-886.

*State,* February 7, 1942; April 1, 1944.

Winborne, B. B. *Colonial and State Political History of Hertford County, North Carolina*. Raleigh, 1906. 398 pp.

HOKE—

Sharpe, Bill. *A New Geography of North Carolina*, IV, 1905-1918.

*State*, November 14, 1942; February 7, 1948.

HYDE—

Sharpe, Bill. *A New Geography of North Carolina*, II, 887-898.

Simmons, Caroline V. "The Settlement and Early History of Hyde County," *Report of the Public Schools of Washington, North Carolina*. Goldsboro, 1907. 106-114.

*State*, March 26, 1938; April 11, 1942; January 22, 1948; August 24, 1957.

IREDELL—

Sharpe, Bill. *A New Geography of North Carolina*, II, 909-928.

*State*, September 8, 1940; January 29, 1944; November 2, 1957.

JACKSON—

Sharpe, Bill. *A New Geography of North Carolina*, III, 1363-1380.

*State*, June 27, 1942; July 3, 1943.

JOHNSTON—

Sanders, William, Jr., and G. Y. Ragsdale. *Johnston County, Economic and Social*. Smithfield, 1922. 95 pp.

Sharpe, Bill. *A New Geography of North Carolina*, II, 929-954.

*State*, September 13, 1941; March 13, 1943; September 8, 1956.

JONES—

Sharpe, Bill. *A New Geography of North Carolina*, IV, 1919-1932.

*State*, October 3, 1942.

LEE—

Sharpe, Bill. *A New Geography of North Carolina*, I, 205-224.

*State*, March 13, 1954.

LENOIR—

Johnson, Talmage C. *The Story of Kinston and Lenoir County.* Raleigh, 1954. 413 pp.

Newsome, A. R. (ed.). "Twelve North Carolina Counties in 1810-1811," *NCHR*, VI, No. 3 (April, 1929), 179-189.

Powell, William S. *Annals of Progress: The Story of Lenoir County and Kinston, North Carolina.* Raleigh, 1963. 107 pp.

Sharpe, Bill. *A New Geography of North Carolina*, III, 1381-1396.

*State*, October 18, 1941; August 14, 1943.

LINCOLN—

Nixon, Alfred. "History of Lincoln County," *NCB*, IX, No. 3 (January, 1910), 111-178.

Sharpe, Bill. *A New Geography of North Carolina*, III, 1397-1418.

Sherrill, S. L. *Annals of Lincoln County, North Carolina.* Charlotte, 1937. 536 pp.

*State*, September 26, 1942; July, 15, 1944.

MCDOWELL—

Sharpe, Bill. *A New Geography of North Carolina*, IV, 1953-1974.

*State*, December 25, 1927; July 19, 1941; April, 15, 1944; December 30, 1944.

MACON—

Sharpe, Bill. *A New Geography of North Carolina*, III, 1419-1444.

Smith, C. D. *A Brief History of Macon County.* Franklin, 1891. 15 pp.

MADISON—

Sharpe, Bill. *A New Geography of North Carolina*, III, 1445-1464.

*State*, April 25, 1942.

MARTIN—

Sharpe, Bill. *A New Geography of North Carolina*, IV, 1933-1952.

*State*, May 30, 1942; December 25, 1943.

Alexander, John B. *History of Mecklenburg County.* Charlotte, 1902. 431 pp.

Blythe, W. Legette, and Charles R. Brockmann. *Hornet's Nest: The Story of Charlotte and Mecklenburg County.* Charlotte, 1961. 511 pp.

Groome, Bailey T. *Mecklenburg in the Revolution, 1740-1783.* Charlotte, 1931. 114 pp.

Sharpe, Bill. *A New Geography of North Carolina,* IV, 1975-2004.

Stenhouse, J. A. *Exploring Old Mecklenburg.* Charlotte, 1952. 50 pp.

Thompson, E. T. *Agricultural Mecklenburg and Industrial Charlotte, Social and Economic.* Charlotte, 1926. 317 pp.

Tompkins, D. A. *History of Mecklenburg County.* Charlotte, 1903. 2 vols.

Writers Project of WPA. *Charlotte, A Guide to the Queen City of North Carolina.* Charlotte, 1939. 74 pp.

Deyton, J. B. "History of the Toe River Valley to 1865," *NCHR,* XXIV, No. 4 (October, 1947), 423-466.

Sharpe, Bill. *A New Geography of North Carolina,* I, 225-253.

*State,* May 9, 1942; June 14, 1952.

Sharpe, Bill. *A New Geography of North Carolina,* III, 1465-1486.

*State,* April 3, 1937; April 18, 1942; May 6, 1944.

Newsome, A. R. (ed.). "Twelve North Carolina Counties in 1810-1811," *NCHR,* VI, No. 3 (July, 1929), 281-294.

Robinson, Blackwell P. *A History of Moore County, North Carolina, 1747-1847.* Southern Pines, 1956. 270 pp.

Sharpe, Bill. *A New Geography of North Carolina,* I, 254-281.

*State,* April 17, 1943; April 17, 1948; September 29, 1951.

Wellman, Manly Wade. *The County of Moore, 1847-1947.* Southern Pines, 1962. 254 pp.

NASH—

Sharpe, Bill. *A New Geography of North Carolina,* I, 282-306.

*State,* November 15, 1942.

NEW HANOVER—

De Rossett, W. L. *Pictorial and Historical New Hanover County and Wilmington, North Carolina, 1723-1938.* Wilmington, 1938. 110 pp.

Howell, Andrew. *The Book of Wilmington, 1730-1930.* Wilmington, 1930. 206 pp.

Reilley, J. S. *Wilmington, Past, Present, & Future.* Wilmington, 1884. 130 pp.

Sharpe, Bill. *A New Geography of North Carolina,* I, 307-328.

Sprunt, James. *Chronicles of the Cape Fear River.* Raleigh, 1914. 594 pp.

———. *Information and Statistics Respecting Wilmington.* Wilmington, 1883. 250 pp.

*State,* March 22, 1952.

Waddell, A. M. *History of New Hanover County, 1725-1780.* Wilmington, 1909. 232 pp.

NORTHAMPTON—

Sharpe, Bill. *A New Geography of North Carolina,* III, 1487-1500.

*State,* February 21, 1942.

ONSLOW—

Brown, J. Parsons. *The Commonwealth of Onslow.* New Bern, 1960. 434 pp.

Sharpe, Bill. *A New Geography of North Carolina,* II, 955-974.

*State,* September 19, 1942; January 29, 1949; March 26, 1955.

ORANGE—

Chamberlain, Hope S. *Old Days in Chapel Hill.* Chapel Hill, 1926. 325 pp.

Lefler, Hugh T., and Paul W. Wager (eds.). *Orange County, 1752-1952*. Chapel Hill, 1953. 389 pp.

Lloyd, A. A. *History of the Town of Hillsboro*. 1945. 20 pp.

Nash, Francis. *Hillsboro, Colonial and Revolutionary*. (reprint), Chapel Hill, 1953. 96 pp.

Sharpe, Bill. *A New Geography of North Carolina*, I, 329-348.

*State*, October 3, 1953.

PAMLICO—

Sharpe, Bill. *A New Geography of North Carolina*, III, 1501-1516.

*State*, January 3, 1942.

PASQUOTANK—

Albertson, Catherine. *In Ancient Albemarle*. Raleigh, 1914. 66-113.

Flora, J. B. *An Historical Sketch of Ancient Pasquotank County, North Carolina, 1586-1793*. Elizabeth City. 1950. 14 pp.

Markham, Frederick P., III. *History of Agriculture, Industry, and Commerce of Early Pasquotank County*. Elizabeth City, 1955. 39-42.

Sharpe, Bill. *A New Geography of North Carolina*, I, 349-367.

*State*, November 17, 1951.

Wood, John E. *Brief Sketch of Pasquotank County*. Elizabeth City, 1955. 15-27.

PENDER—

Bloodworth, Mattie. *History of Pender County, North Carolina*. Richmond, 1947. 240 pp.

Sharpe, Bill. *A New Geography of North Carolina*, III, 1517-1534.

*State*, May 16, 1942; June 17, 1944.

PERQUIMANS—

Albertson, Catherine. *In Ancient Albemarle*. Raleigh, 1914. 144-133.

Sharpe, Bill. *A New Geography of North Carolina*, IV, 2005-2022.

*State,* August 1, 1942; May 28, 1949.

Winslow, Ellen G. *History of Perquimans County.* Raleigh, 1931. 488 pp.

PERSON—

Foushee, Alexander R. *Reminiscences, A Sketch and Letters Descriptive of Life in Person County in Former Days.* Durham, 1921. 81 pp.

Sharpe, Bill. *A New Geography of North Carolina,* II, 975-990.

*State,* April 3, 1943; August 10, 1946; May 21, 1949; March 10, 1956.

PITT—

King, Henry T. *Sketches of Pitt County.* Raleigh, 1911. 263 pp.

Pitt County Club, University of North Carolina. *Pitt County, Economic and Social.* Chapel Hill, 1920. 78 pp.

Sharpe, Bill. *A New Geography of North Carolina,* III, 991-1012.

*State,* January 21, 1937; August 30, 1941; August 21, 1943; October 5, 1957.

POLK—

Patton, Sadie S. *Sketches of Polk County.* Asheville, 1950. 161 pp.

Sharpe, Bill. *A New Geography of North Carolina,* III, 1535-1552.

*State,* September 12, 1942; June 24, 1944; June 8, 1946.

RANDOLPH—

Blair, Joseph A. *Reminiscences of Randolph County.* Greensboro, 1890. 57 pp.

Burgess, Fred. *Randolph County, Economic and Social.* Chapel Hill, 1924. 90 pp.

Sharpe, Bill. *A New Geography of North Carolina,* II, 1013-1042.

*State,* November 16, 1940; February 13, 1943; July 14, 1956.

RICHMOND—

Sharpe, Bill. *A New Geography of North Carolina,* I, 368-385.

*State,* October 24, 1953.

ROBESON—

Lawrence, Robert C. *The State of Robeson.* New York, 1939. 279 pp.

Sharpe, Bill. *A New Geography of North Carolina,* I, 386-410.

*State,* November 29, 1952.

ROCKINGHKAM—

Craig, Marjorie (ed.). "Home-life in Rockingham County in the 'Eighties and 'Nineties," *NCHR,* XXXIII, No. 4 (October, 1956), 510-528.

Newsome, A. R. (ed.). "Twelve North Carolina Counties in 1810 and 1811," *NCHR,* VI, No. 3 (July, 1929), 294-301.

Rockingham County Club, University of North Carolina. *Rockingham County, Economic and Social.* Chapel Hill, 1918. 84 pp.

Sharpe, Bill. *A New Geography of North Carolina.* I, 411-437.

*State,* March 28, 1953.

ROWAN—

Brawley, James S. *The Rowan Story, 1753-1953.* Salisbury, 1953. 402 pp.

Chamberlain, Hope S. *This Was Home.* Chapel Hill, 1938. 328 pp.

Ervin, Samuel J., Jr. "A Colonial History of Rowan County, North Carolina," *JSHP,* XVI, No. 1 (1917), 1-54.

Hammer, Carl, Jr. *Rhinelanders on the Yadkin.* Salisbury, 1943. 130 pp.

Rumple, Jethro. *History of Rowan County.* Salisbury, 1881; reprint, Raleigh, 1929. 619 pp.

Sharpe, Bill. *A New Geography of North Carolina,* I, 438-463.

*State,* April 11, 1953.

RUTHERFORD—

Griffin, Clarence W. *The History of Old Tryon and Rutherford Counties, 1730-1936.* Asheville, 1937. 640 pp.

———. *History of Rutherford County, 1937-1951.* Asheville, 1952. 136 pp.

Price, R. E. *Rutherford County, Economic and Social.* Chapel Hill, 1918. 76 pp.

Sharpe, Bill. *A New Geography of North Carolina,* IV, 2023-2050.

SAMPSON—

Bass, Cora. *Sampson County Yearbook.* Clinton, 1957. 156 pp.

Sampson County Club, University of North Carolina. *Sampson County, Economic and Social.* Chapel Hill, 1917. 60 pp.

Sharpe, Bill. *A New Geography of North Carolina,* III, 1553-1572.

*State,* March 1, 1941; November 6, 1943.

SCOTLAND—

Sharpe, Bill. *A New Geography of North Carolina,* IV, 2051-2070.

*State,* November 21, 1942; September 23, 1944.

STANLY—

Sharpe, Bill. *A New Geography of North Carolina,* III, 1573-1592.

*State,* February 13, 1937; August 5, 1942; September 11, 1943; May 27, 1944.

STOKES—

Newsome, A. R. (ed.). "Twelve North Carolina Counties in 1810 and 1811," *NCHR,* VI, No. 3 (July, 1929), 302-304.

Sharpe, Bill. *A New Geography of North Carolina,* IV, 2071-2092.

*State,* October 31, 1942.

SURRY—

Hollingsworth, J. G. *History of Surry County.* Greensboro, 1935. 280 pp.

Newsome, A. R. (ed.). "Twelve North Carolina Counties in 1810 and 1811," *NCHR*, VI, No. 3 (July, 1929), 302-304.

Sharpe, Bill. *A New Geography of North Carolina*, III, 1593-1614.

SWAIN—

Sharpe, Bill. *A New Geography of North Carolina*, I, 464-486.

*State*, July 18, 1942.

TRANSYLVANIA—

Sharpe, Bill. *A New Geography of North Carolina*, IV, 2093-2120.

*State*, December 10, 1938; June 20, 1942; June 19, 1943.

TYRRELL—

Sharpe, Bill. *A New Geography of North Carolina*, IV, 2120-2140.

*State*, June 26, 1942.

UNION—

McNeely, R. N. "Union County and the Old Waxhaw Settlement," *NCB*, XII, No. 1 (1912), 6-20.

Sharpe, Bill. *A New Geography of North Carolina*, II, 1043-1058.

*State*, February 5, 1938; October 10, 1942; December 1, 1956.

Winchester, George T. *A Story of Union County and the History of Pleasant Grove Camp Ground.* Mineral Springs, N.C., 1937. 104 pp.

VANCE—

Peace, Samuel T. *"Zeb's Black Baby," Vance County, North Carolina.* Henderson, 1955. 457 pp.

Sharpe, Bill. *A New Geography of North Carolina*, I, 487-507.

*State*, April 27, 1954.

WAKE—

Amis, Moses. *Historical Raleigh with Sketches of Wake County and Its Important Towns.* Raleigh, 1902; revised and enlarged, 1913. 289 pp.

Battle, Kemp P. *The Early History of Raleigh*. Raleigh, 1893. 144 pp.

Chamberlain, Hope S. *History of Wake County*. Raleigh, 1922. 302 pp.

Sharpe, Bill. *A New Geography of North Carolina*, IV, 2141-2182.

Swain, David L. *Early Times in Raleigh*. Raleigh, 1867. 83 pp.

Waugh, Elizabeth. *North Carolina's Capital: Raleigh*. Raleigh, 1967. 216 pp.

Writers Program, WPA. *Raleigh: Capital of North Carolina*. New Bern, 1942. 170 pp.

WARREN—

Montgomery, Lizzie W. *Sketches of Old Warrenton, North Carolina*. Raleigh, 1924. 451 pp.

Sharpe, Bill. *A New Geography of North Carolina*, IV, 2183-2204.

*State*, August 3, 1940; December 18, 1943.

Wellman, Manly W. *The County of Warren, North Carolina, 1586-1917*. Chapel Hill, 1959. 282 pp.

WASHINGTON—

Sharpe, Bill. *A New Geography of North Carolina*, III, 1615-1640.

*State*, June 13, 1942; March 26, 1949.

WATAUGA—

Arthur, J. P. *History of Watauga County*. Richmond, 1915. 364 pp.

Sharpe, Bill. *A New Geography of North Carolina*, II, 1059-1082.

*State*, October 6, 1956.

Whitener, Daniel J. *History of Watauga County*. Kingsport, Tenn., 1949. 112 pp.

WAYNE—

Byrd, Sam. *Small Town South* [Goldsboro]. Boston, 1942. 237 pp.

Daniels, Frank A. *History of Wayne County*. Goldsboro, 1914. 43 pp.

Newsome, A. R. (ed.). "Twelve North Carolina Counties in 1810 and 1811," *NCHR*, VI, No. 3 (July, 1929), 304-309.

Sharpe, Bill. *A New Geography of North Carolina*, I, 508-528.

*State,* November 21, 1953.

WILKES—

Cox, A. B. *Foot Prints on the Sands of Time.* Sparta, 1900. 142-147.

Crouch, John. *Historical Sketches of Wilkes County.* Wilkesboro, 1902. 141 pp.

Hayes, Johnson J. *The Land of Wilkes.* Wilkesboro, 1962. 577 pp.

Sharpe, Bill. *A New Geography of North Carolina*, II, 1083-1102.

*State,* April 12, 1941; January 22, 1944; January 28, 1956.

WILSON—

Sharpe, Bill. *A New Geography of North Carolina*, IV, 2205-2228.

*State,* March 29, 1941.

YADKIN—

Sharpe, Bill. *A New Geography of North Carolina*, IV, 2229-2248.

*State,* October 24, 1942.

*Yadkin County Record Book.* Yadkinville, 1939. 97 pp.

YANCEY—

Sharpe, Bill. *A New Geography of North Carolina*, III, 1641-1666.

*State,* May 2, 1942.

Teacher Training Class of Burnsville. *History and Geography of Yancey County.* Burnsville, 1930. 70 pp.